TOWARDS THE END OF ISOLATIONISM: CHINA'S FOREIGN POLICY AFTER MAO

TOWARDS THE END OF ISOLATIONISM: CHINA'S FOREIGN POLICY AFTER MAO

Michael Yahuda

St. Martin's Press   New York

All rights reserved. For information, write:
St. Martin's Press, Inc., 175 Fifth Avenue,
New York, NY 10010
Printed in Hong Kong
First published in the United States of America in 1983

Library of Congress Card Catalog Number 83—42610

ISBN 0—312—81141—1

For my father
and in memory of my mother

Contents

PART TWO: FOREIGN POLICY AFTER MAO

Preface

This book seeks to examine the continuities and changes in China's foreign policy since the death of Mao Zedong in September 1976. To this end it suggests that this can best be done by distinguishing between the geopolitical and societal dimensions of China's foreign relations. The former is concerned with questions of power relations and national security, while the latter focuses on the impact on Chinese society of China's economic and cultural interactions with the outside world. In practice the two dimensions may be closely related; but for the purposes of analysis it is useful for example, to separate discussion of China's relations with the two superpowers from discussion of China's capacity to absorb advanced Western technology or the challenges that might be presented to social values from increased contact with the world as envisaged by the policy of the 'open door'.

The book is divided into two parts. The first considers the character of Mao's legacy in foreign affairs and the second examines the developments since his death. Both parts analyse the geopolitical and societal dimensions separately.

Since the death of Mao, China has embarked on a series of domestic changes that constitute a disavowal of most of the ideological concerns and policies associated with Mao for the last twenty years of his life. In July 1981 the Central Committee of the Communist Party of China issued a considered verdict on its history since the establishment of the People's Republic of China in 1949.[1] The document also included a separate section on Mao himself. This praised his contribution to the Chinese revolution but it also criticised severely many of his policies from the late 1950s. In particular it criticised him for having initiated the Cultural Revolution which was condemned as a calamity without a single redeeming feature.

Strangely, despite the significance of foreign relations to

China's development over this period of more than thirty years, hardly any space was found in this 30,000 word document for comment or analysis of foreign affairs. For example, neither the Sino-Soviet alliance of the 1950s nor the tilt to the United States in the 1970s (both of which might be thought to have been of considerable importance in China's history since 1949) was explicitly mentioned. Aspects of foreign affairs are referred to at various points *en passant*, but no one reading the resolution would realise that there had ever been any controversies or major changes in the conduct of China's foreign policy over this long period. It is true that Mao's approach to foreign affairs was put in a positive way, but nowhere was it summarised, let alone discussed in any depth. Interestingly, the nearest the document came to detailed comment concerned Mao's foreign policy performance during the Cultural Revolution. Having subjected him to withering criticism for his theories and policies during this period, the resolution simply endorsed Mao's foreign policy without note or explanation:

> In his later years, he still remained alert to safeguarding the security of our country, stood up to the pressure of social imperialism, pursued a correct foreign policy, firmly supported the just struggles of all peoples, outlined the correct strategy of the three worlds and advanced the important principle that China would never seek hegemony.[2]

In effect this official history declared that whatever mistakes may have been committed by the Party leaders in general and by Mao in particular since the founding of the PRC, they did not lie in the field of foreign relations.

This minimal reference to foreign affairs reflects a general reluctance by China's authorities to discuss openly differences and disputes on foreign policy that have taken place at various times between the leaders. Frequently, very detailed and politically damaging accounts of leadership disputes on domestic questions have been disseminated within the country and even to the outside world. But even when foreign policy differences were known to have been involved, they have been deliberately excised from the later accounts. The clearest

example of this is the Lin Biao affair. The materials which
the Chinese authorities released on this included a great deal
of information on inter-leadership relations, and on the
Chinese political process as well as on the substance of the
case itself. Much of this was highly damaging to the integrity
and authority of the regime and its surviving leaders. But
even though Lin and his close associates were known to have
opposed the opening to the United States, precious little was
released on this dimension of Lin's conflict with Mao and
Zhou. Similarly, many of the leaders who were disgraced in
the early stages of the Cultural Revolution such as Luo Ruiqing,
Liu Shaoqi and Peng Zhen, had disagreed with aspects of
Mao's initiatives in foreign affairs in 1965–66. But their
otherwise voluminous indictments during the Cultural Revolution left out virtually all mention of this.[3]

This peculiar reticence on foreign affairs extends even
further. There has not been any general attempt by Chinese
officials or scholars to survey their country's foreign policy
over the more than thirty years since the establishment of
the PRC. The reports on the work of the government given to
meetings of the National People's Congress do contain sections
on foreign affairs, but these are usually very brief and by their
nature they are not analytical or sufficiently detailed to be of
much interest. There have been a few sporadic attempts to
assess the foreign policy contributions of certain leaders, the
most notable of which was by the research division of the
Ministry of Foreign Affairs on the second anniversary of
Zhou Enlai's death.[4] But, to my knowledge, there has never
been a similar assessment of Mao. This is distinctly odd in
view of the constant claims by Chinese officials to disbelieving
foreigners that their foreign policy has always been consistent
and principled. In fact there can be few countries whose
foreign policy has been more marked by volatility and change
than China. As I shall argue in this book, if there is a consistency underlying China's foreign policy it is to be found in the
geopolitical thought which has guided it, rather than in the
didactic principles constantly invoked by its officials. The
absence of Chinese accounts of their foreign policy is all the
more striking in view of the veritable stream of Soviet publications which seek to demonstrate, in considerable detail, the

claim that Soviet foreign policy has always followed Leninist principles.

There are signs, however, that aspects of this may be about to change. In 1981 the Chinese Academy of Social Sciences began publication of the journal *International Studies* which has carried scholarly articles on aspects of Chinese foreign affairs. So far these have been little more than background papers to current policies. For example, issues one and two published articles on the Sino-Soviet border dispute and the initial involvement of the United States in the Taiwan issue in 1949–50. However, there has also been a lengthy article on Zhou Enlai's diplomatic style. It is to be hoped that the scope of the journal will soon be enlarged to facilitate a deeper understanding of Chinese perceptions of foreign policy issues. This book is an endeavour to contribute to that understanding.

The original title of the book was simply *The End of Isolationism*. On reflection, however, it seemed appropriate to qualify such a claim by adding the word *'towards'* at the beginning. Even though important changes have occurred since the early 1970s and especially since the end of that decade which have significantly expanded and deepened the extent of China's interchanges with the outside world, it still cannot be said that China's relative isolation is at an end. As will be argued in Chapter 4, China is still far from sharing the patterns of interdependency with other countries that characterise the international relationships of most states in world affairs. The processes of policy making in the Chinese government still remain obscure in many respects. Changes in Chinese policy arise from internal developments that continue to be unknown and perhaps unknowable to the outside world. Even in foreign affairs, incidents can still occur whose causes remain unfathomable and certainly unprovable. For example, in the spring of 1978 many armed Chinese fishing boats suddenly appeared in the waters of the Senkaku Islands (or in Chinese Tiaoyudai) claimed by both China and Japan. The boats proclaimed China's sovereignty over the islands, and the incident was perceived in Tokyo as an anti-Japanese demonstration. Just as suddenly the boats withdrew and the embarrassing incident was smoothed over by both sides. Even more than four years later, despite many speculations about the causes of the incident, nothing has been proved.

Similarly, although travel to and from China has expanded considerably, the Chinese authorities are still able to exercise controls over the extent of discourse between Chinese and foreigners. The growth of foreign economic relations has given rise to acute problems of absorption of foreign technology in China. The interchange with the foreign business community (especially with Overseas Chinese and those from Hong Kong and Macau) has been linked with the widespread incidence of corruption. Important political forces in China have perceived Western cultural influences as dangerous 'bourgeois liberalism' corrupting writers and young people. The policy of the 'open door' cannot be said to have found universal favour in China and it cannot be said to be irreversible.

Nevertheless, compared with a decade ago, China has made giant strides towards ending its isolation. The value of trade trebled between 1972 and 1975 and trebled again between 1977 and 1981, so that its value is now 16 per cent of the country's estimated GNP. The development of particular regions and sectors of industry have become linked with that trade. Thousands of Chinese students are studying in Western countries (7000 in the United States alone). Academic and cultural exchanges have expanded enormously. There is a growing interest in foreign countries and cultures in China. The Academy of Social Sciences which was founded in 1977 now has separate institutes for the study of certain countries and regions such as the United States, the Soviet Union, Japan, Western Europe, South Asia and Southeast Asia. It also has one for the translation of foreign literature. As we shall see, China's diplomacy has acquired greater sophistication and subtlety.

In sum, the trend towards greater involvement and interchange with the outside world is unmistakable, but whether it will continue and in what forms remains yet to be seen.

Finally, it is a pleasure to record my gratitude to Robert Catley, Greg O'Leary and Andrew Watson for their helpful comments on sections of the book. Mrs Barbara Bray provided invaluable research assistance in the writing of Chapters 4 and

5. I am also grateful to Mrs Jenifer Jefferies for typing the manuscript. Of course, I alone am responsible for any failings or errors in the book.

Michael B. Yahuda.
Adelaide.

Abbreviations

ASEAN	Association of South East Asian Nations
CC	Central Committee (of the Communist Party of China)
c.i.f.	cost, insurance and freight
CMEA	Council for Mutual Economic Assistance (Comecon)
CPC	Communist Party of China
CPI	Communist Party of Italy
CPSU	Communist Party of the Soviet Union
EEC	European Economic Community
f.o.b.	free on board
GDP	Gross domestic product
GNP	Gross national product
ICBM	Intercontinental ballistic missile
JPRS	Joint Publications Research Services
KMT	Kuomintang
LDC	Less developed countries
NATO	North Atlantic Treaty Organisation
NPC	National People's Congress
PKI	Parti Kommunisti Indonesia
PLA	People's Liberation Army
PRC	People's Republic of China
SWB/FE	Summary of World Broadcasts, (Part Four) The Far East (Published daily by the British Broadcasting Corporation)
SW	*Selected Works of Mao Tse-tung*, Vols 1–5, Beijing, Foreign Language Press 1960–65 and 1977.

Abbreviations

1

Introduction

(The important and far-reaching changes in China's domestic affairs since the death of Mao Zedong have been reflected in its external relations) but not as much as might be thought at first sight. China's leaders have adopted what they call an 'open door' policy towards the outside world as a vital part of their programme for modernising the country. The 'open door', in contrast with the more 'closed door' of the previous two decades, involves mainly expanded foreign economic relations but also a wide range of scientific, cultural and other exchanges with Western countries in particular. Yet with regard to power relations and security questions the changes are far less evident. These are still marked by the attempt to establish an anti-Soviet coalition combined with what might be called a subtle alignment with the United States as initiated by Mao Zedong and Zhou Enlai at the beginning of the 1970s.

The contrast between these elements of change and continuity calls for an explanation. It is something of a truism to assert that there are complex processes of interaction between domestic and foreign policies. How, then, can the contrast between radical domestic change and relative continuity in the strategic dimensions of foreign policy be accounted for? In the first place, it is important to appreciate another possible truism of international politics: that the politics *between* states operate on a separate basis from those that take place *within* states. Relations between sovereign states are concerned ultimately with the maintenance of their independence and security in a context in which great powers exist and play a predominant role in determining the general conditions of peace or war, security or insecurity in the world as a whole.[1]

The international environment in which a state is located does not necessarily change in accordance with changes in its domestic arrangements. To be sure, different leaders or governments of the same state may hold divergent views of the character of the international environment of their particular state. But it is usual for such leaders and governments to find in time that they face similar geopolitical realities and international constraints upon their behaviour as their predecessors. This surely has been the experience of the American Presidents Carter and Reagan. Despite coming to office with very different views of the goals and priorities of the foreign policy of the world's most powerful state, they have found it necessary to modify these in the light of the realities of international politics. Second, if much of international politics takes place in a separate (albeit related) arena from those of the domestic state, it is possible that a new set of leaders may choose to introduce great changes in the domestic arena without seeking to alter the international orientation of their state. In other words, they may identify a need for major domestic reforms while perceiving that their country's national security interests *vis à vis* other states have remained unaltered.

Finally, it is possible to distinguish between the foreign economic interests and the national security interests of a state. For many states foreign trade is so important to their general economic well-being that the distinction might be thought to be so fine as to be without value. But even in the case of trading countries like Britain and Japan there are certain national security questions which transcend the issues of foreign economic relations. Japan's claims to the 'four northern islands' at the southern tip of the Kurile Islands chain have soured its relations with the Soviet Union and severely restricted Japan's participation in the economic exploitation of Siberia. This claim has also damaged Japan's preference for a policy of 'equi-distance' between the major powers (albeit under the American security umbrella) — a policy which is more fitting for a trading nation. British trading opportunities with the Soviet Union and Eastern Europe have been tempered by obvious strategic considerations. Economic interests, in other words, compete with other interests in what may be conceived as the amalgam of national security interests.[2] In the case of huge continental countries, such as China, foreign economic relations necessarily rank lower in the order of strategic priorities than resource-poor trading countries like Japan. Interestingly, both the United States and the Soviet Union have tried in vain to induce change in China by economic pressure. Throughout the 1950s and 1960s China was subject to an American trade embargo; and in 1960 the Soviet Union abruptly withdrew all its assistance when China was in the throes of a great economic depression. There can be no question that these measures did inflict harm on the country, but the consequence of these acts was in both cases to increase Chinese resolve to pursue their independent course.

Two dimensions of China's foreign relations

In considering the degree of change and continuity in China's foreign policy after Mao, it is useful to distinguish between two dimensions of the country's interactions with the rest of the world. The first might be called societal and the second strategic. The first concerns those aspects of external relations which impinge directly upon Chinese society and those aspects of political, social and economic change at home which affect China's orientation to the outside world. Strategic relations, by contrast, are concerned with the management of China's national security interests in response to perceived changes in global and regional balances of power. The two dimensions are by no means independent of each other and there is usually a considerable degree of overlap between them. Indeed, the ways in which successive Chinese leaders have perceived strategic interests have been influenced by their experiences within China, by their preferences among the social priorities for domestic development and by their domestic political alignments.

Nevertheless the distinction is useful in many respects. First, it enables analysis to focus more clearly on the particular issues of foreign relations concerning alliances and questions of peace and war. Instead of analysing major developments piecemeal, in which all the various main factors influencing decision-making are considered as a complex whole, it should be possible to examine whether Mao had a distinctive pattern of geopolitical thought which underlay much of China's foreign policy-making in this domain. If this was so, it should be possible to consider the extent to which his successors have continued along his path. Second, the distinction draws attention to an important aspect of decision-making in China's political system. Unlike the societal dimension, strategic/ diplomatic decisions, such as with whom to ally or whom to oppose in international relations, do not require the active participation of significant elements within Chinese society either for the making of decisions or for their implementation. These decisions appear to be confined to the highest levels of the Political Bureau assisted by a small number of official experts from the Ministry of Foreign Affairs and related organisations. When there have been disagreements about these questions, either for substantive or factional reasons, these have been confined to the senior levels. Societal dimensions of foreign relations, by contrast, involve broad elements of the Chinese people, if not always in the initial making of the decisions then certainly in their implementation. The expansion of foreign economic relations or of cultural exchanges, for example, necessarily brings broader elements of Chinese society into play and may lead to consequences that were undesired or unforeseen by the central leaders.

However, the distinctions between the levels of decision-making are important. Such evidence as is available indicates that it was Mao who took the decision to intervene in the Korean War.[3] Likewise, the decision to tilt to the United States in 1971/72 was taken by Mao and Zhou. Although this led to a rapid increase in trade, there is no evidence to suggest that this was a major consideration for Mao at the time, and it certainly did not commit him to the kinds of open-door modernisation pursued by his successors. It was entirely possible for him to have pursued a more closed-door, self-reliant policy while simultaneously cultivating a strategic alignment with the United States in order to contain Soviet 'hegemonism'. Similarly, the considerations which affected the decision to attack Vietnam in February–March 1979 and to maintain military and diplomatic pressure on that country for the following months and years belong entirely to the strategic domain. An argument can be made that the conse-sequences of these actions have had profound 'societal' implications and that these and the anticipation of them may have constrained Chinese actions. Yet these possible con-straints do not in themselves explain China's actions or suggest the extent of the 'societal' costs China's leaders may have been prepared to pay.

Third, by distinguishing the societal dimension for separate analysis, it becomes possible to examine the significance of external influences upon the country's economic development. It also facilitates discussion of the relationship between this aspect of foreign relations and the strategic dimension.

Thus the negotiation of the Sino-Soviet Alliance in the winter of 1949–50 when Mao spent seven uncomfortable weeks in Moscow belonged very much to the strategic dimen-sion of foreign policy, but the adoption of the Soviet model for economic development in the early 1950s belonged rather to the societal dimension. Chinese success in absorbing what has been called 'the largest technological transfer in history' was to a considerable extent the result of almost blind copying of many related Soviet institutions such as the economic planning system, the organisation of education, health and various state and urban bureaucracies. So intent were Chinese people bent on learning from, or rather imitating, their Soviet 'elder brother' that by the mid-fifties Mao in particular was beginning to voice his concern at this psychological dependency. Interestingly, it was the societal relationship which had made China dependent upon the Soviet Union in the early fifties. On the strategic plane after the performance of its armed forces in the Korean War (1950–53), the People's Republic of China (PRC) had proved itself to be a great power in its own right and thereafter it acted as very much the independent ally of the Soviet Union.

The experience of the absorption of Soviet technology in the 1950s raises important questions about China's capacity to absorb advanced technology from the West in the 1980s. Unlike in the earlier period, the current attempt in China at technology absorption is marked neither by an ideological affinity nor by institutional similarity with the foreign sup-plier. As will be discussed in Chapter 4, important problems have already arisen with regard to the major industrial plants imported in the 1970s and significant changes in policy have taken place as a result. It remains to be seen how successful these will be and what consequences, if any, will accrue to the strategic dimension of foreign policy.

Finally, the distinction facilitates discussion of the relationship between the pursuit of socialism (however it has been variously defined in China) at home, and such challenges as may be posed to it by foreign influences. Another aspect of the societal dimension of foreign relations is the impact on Chinese society of the effects of contacts with Westerners and their culture on the Chinese way of life. These contacts necessarily affect perceptions of lifestyles, personal ambitions, education and career preferences and so on. Much of this is unwelcome to the Communist Party and its leaders. Their dilemma is how to practise an 'open-door' policy in which only what they regard as desirable influences are imported into the country.

China's leaders have been particularly alert to the significance of cultural values and they have proved to be unusually active in the attempt to inculcate desired social norms among the Chinese people. Domestic arguments and conflicts about the priorities of socialist development, or even as to what is and is not truly socialist, may have profound implications for the extent to which Chinese society is isolated from or integrated with the social developments in other countries. But none of this need *necessarily* affect strategic thinking about the relative military threats of the two superpowers and the appropriate diplomatic measures to counter them. Indeed it can be argued that towards the end of his life Mao stood for a variant of 'socialism in one country', by which foreign policy was designed to ensure that China could have the necessary security to continue its domestic struggles to maintain and develop revolutionary socialism.[4] In that sense any foreign policy that could secure the socialist homeland was acceptable.

It could be suggested that such attitudes indicate the persistence of sino-centricity. However, it would be surprising if there were no signs of its persistence. For thousands of years the Chinese state developed more or less autonomously. Foreign trade was negligible and regarded as a source of interesting exotica. China's size and abundance of resources meant that through internal trade it was largely self-sufficient. Foreign influences such as Buddhism or even alien 'barbarian' invaders were absorbed and sinicised over time. This culture-based 'sino-centricity' was shattered by the 'century of shame and humiliation' imposed by the West and later by Japan from 1840 until the Communist-led 'Liberation' in 1949. During this process China's 'culturism' was replaced by nationalism.[5] But sino-centric attitudes persist albeit in new forms and in a totally transformed international system. There are complex ambiguities in the drive for modernisation in the sense that China's leaders seek to modernise in some ill-defined 'Chinese way'. Also, from the outset, the successive leaders of the PRC have sought to reassert China's greatness and establish a Chinese centrality in world affairs. In one sense China shares many of the problems and attitudes of other Third World countries in seeking to develop economically while still asserting an independent identity. In another sense China belongs to the world of great powers, but with a declaratory position which eschews the policies traditionally associated with great powers. The distinction between the societal and strategic dimensions of foreign relations should facilitate examination of these issues.

The distinction between these two dimensions of China's foreign policy is similar to that which writers on the foreign policies of Western countries used to draw between 'high' and 'low' levels. The highest level concerned military threats to national security, or at least they involved a major military element. However, a critical threat to the nation's well-being, or a significant non-military international commitment (such as the British decision to enter the European Economic Community) might also belong to this level. High policy was typically centred on issues of major importance to national security and the relevant decisions would be made by governmental leaders. The lowest levels involved policy questions which did not immediately affect the survival of the overall well-being of the state and which could be decided on a case-by-case basis in relative isolation from larger issues. Low policy typically would be decided upon below the Cabinet level of government, often by officials dealing directly with the relevant foreign organisations in a semi-autonomous way. The point of these distinctions was to highlight those aspects of foreign policy in which the executive branches of government in Western democracies were most clearly dominant and to separate them from those aspects in which discrete groups in the polity could play a more effective role.[6] In recent years, however, the distinction has become increasingly blurred in the Western democracies, partly because of the growing importance of economic inter-dependencies which have transformed the traditional considerations of national security and partly because of the proliferation of political and economic groups with special interests to protect or promote in areas where domestic and foreign concerns overlap. Moreover in Western Europe in particular there are signs in the early eighties of a breaking-up of the national consensuses which had hitherto sustained the various executives in their monopoly of decision-making on national security questions affecting nuclear weapons in particular.

Although China is very far from being a democracy in the Western sense, and it is not worth trying to distinguish between the executive and other branches of government, there is nevertheless a point to distinguishing between the 'high' and 'low' levels of decision-making. The strategic dimensions of policy have been decided only by a very few men within the Political Bureau. Although factional and other political factors were sometimes involved,[7] purposive consultation, and still less active participation in policy-making, has never reached far down the Party hierarchy. Indeed on several occasions it would seem that critical decisions were taken by only one or two men. It should be noted that China is by no means unique in this regard. This has also been true of the Western democracies at times of crisis.

The distinction between the societal and strategic dimensions of Chinese foreign policy, however, is more analytical than real. In practice, of course, there is usually a considerable overlap between them. Consider, for example, the issue of national defence: China's military capabilities relative to its adversaries and its defence postures lie at the heart of the management of strategic relations; but at the same time defence needs place great demands on national budget allocations and make major claims on China's scarce resources of skilled personnel, energy, heavy industry and advanced technology. Chinese debates about its defensive posture also involve debates about the character of socialist development desirable for the country. Typically, those who have stressed the significance of a people's army above the demands of a more professionalised army have also stood for a pattern of socialist development which emphasised mass activism and 'politics in command' at the expense of heirarchical organisation and 'experts in command'. These have not on the whole set a premium on the acquisition of advanced conventional weaponry. However, those who have stressed the need for a more professionalised armed forces have tended to press for the acquisition of advanced weapons systems from abroad. Thus, in addition to competing for scarce resources with other economic sectors and with the necessity to divert resources to agriculture and light industry to meet the needs of China's burgeoning population, the military 'modernisers' also presuppose particularly close strategic relations with countries able to supply the advanced military technology. Thus defence issues span nearly all aspects and levels of policy. Nevertheless, the distinction between the two dimensions of foreign policy is still analytically useful and it will be used here both for the purpose of assessing Mao's legacy and for examining the changes and continuities of the post-Mao era.

Some historical and comparative perspectives

The reasons for this dualism in China's foreign relations transcend organisational divisions in Chinese politics and issues of power politics. They reflect some of the historical problems in China's adjustment to the challenges first posed by the impact of the West.

In its response to the modern world China shares many of the attributes common to other Third World countries. The particularities of China's experience of a century of 'shame and humiliation' at the hands of Western and other imperialists may differ from those of other countries in the Third World, but in general the characteristics of the imperialist challenge and the Chinese struggle for independence are broadly comparable. The imperialist challenge was not that of superior military power alone; it also entailed the destruction of the traditional domestic order by incorporating the country within the modern world of the industrial revolution and that of nationalism and popular sovereignty. Like their equivalents elsewhere in the Third World, Chinese nationalists from the end of the nineteenth century, drawing on ideas derived from the West, had sought in different ways to establish a strong unified state with a new political order which would be able to preside over an effective programme of economic development. Like other Third World leaders, the rulers of the PRC have in effect sought to forge a new national identity around an imported ideology in order to modernise the economy to ensure that the country would be sufficiently powerful to sustain its independence against threats to its sovereign territory.

China is far from unique in seeking to draw a balance between the one extreme of modernising the economy through dependence on external sources and the other extreme of autarkic development. The first leads to the loss of independent control over social and other developments, leading in effect to a kind of new colonialism in which the local rulers and elites become the agents of foreign domination. The second, however, leads to an isolation in which the country's level of scientific and technological development falls so far behind that of its adversaries that its special identity may become vulnerable to external erosion. Mao's concept of the balance to be drawn between these unattractive extremes was subsumed within the term 'self-reliance', according to which one should depend on one's own resources and values in the first instance and use external sources selectively to supplement these. In practice, however, even in Mao's day the concept was subject to a number of interpretations which could allow, for example, for significant variations in the role of foreign trade in economic development.[8] During Mao's leadership of the PRC there were three separate periods of large injections of foreign technology: 1950—59, from the Soviet Union; 1963—65 and 1973—76 from Western and Japanese sources. The argument about the different interpretations of self-reliance was forcibly expressed during the last

three years of Mao's life when 'modernisers' such as Deng
Xiaoping wanted to extend foreign participation in the Chinese
economy by the sale of oil and coal while 'nativists' such as
the Gang of Four sought a more isolationist policy in which
China would depend on its own resources and maintain its
socialist identity without foreign adulteration. In essence this
is a problem which all third world countries face, but few like
China have the traditions, the power, size and wealth of
resources to contemplate autarky as a feasible option.

If, in the Islamic world, this problem has manifested itself
as a conflict between Westernisation and Islamic fundamental-
ism, in China it is possible to argue that the problem has taken
different forms at different periods in modern Chinese history.
Beginning in the 1860s and continuing into the 1880s there
were high Confucian officials who sought to copy Western
industrial techniques of armament manufacture to strengthen
China against Western armies in order to preserve the traditional values of the Chinese system. Known as 'self-strength-
eners', their approach was summed up in the famous slogan
of Zhang Zhidong (Chang Chih-tung): 'Chinese learning as
essence (*ti*) and Western learning for practical application
(*yong*).' The movement of these conservative reformers —
perhaps China's first modernisers — failed to achieve its
objectives.[9] In a sense their very slogan may be said to have
epitomised their dilemma rather than to have pointed the
way to resolving the problem. Chinese conditions and traditional Confucian values as articulated by less enlightened
officials and gentry groups militated against the application
of 'Western learning' (advanced weaponry, industrial technology, Western languages, etc.) and in so far as the latter could
have been 'used' it necessarily would have threatened the
integrity of that 'Chinese essence' it was meant to protect.

Nevertheless, the sentiments and indeed the dilemma underlying the resolve of these early modernisers could be found in
different ways in the attitudes and approaches of first the
Kuomintang and then the Communist governments. The
Kuomintang government in the decade before the Japanese
invasion of China proper in 1937 had tried to promote a
degree of industrialisation. Chiang Kai-shek sought to resurrect an appeal to remnant Confucian values as a kind of

Chinese 'essence' which would provide an ideology that would bolster the authority of his regime and that would facilitate industrialisation. The attempt to revive and breathe life into Confucianism through what he called the 'New Life Movement' in retrospect has been condemned as foredoomed to fail. It has been argued that the attempt to revive and breathe life into Confucianism, once the underlying social structures and global vision which had given it meaning and universalism no longer existed, could not but result in a particularistic authoritarianism of a Fascist kind.[10] Yet had Chiang Kai-shek won the civil war this or a variant of this might well have provided a nationalistic ideology around which Chinese unity would have found spiritual expression.[11]

At least since the Yen'an days of the 1940s 'modernisation', in the technological sense of the term, has been an explicit component of the revolutionary goals sought by all the Communist leaders including Mao. However, the fundamental tensions between revolutionary values and the practicalities of modernisation began to appear as China broke with the Soviet model in the mid-fifties. Interestingly, as late as 1956 Mao rejected the validity of the slogan of 'Chinese learning for essence, Western learning for practical application' on the grounds that the so-called Chinese essence was now universal Marxist theory which had come from the West; but less than ten years later he appeared to reverse himself and accepted it.[12] By that stage one dimension of the political struggle in China may be seen as a conflict between those who sought modernisation by stressing the roles of centralised organisation, material incentives, business efficiency and expertise and those who argued that in the long run China's economic development would be better served by giving primacy to the revolutionary politics of class struggle, mass line democracy and the inculcation of socialist consciousness. The former, who for convenience will be called the 'modernisers', were far readier to open China's doors to foreign participation in the Chinese economy than were the latter, who might be called the 'revolutionaries'. A nativist position appealed more to the 'revolutionaries' because any increase in foreign influence within Chinese society might threaten their programme.

It would be wrong and unfair to characterise Mao as a

xenophobe. He constantly argued in favour of learning from positive advanced foreign experience. But he was against blind copying or what he called 'dogmatism': 'Blindly rejecting foreign things is like blindly worshipping them. Both are incorrect and harmful'. Instead Mao favoured a synthesis:

> We must learn good things from foreign countries and also learn good things from China. Half bottles of vinegar are no good: we must change two half bottles into two whole bottles. We must master both Chinese and foreign things and combine them into an organic whole.[13]

Yet, once Mao had accepted the view in the mid-sixties that China was the only true centre of socialism in the world, and that that socialism could only be preserved through continuous revolution, the question of mixing half the Chinese bottle with some foreign variety could hardly arise.

That these considerations are not simply abstract speculations can be seen from the way the *ti—yong* dilemma has found expression in Chinese semantics and ordinary language usage. The word *yang* which originally meant 'ocean' was applied to the Western invaders from across the oceans. Hitherto invasions had come from the lesser civilised peoples to the north. *Yang* can now imply on the positive side 'modern, industrialised and strong'; but it also has the negative connotation of 'foreign, alien and Westernised'. Thus it is at once a desirable good and a corrupting influence on inferior, less developed societies.

Tu implies positively 'native and indigenous'; but negatively it denotes 'backward and primitive'. It suggests simultaneously a positive identification with Chinese common people and a negative phenomenon to be overcome. Seen in this light, Mao's injunction to the Chinese people to be both red and expert can be read as implying that they should be both *tu* and *yang*. It suggests an association between 'red' and 'native' on the one hand, and 'expert' and 'foreign' on the other.[14] Indeed for Mao's China the semantic associations can be extended still further. The red native is associated with the Communist cadre of peasant origins with the background of the idealised simple guerrilla soldier. The foreign expert is associated with the bourgeois urban intellectual with the background of academic training in the West or revisionist Russia. Thus in periods of high mass mobilisation when Mao sought populist solutions to China's problems, such as the Great Leap Forward of 1958 and the Cultural Revolution (especially during its first two years 1966—68), the red and native were exalted over the expert and foreign.

The xenophobia and anti-intellectualism of the Cultural Revolution has often been compared with that of the Boxer Uprising of 1899—1900. But the tension between *tu* and *yang* is not unique to China and, like the pursuit of power and modernity, this is shared by many other developing countries with a strong sense of nationalism. The distinctiveness of the PRC derives partly from China's size and history as well as the intensity of its leaders' commitment to socialism and self-reliance and partly from China's significance as a global power.

The PRC as a global power

If in some respects China shares the attributes of other Third World countries, there are others in which it is clearly distinctive. None more so than in its position as a great power of global significance. The PRC is the only power which by its independent actions over the last three decades has been able to exercise a major influence on the strategic central balance between the two superpowers. Its shift of alignment from the Soviet Union to the United States, and the general recognition of strategic tripolarity, have had profound implications for the international system. But China's strategic significance is complex and somewhat paradoxical. The PRC lacks the capacity to project its forces far beyond its borders and in strictly military terms China cannot be considered to be more than a regional power — and a rather limited one at that. Yet the PRC is the only state to have been threatened at different times with nuclear attack by both the superpowers and it is the only country to claim invincibility to invasion by either.

The PRC has also demonstrated a high degree of autonomy in world affairs without developing long-term dependencies. This has facilitated very significant changes in its foreign policy orientations. It is true that the foreign policies of all countries are subject to innumerable changes over a lengthy period of 20—30 years, but since the Second World War no major country has changed its fundamental alignments and world roles to the extent of China. Under Mao's leadership the PRC has shifted from a close alliance with the Soviet Union in the 1950s to a *rapprochement* with the United States in the 1970s. In the 1960s the PRC challenged the generally accepted international order by seeking a revolutionary international united front from *below* (i.e. with popular movements) against American imperial power; but in the 1970s China has sought an anti-Soviet international united front from *above* (i.e., with those who wield state power) which has led many to consider that the PRC has been transformed into a conservative power with respect to the international system. These 30 years or more have also witnessed the transformation of China's international status from a position of weakness and isolation to the rank of a great power.

China's rise to great power status and its major foreign policy changes have not only altered China's role in world affairs, but they have contributed to the transformation of international politics in general and East—West relations in particular. Sino-American enmity in the fifties and sixties involved the United States in two major wars in Asia and in maintaining a strategic readiness to fight what used to be called 'two and a half wars' — i.e., a war each in Asia and Europe (against China and Russia respectively) and half a war elsewhere. Since the end of the 1960s it has been the Soviet Union which has been faced with the prospect of war on two fronts. As seen from Moscow, the world's most populous country is aligned with the world's most powerful country in combination with the most economically advanced countries of Asia and Europe against the Soviet Union. Something like a quarter of the Soviet military might has been deployed in the Far East near the borders with China. China's realignment has also had a profound impact on its region: changing close allies like Vietnam into bitter enemies, and hostile relations with several Southeast Asian countries into those of friendship. But it has also altered other aspects of international politics. There are few areas of the world which are unaffected by the ramifications of the Sino-Soviet enmity. Moreover by complicating the Soviet position in the Third World, China has undoubtedly helped the United States. Despite Sino-American differences on many Third World issues, there is a sense in which they parallel each other. China makes it much more difficult for the Soviet Union to present itself as a 'natural ally' of the Third World. This is a far cry from the fifties when the Third World was presented by the Chinese as an associate of the socialist camp against United States imperialism.

Despite these immense changes there have also been significant continuities in China's foreign relations over this period. These include continuities in strategic perspectives, the goals of foreign policy and unresolved tensions and problems. However, perhaps the most significant element of continuity derives from China's relative weakness as against its super-power adversaries. This has placed China in essentially a reactive position so that its leaders have had to respond to the threats and challenges of others. Thus China's shift of alignment from East to West may be seen as the reaction to the change in the direction of the main threat from West to East. In this sense Peking has been continuously preoccupied with defending China's independence and national security against more powerful military adversaries. Seen in this per-spective, it can be argued that China's foreign policy goals have remained relatively constant. These would include the drive for great power status; the resolution of border problems and the consolidation of territorial unity despite conditions of perceived insecurity; the maintenance of military independ-ence and of China's cultural and economic integrity against corrupting alien influences; and ensuring an external environ-ment which would allow economic development and the building of a socialist society. However, as has already been suggested, these goals may be seen to mask considerable ten-sions and ambiguities between the claims of 'revolution' and 'modernisation'.

The shift of alignment from East to West was by no means a smooth or a rapid process. There was an intervening period in which China opposed both superpowers — or rather both superpowers were perceived as colluding together against

China and its independent aspirations which included the desire to develop a nuclear weapons capability. During this period the PRC sought to establish an international united front centred upon Third World radicalism and anti-imperialism. Therefore in assessing China's behaviour as a global power it is useful to distinguish between three phases of China's foreign policy which roughly coincide with each of the three decades from the fifties to the seventies: The Sino-Soviet Alliance, Third World Radicalism and Alignment with the West.

These different phases can be understood as Chinese reactions to the perceived changing challenges of the superpowers and to the emergence of multi-polarity in the international system in which China played a part. But they can also be related to domestic developments within China. The fifties was broadly the period in which China followed the Soviet model and relied to a considerable extent upon trade with the Soviet bloc. The Sino-Soviet rupture was in part related to the Chinese abandonment of many of the features of the Soviet model and the ending of Soviet aid. The sixties, therefore, was a time in which China developed its own model of self-reliance almost to the point of autarky. The opening to the West in the seventies was pursued primarily for strategic reasons, but it also facilitated access to Western advanced technology. In other words, these three periods roughly coincided with significant domestic political—economic reorientations. The shift from one period to another involved significant societal changes and they became important factors in leadership factional conflicts. That was especially true of the development of the Sino-Soviet conflict and of the opening to the United States.

Domestic politics and foreign policy

There is an interpretation of Chinese foreign policy which asserts that the main explanation for its various fundamental changes of alignment is to be found in the changes which took place in China's domestic political order. In this view, for example, the pursuit of radical mass mobilisation politics at home has led to the promotion of revolutionary policies abroad. In particular, proponents of this view cite the Great

Leap Forward of 1958 as the origin of a more radical leftist foreign policy and the early phase of the Cultural Revolution (1966–68) as the source of the revolutionary isolationism in foreign affairs of that time. Such an explanation is too mechanistic. It is one thing to allow for the influence of domestic politics in foreign policy as an important factor among others, and it is quite another to allot it such a deterministic role. Actually the theory that moderation or radicalism at home leads respectively to moderation or radicalism abroad simply does not hold true in many instances. For example, the radical high tide of collectivisation in the latter half of 1955 coincided with the moderate phase of Chinese foreign policy associated with the Bandung Conference and its aftermath. And the moderate economic retrenchment of 1959–61 coincided with the immoderate sharpening of the Sino-Soviet dispute and with a rather radical style of foreign policy in Africa and Asia. Generally speaking, as the weaker power whose leaders perceived their country to be under perpetual threat from one or other of the superpowers, China's foreign policy necessarily tended to react to external pressures rather than to initiate developments which it could not hope to control.[15] Moreover, given the centralisation of decision-making on foreign affairs and its organisational seclusion from the domestic society, it is difficult to see why the conduct of foreign affairs could not be relatively independent of the domestic order. Chinese officials and intellectuals have always claimed that Mao Zedong and Zhou Enlai monopolised the main decision-making in foreign affairs. The accounts of those who had negotiated with the Chinese on matters of high politics such as Nikita Khrushchev and Henry Kissinger very much substantiate that claim.[16]

This is not to argue that divisions in the leadership because of factional maneouvring, or of differences over the proper lines of development of Chinese society, or indeed of disagreements as to how best to respond to a foreign threat, did not affect foreign policy. It is difficult, however, to see by what process, let us say, the radicalisation of Chinese society would *necessarily* lead to the radicalisation of foreign policy. Domestic changes in themselves could not alter China's external strategic environment — at least in the short run. Moreover, there are few countries in the world whose society has been more insulated from foreign influences than China. China has been relatively free from the complex web of interdependencies which characterise the external relations of other great powers. In Mao's day the PRC not only avoided imposing dependencies on others, but after the break with the Russians it strenuously eschewed policies which would have made China dependent on others, either. The extent to which this may be said to have been changed by Mao's successors will be examined in part two of this book. Given the relative insularity of Chinese society there was little reason for arguments about foreign policy to percolate very far down from the top leadership. Once a foreign policy line had been determined then strenuous efforts would be made to propagandise it among the Chinese people; so that Chinese people were remarkably well informed about their country's declared position on foreign affairs, but they knew little of the alternatives which had been discussed among the leaders and still less were they in a position to assess their respective merits. As has been noted before, despite the wealth of material on discord about domestic politics which has come out from China over the last two decades, there is very little indeed on disagreements on foreign policy matters. This may have been the result of a deliberate policy to preserve national security secrets. But in view of the considerable evidence available on disputes about sensitive military affairs a more likely explanation is that foreign policy questions involved only the highest of leaders, and other levels of decision-makers were simply excluded from the foreign policy process.

On the one occasion when foreign policy questions were debated among the 'masses' it was apparent that their understanding of the outside world was minimal and that the focus of their concerns was exceedingly narrow. Thus during the early stages of the Cultural Revolution some of the Red Guards sought to identify revisionist aspects about the conduct of Chinese foreign policy in the same way that they had identified them on domestic questions. They concentrated on only three main issue areas:

(1) Certain leaders were alleged to have been conciliatory

on matters of high principle in negotiating with the Russians in the early sixties. These leaders were also accused of having promoted the policy of 'three reconciliations and one reduction' (*san he yi shao*) i.e., reconciliation with revisionism (the Soviet Union), imperialism (the United States) and reactionaries (India) and reduction of aid to the Third World. This paralleled a similar charge that within China they had encouraged capitalism in agriculture through 'the three freedoms and the one contract' (*san zi yi bao*).

(2) Overseas Chinese, in the view of radical Red Guards, should have been mobilised to spearhead revolutionary struggles in Southeast Asia. The relevant Chinese leaders who had not done so were castigated for revisionism.

(3) Chinese diplomats were upbraided for not maintaining a spartan revolutionary lifestyle.

All this simply adds up to a charge that certain leaders had betrayed the course of revolution abroad as well as at home, but this does not constitute a coherent foreign policy. Indeed these points betray little or no understanding of the world outside China.

In a general sense the official propaganda organs during the first two years of the Cultural Revolution presented China as an isolated revolutionary bastion of socialism. The outside world was depicted in the stark Manichean terms of goodies and baddies as ostensibly applied domestically within China. Thus 90 per cent of the people of the world supposedly revered Mao as in China. Perhaps impressionable young Chinese were taken in. But outside China, while Mao may have been respected by some, the so-called Maoists were always a tiny minority even in radical circles and there was never any question of a mass following. The upheavals of the Cultural Revolution, accompanied by a degree of xenophobia, led to many diplomatic incidents. These caused irritation and bewilderment, but they never seriously threatened the fundamentals of the strategic aspects of foreign policy.

In the wake of the Soviet invasion of Czechoslovakia in August 1968 the PRC immediately took steps to resume normal diplomatic behaviour. Rapid overtures were made to normalise relations with Third World governments and

capitalists states of the second rank. But the first countries
to be wooed were those bordering the Soviet Union, such as
Iran and Turkey, or those of particular concern to the Soviet
Union in the Balkans, such as Romania and Yugoslavia. The
overriding significance of the strategic dimension may be
gauged from the fact that only weeks before the Shah had
been pilloried in China as the reactionary butcher of the Iran-
ian people, while Yugoslavia has been regarded as the ultimate
hotbed of revisionism.

Until the recent post-Mao reforms the PRC had a command
economy in which the only economic organisations concerned
with foreign trade as with other aspects of foreign economic
relations were highly centralised.

It can be argued that there were many organisations at
various levels in China which were greatly affected by the
consequences of particular foreign policy decisions, but there
is little evidence to suggest that they played a role as active
participants in the making of those decisions. Moreover, unlike
decision-making in the domestic arena, China's leaders did
not even have to depend upon a wide range of bureaucracies
to carry out their foreign policies. The administrators of
Fujian Province, for example, were doubtless affected by the
Chinese troop movements associated with the various crises
concerning Taiwan and the offshore islands in the 1950s, but
there is no evidence or reason to suggest that Mao felt called
upon to deliberate with them over his various options at the
time. They may have been required to play a part in facilitat-
ing the logistic exercises attendant upon the troop movements,
but they would have had no leeway in interpreting their
superior orders, whereas as provincial administrators they
played an altogether different role in implementing domestic
policies related to their own province.

This does not mean that domestic politics did not impinge
on foreign policy. Foreign policy questions were frequently
the subject of disputes in the leadership. Three broad types
of leadership disputes may be identified: differences of
opinion regarding domestic priorities and the appropriate
foreign policy to sustain them; conflicts of interest in which a
specific foreign policy may be regarded as enhancing or threatening a cherished domestic interest; and factional conflict in
which a foreign policy issue may be used in order to discredit

or advance a particular faction. To be sure, aspects of all three may be involved in any particular issue; nevertheless it is useful for analytical clarity to distinguish between them.

Perhaps the most significant differences of opinion to emerge during Mao's leadership centred on relations with the Soviet Union. There were those whose view of the Communist Party and its role differed from Mao's and who were more attached to the traditional Communist view of the significance of relations with other Communist Parties. Perhaps the most striking example after 1949 concerns those who were loath to go as far as Mao in 1966 in condemning the Soviet Party as not only revisionist, but as actively counter-revolutionary. In so doing Mao deliberately cut off relations with other East Asian Communist Parties. The most notable exponent of the contrary view attaching significance to inter-Party links and to the organisational importance of the Party was Liu Shaoqi who until that point ranked second to Mao.[17] Another current of opinion which surfaced in the early sixties was advanced by those who took a more liberal view than Mao on cultural matters generally and towards intellectuals in particular. They were keen to develop more contacts with western countries. The best-known advocate of these views was the then Foreign Minister, Chen Yi — the forthright scholar/general — who at that time spoke out in favour of greater intellectual freedom and who was said to have been the initiator of the policy of cultivating relations with the West Europeans and Japan after the break with the Soviet Union in 1960.[18] Yet another alternative current of opinion advocated that China should follow a more export-orientated pattern of economic development. Chen Yun — a very prominent leader in the forties and fifties whose star was dimmed but not eclipsed from the Great Leap Forward until the end of the Cultural Revolution and who has since re-emerged to rank fifth in the post-Mao hierarchy — is regarded as the main proponent of this view.[19]

Differences involving conflicts of interest tended to arise in a context in which a change in foreign policy was perceived as challenging a cherished interest. The best-known examples of such occurrences involved the leaders of the armed forces. Thus the beginnings of the break with the Soviet Union in 1958 involved national security questions and the appropriate character and role of the armed forces. There is evidence to suggest that some of the most senior commanders sought to continue the professionalisation of the People's Liberation Army (PLA) along Soviet lines and therefore they challenged the direction of policy which exacerbated the rift with the Soviet Union.[20] Another example concerns the then Chief of the General Staff, Luo Ruiqing, who in 1965 promoted greater professionalism and advocated a different defence strategy to that favoured by Mao and Lin Biao, and who therefore differed with Mao on the proper response to the massive American intervention in the Vietnam War in 1965.[21]

Perhaps the best-known examples of factional conflict involving foreign policy issues occurred during the Cultural Revolution. All political issues at that time became enmeshed in the factional intrigues for the political succession to Mao. Thus Lin Biao and his faction opposed the *rapprochement* with the United States at a time in which his domestic political base was being undermined by Mao. It is difficult, even over 10 years after the event, to separate his opposition to the new foreign policy line from his struggle to retain power. Moreover the difficulty is further compounded by the fact that the struggle for power involved a major political and ideological issue: Mao, having rediscovered some of his Leninist concerns, sought to demote the armed forces from their highly visible political role in running the country and he was actively engaged in restoring the Communist Party as an effective organisation. This involved the restoration of many of those leaders who had been purged as revisionists during the early stages of the Cultural Revolution. Interestingly, the Chinese authorities have released much material recounting Lin Biao's bizarre alleged plots to assassinate the Chairman, but no official documentation has been released concerning the foreign policy issue and only very little on the clash of principles between Mao and Lin.[22] A better-documented account exists of the opposition by the Gang of Four and their associates to Deng Xiaoping's plan to acquire Western technology in exchange for Chinese raw materials. Dubbed as an example of the latter's alleged 'national betrayal' this played a part in the Gang's campaign against Deng and the other modernisers in their bid for power. Even in this case it is possible to argue that this was not just cynical manoeuvring

on behalf of the radicals, but that it was a part of the rear-
guard struggle to hold onto the 'newborn things of the
Cultural Revolution'. In other words, they may have believed
in their radicalism and that it was necessary to struggle for
power in order to sustain it. Nevertheless it is clear in retrospect that, unlike the previous years, the Cultural Revolution
period was one in which the factionalism inherent in Chinese
politics reached its apogee. That factionalism then spilt over
into foreign affairs, an arena which Mao Zedong and Zhou
Enlai had hitherto kept relatively free from such influences.

Despite these various domestic influences on foreign policy,
it is nonetheless clear that unlike the domestic arena, Mao's
hold of the reins of foreign policy was never broken. There
are no examples known to Western scholars where Mao was
overruled by his colleagues on a foreign policy issue. Even in
the 1959—62 period, when in the wake of the disasters of the
Great Leap Forward Mao was ignored by his colleagues on
many important domestic issues, the evidence suggests that
his was the decisive hand at the helm of foreign policy. He
was subsequently to complain of those years when his colleagues supposedly treated him as an ancestor at his own
funeral; yet it was he who at this time was steadily propelling
the division with the Soviet Union.[23]

Much of the argument about the supposed domestic sources
of foreign policy changes by Western scholars may arise out
of the attempt to extend to China approaches based on the
American experience of foreign policy making, where indeed
this may apply. In China, however, it seems more likely that
the opposite might apply. In other words, the broad strategic
orientations of foreign policy have played a large part in
shaping the patterns of domestic change. Thus the Sino—
Soviet alliance led to the adoption of the full Soviet model.
The strategic break with the Soviet Union led to isolation and
the strategic alignment with the West paved the way for the
emphasis on modernisation. Reality, however, would appear
to be too complex for either argument to carry ultimate con-
viction. But it is surprising that the second argument has yet
to be developed in the scholarly literature when the field is
replete with attempts to substantiate the first.

The three phases of China's foreign policy

The foregoing discussion may be summarised to suggest that despite various domestic influences on the making of foreign policy, the dominant factors which caused changes in China's foreign policy on the strategic plane were the policies of the two superpowers and China's attempt to maintain its independence and become a great power — as interpreted primarily by Mao. His legacy in what I have called here the strategic and societal dimensions of foreign policy will be examined separately in the next chapters, but it may be useful first to survey briefly the main phases of China's foreign policy and consider the relationship between the two dimensions.

The Sino—Soviet alliance

China's alliance with the Soviet Union in the 1950s was the period in which the 'strategic' and 'societal' dimensions of its foreign policy were most closely interlinked. Their strategic association was an important and critical factor in establishing limits to American military actions during the Korean War and still later the Soviet nuclear shield provided deterrence against American threats. The Soviet Union also extended invaluable military assistance both in terms of equipment and advice towards the modernisation of the armed forces. It is a measure of the significance of the Soviet support that the technological levels of China's conventional forces at the beginning of the eighties were not much in advance of those established by the end of the fifties when Soviet assistance came to an end. The Soviet impact on the 'societal' level was even more marked. The core of China's heavy industry was built up through Soviet aid; the economic planning system and its priorities were copied directly from the Soviet Union, as was much of the state administration in the urban sector. The organisation of education, culture, health, sports, trade unions and welfare, for example, were entirely modelled on their Soviet equivalents. Thousands of Soviet advisers were located in ministries, factories and research organisations. Russian was the first foreign language taught at schools and thousands of Chinese students were sent to Russia, while a whole generation of officials imbibed Soviet administrative practices.

It would seem that the close interlocking of the 'strategic' and 'societal' planes which was such a marked feature of the alliance with the Soviet Union amounted to a kind of dependency. The break-up of the alliance in the late fifties and early sixties may be seen as a reaction to that dependency. Mao in particular was irked by this even before cracks in the alliance began to be visible in 1956.[24] By the mid-fifties an independent set of Chinese strategic concerns began to emerge, but it was only once Mao began to develop an independent Chinese way to socialism in 1958 coupled with a diverging set of strategic attitudes towards the United States that Sino-Soviet relations began to move towards a rupture. Interestingly, Chinese economists in the late seventies looked back to the fifties as a period of genuine economic achievement. While disparaging much of Mao's subsequent economic policies, they have neither praised the Soviet factor in that earlier period nor commented directly upon the end of the dependency relationship. Judging by the CPC (Communist Party of China) Central Committee's official review of its history and its verdict on Mao of 1981,[25] it is the nationalistic element in Mao's approach which is implicitly affirmed even while his political values and economic methods were openly rejected. In the late seventies Chinese officials let it be known that they had come to reject as fallacious many of the arguments which had been put forward by their side in the famous ideological polemics with the Soviet Party in the early sixties. 'Revisionism' was no longer to be part of their political lexicon. Nevertheless at the same time Mao was praised for his role in having protected China's unity and having enhanced its national dignity while elevating the country into one of the world's major powers. These leaders have in effect placed the Sino-Soviet conflict exclusively on the strategic plane. They have tended to emphasise a point made repeatedly by Mao in the latter half of the fifties (even though it was not made public at the time) that one of the main problems of the Soviet leaders was their 'great nation chauvinism'. The perspectives and problems of the post-Mao leaders, however, will be discussed at length in Part Two.

To return to the Sino-Soviet alliance, perhaps the most interesting question in retrospect is not why it split up, but why China's leaders should have started out by transforming their country into almost a Soviet dependency. After all, their revolution had been genuinely novel and independent and under Mao's leadership they had pursued their own strategy, often against Stalin's advice.

The dependency (which will be examined more closely in the next chapter) was more a product of the circumstances of the Cold War and the pressures of both the Soviet Union and the United States than it was the choice of Mao. In the summer of 1949 Mao had declared that the New China would lean to the side by the Soviet Union, but at the same time he envisaged that China would be an independent member of an extensive united front centred on the Soviet Union, trading freely with the Western world while posing as a unique revolutionary model to the peoples of Asia. Moreover, it was to be a new China with its sovereignty, unity, territorial integrity and essential dignity restored. At the same time it was also true that Mao, as well as some of his less aggressively independent colleagues, chose to copy much of the Soviet model. They were conscious of their inexperience in running cities, let alone running a huge state and transforming the economy along socialist lines. The prestige of Stalin and the Soviet Union was very high. At that time the Soviet way was regarded as the only one. The notion of different paths to socialism had yet to be formulated even by the Yugoslavs. Nevertheless Mao clearly anticipated that he would have much more room for manoeuvre than subsequently proved to be the case. Throughout 1949 the American Administration proved impervious to the various diplomatic feelers which Zhou Enlai in particular sent in its direction. Zhou's position can be summed up in his crisp observation to an American emissary at the time: 'we shall lean to one side, but how far depends on you'.[26] Meanwhile the American Administration, imbued with the spirit of the Cold War and fearful of a domestic backlash to the 'loss of China' proceeded to pressurise its European allies not to recognise the PRC.

Stalin, for his part, was deeply suspicious of the new China whose liberation he had tried to thwart. In Mao's words of 1962:

> After the victory of the revolution he next suspected China of being a Yugoslavia, and that I would be a second Tito. Later when I went to Moscow to sign the Sino-Soviet Treaty of Alliance and Mutual Assistance, we had to go through another struggle. He was not willing to sign a treaty. After two months of negotiations he at last signed. When did Stalin begin to have confidence in us? It was at the time of the Resist America, Aid Korea campaign from the winter of 1950. He then came to believe that we were not Tito, not Yugoslavia.[27]

Perhaps Stalin had been informed of Zhou's approaches to the Americans. In any case from his perspective, the harshly realistic and suspicious Stalin had every reason to regard Mao's total victory as a mixed blessing. A proud and fiercely independent China, full of revolutionary vigour which was beyond his powers to control, would inevitably pose problems to the Soviet Union. Ever since the Yalta Conference of 1945 Stalin had consistently sought to recover and consolidate the areas in the Far East which had been lost earlier in the century, especially as a result of the Russian defeat by Japan in 1905. Aspects of this figured in the Sino-Soviet treaty. Stalin kept his commitments to China under a tight rein and it was not until after his death when the political balance between Mao and Stalin's successors changed in favour of the former.

In so far as Stalin had been apprehensive lest Mao and his colleagues should succeed in improving Sino-American relations he must have perceived the Korean war as very much to his advantage. Truman's reaction of imposing a tight trade embargo on China, and of interposing the American Seventh Fleet between the mainland and Taiwan island, ensured that the Sino-American conflict would not be easily resolved. The open armed conflict between China and America confirmed this still further. There is evidence to suggest that he delayed military supplies to the Chinese forces in Korea for some time.[28] Perhaps startled by the not entirely welcome sweeping victories of the Chinese in the early stages of their intervention, he was prepared to be more forthcoming once the stalemate between the two sets of combatants developed along the 38th Parallel, and it would have been a useful reminder to the Chinese of their dependence on the Soviet Union.

Nevertheless China's relative success in Korea turned out to be a major factor in the emergence of the new China as a significant independent power in world politics in its own right. Noting that the ceasefire agreement was not concluded until after Stalin's death in March 1953, some have suggested that he may have been instrumental in having delayed it. But the evidence is circumstantial at best, and that hypothesis implies a greater degree of Soviet control over Chinese decision-making than appeared to be the case. A more likely hypothesis is that the Chinese would have had every incentive to speed up the agreement after Stalin's death, partly because of the greater pressure from the incoming Eisenhower Administration, and partly because of their uncertainties about the new Soviet leaders.

The void left by Stalin improved China's relative political 'weight' in Moscow. It was only then that it became possible to elicit Soviet support for the projected First Five Year Plan. The Minister in charge of the plan had been kicking his heels in Moscow continuously for 8 months from August 1952, but it was not until 8 months later, in March the following year when Zhou Enlai came to attend Stalin's funeral (where he was significantly the only foreign pallbearer of the coffin), that an agreement was reached. And it was not until September that some of the details of the agreement were made public. Further Soviet assistance was announced during the visit to Peking by Khrushchev and Bulganin the following year. The plan which was supposed to have started on 1 January 1953 was not made public until 1955. The core of the plan was the Soviet-supplied heavy industrial enterprises. Yet it was in 1955–56 that the Chinese began to move away from the Soviet model. Nevertheless the basis for China's industrialisation continued to be this Soviet assistance which was being supplied right up to 1960.

The foregoing discussions suggest very strongly that China's economic dependence upon the Soviet Union did not in any significant sense lead to Soviet controls over China. On the contrary, it was Stalin's very limited assistance and tough bargaining which tied China more closely to the Soviet Union. The provision of substantial Soviet aid was a consequence of China's increased independence and greater political leverage in Moscow. Sino-Soviet economic relations were a product of their political and strategic relationship rather than vice-versa. If in the middle fifties Mao was irked by the slavish imitations of Soviet practices and institutions in China, it was not because these had been imposed on his countrymen from the outset, but rather because they so readily and voluntarily submitted themselves to the foreign orthodoxy to the neglect of their own revolutionary traditions and sense of independence. By the late fifties Mao was not only asserting that many of the Soviet approaches were unsuited to China's needs and conditions, but he was querying the Soviet refusal to learn from China.[29]

It was also in the wake of the Korean War and the Geneva Conference of 1954 (where China for the first time in modern history had played an active part as an acknowledged truly independent great power in shaping the pattern of world order) that China's foreign policy began to develop new approaches and dimensions which drew it away from the close embrace of the Soviet community. These were the policies commonly associated with the 'Bandung Phase' of China's foreign relations.

The 'Bandung Phase' (so named because of Zhou Enlai's diplomatic performance at the first conference of Afro-Asian countries held in Bandung in 1955), was characterised by a readiness to deal with all governments regardless of their political hue and to solve all problems with moderation and diplomacy. It was as a result of Bandung that the first offshore island crisis with the United States was settled and moves begun which led to Sino-American ambassadorial talks being held first at Geneva and then at Warsaw. The 'Bandung Phase' may also be seen as the fruit of the diplomacy conducted with India and Burma in 1954, when India and China signed an agreement which introduced the famous 'Five Principles of Peaceful Co-existence' that the Chinese have claimed ever since has determined their intergovernmental relations (people-to-people diplomacy and inter-Party relations have been regarded as unaffected by those principles — not always to the satisfaction of all the other governments concerned).

The 'Bandung Phase' had, however, had a deeper significance in that it marked the beginning of the Third World dimensions of the PRC's foreign policy. For China's leaders, and especially for Mao, this signified recognition that the nationalist leaders (regardless as to whether or not they were bourgeois) of the newly independent Third World countries were potential allies of the Chinese in the alignment against imperialism. Moreover it was from this time that China's leaders emphasised that China and the Third World countries shared a common history of colonialism and a common need to develop their industrially backward countries. Neither of these points was true for the Soviet Union. Mao also began to argue that the spearhead of imperialism was directed in the first instance against the countries of the Third World rather than the countries of the socialist camp. The full import of this approach was not to become clear until later in the fifties and early sixties. Meanwhile, basking in the glow of the aftermath of its recent diplomatic triumphs while concentrating domestically upon the economic programme of the First Five Year Plan, the PRC leadership put great store by the evident relaxation of international tensions which it was experiencing. Zhou Enlai reported to the National People's Congress in June 1956, in words remarkably similar to those of Khruschev: 'even within United States ruling circles, some people who are more sober minded are beginning to realise that there is no future for the policy of cold war and the policy of strength'.[30] Later the Chinese criticised Khruschev for this. But one important difference between Zhou and Khruschev was that Zhou held that these people were not the real holders of power, whereas for the latter these people were at the very top and that they needed to be treated with moderation lest they be pressured to take up more hawkish positions. The Chinese view was that of emergence of relatively pacific groups in the American leadership was not the result of any sudden enlightenment about the dangers of nuclear war. Instead this was the result of stepped-up countervailing pressure by the socialist camp, the newly independent countries and the internal contradictions in the imperialist camp. Thus Zhou's report cited above went on to observe that the debate between the hawks and the doves in Washington showed that they were 'in an acute dilemma in which both peace and war are difficult alternatives'.

These and other disagreements with the Soviet Union which were growing in the late fifties may be seen as reflecting some of the very great differences between the two countries. Unlike China, the Soviet Union was already a highly industrialised country, which had been one of the great imperialist powers of the nineteenth century, with a different revolutionary tradition in the twentieth century and which by the latter fifties was developing different strategic interests from China. Superficially, their leaders shared the same ideology and outlook on world affairs, but in fact there were important differences which their common Marxist—Leninist language at first tended to minimise and later to exacerbate. Beginning with Stalin, and perhaps even earlier with Lenin, Soviet leaders have tended to place their revolution and their country as the most important factor in effecting the roll-back of imperialism and the promotion of socialist change across the world. They have tended to portray the future of the world as determined by the struggle between the forces of socialism centred upon the Soviet Union and those of imperialism, which since 1945 have centred on the United States. Therefore the continued strength and security of the Soviet Union has been regarded as the first priority of Communists throughout the world. True proletarian internationalism consists in the Soviet view of being closely linked to the Soviet Union, following its experience and sheltering under its protective umbrella. The Chinese revolution, however, had many of the characteristics of national liberation; unlike its Soviet predecessor, none of its leaders ever thought that the revolution would fail or lose its way if it remained confined to China and did not immediately spread elsewhere. Furthermore, proletarian internationalism for Mao never meant that one Party would lay down the lines for others to follow, or that one Party would sit at the fulcrum of a tightly organised alliance with centrally co-ordinated networks radiating outwards. For him proletarian internationalism meant mutually supportive, popular, independent, revolutionary activity. United fronts rather than formal alliances were his preferred mode of co-operative endeavours.

One of the consequences of China's membership of the socialist camp and the similarity of its organisational structures and ideology to those of the other members of the camp was that fundamental challenges to the system in other parts of the camp necessarily had profound implications for China too. This may be seen in terms of the dichotomy suggested in this book as belonging to the 'societal' plane. Thus the debunking of Stalin and the assault on the cult of personality in the Soviet Union in early 1956 became an important factor in the curtailment of Mao's exalted role later that year at the Eighth Party Congress. Likewise the upheavals in Poland and Hungary in that year made their mark in China and were a contributory factor to the development of Mao's distinctive theorising about classes in socialist society and the launching of the Hundred Flowers movement in the first half of the following year.[31]

The turning point in China's foreign policy took place towards the end of the fifties. During this time there was a growing strategic association between the Soviet Union and the United States at a time in which the United States was pursuing a harder line against China and playing a more interventionist role in the Third World. China's overtures towards the United States in 1955 and 1956 had come to naught. The United States had unilaterally downgraded the ambassadorial talks at Geneva, and the Secretary of State, Dulles, had rejected Zhou's offer to have a group of respected journalists visit China. Instead it was decided in Washington in February (and carried out in May 1957) to deploy nuclear-tipped surface-to-surface Matador missiles in both South Korea and Taiwan. On 28 June 1957 Dulles delivered a major speech on Sino-American relations in San Francisco, in which he put an end to any remaining prospects for improving relations by declaring that the American Administration would do all it could to contribute to the passing of the Communist Government in China.

It was against this backcloth that China's leaders, not surprisingly, developed a new foreign policy which saw no merit in seeking to conciliate the United States. On the contrary, they developed a policy of opposition to American attempts to impose their vision of order on world politics and they identified their country with those people and movements in the Third World who were prepared to resist those attempts. If these developments are examined through the perspectives of Peking, the Chinese responses become clearer and more understandable without having to resort to doubtful explanations of the domestic sources of foreign policy. To be sure, changes in China's domestic arrangements may very well affect the 'style' of its foreign policy. But style should not be confused with substance.[32]

From a Third World united front to revolutionary isolation

China's foreign policy during the sixties was characterised by growing opposition to both the superpowers, and by attempts to associate the Third World and the medium capitalist powers in a common united front against them. With the failure of these attempts China, during the first few years of the Cultural Revolution, turned towards a more isolationist position of a revolutionary bastion against imperialism, revisionism and all reactionaries. The rupture with the Soviet Union was a drawn-out process. Thus it was not until the spring of 1966 that Mao broke Party relations with the CPSU (Communist Party of the Soviet Union). Yet it was in July 1963 after the signing of the nuclear test ban treaty between Russia, America and Britain that China declared that the Soviet Union was conspiring with these powers against it. An editorial in the *People's Daily* of 3 August was quite explicit:

> It is most obvious that the tripartite treaty is aimed at tying hands. The U.S. representative to the Moscow talks has said publicly that the United States, Britain and the Soviet Union were able to arrive at an agreement, because 'we could work together to prevent China getting a nuclear capability' . . . This is a US—Soviet alliance against China pure and simple.

Chinese official statements also claimed that the Soviet position facilitated American offensive designs against the Third World. In Mao's perception, the Soviet Union, having failed to subordinate China to its strategic designs in 1958—59, was seeking to coerce and manipulate the PRC into its framework of collusion and contention with the United States so that Russia could achieve certain great-power objectives. At the same time he argued that the American government was engaged in a large-scale imperialist offensive directed against the Third World and that, although not a primary target at this stage, China was the main obstacle to this. Not only were the Russian leaders said to be conniving at this, but together with reactionaries or those confused by the Soviet socialistic rhetoric, there were various elements who were instrumental to sowing division in the Third World which served the predatory interests of the superpowers.

1962 was a critical year in the establishment of this picture in Mao's eyes. Just as China was emerging from the great crisis after the failure of the Great Leap Forward it was confronted with three major challenges from different directions of its vulnerable borders; In Xinjiang tens of thousands of Kazakhs crossed the border to the Soviet Union; in the southeast there was an invasion scare from Taiwan; and in the southwest an actual border war was fought with India. Both the Soviet Union and the United States came to the aid of India, thus proving to Chinese satisfaction an unholy relationship between reactionaries (India's ruling circles), revisionism (the Soviet Union) and imperialism (the United States).

The Chinese response was to try and establish two kinds of international fronts against the United States from which the Russians would be excluded. One was directed towards the small and medium capitalist countries who were portrayed as wishing to assert their national independence against American attempts to control them. A *People's Daily* editorial of 21 January described them as belonging to the 'second intermediate zone' (the 'first' consisted of the Third World) between America and the Soviet Union. They were said to have a 'dual character', while their ruling classes are exploiters and oppressors, these countries themselves are subject to U.S. control and bullying'. Apart from gaining diplomatic recognition by De Gaulle's government, increasing trade and importing some

30 major industrial plants, the Chinese had little to show for the initiative.

The other international front was directed towards the Third World. China's efforts culminated at the second Afro-Asian summit in Algeria in 1965. However these too were unsuccessful. By 1966 China had become rather isolated as two of its major associates in Afro-Asia, Sukarno and the PKI (Parti Kommunisti Indonesia) in Indonesia and Nkrumah in Ghana, had lost power because of domestic coups. To be sure the diplomatic picture was less bleak in the sense that many of the newly independent countries in the Third World had extended diplomatic recognition to the PRC rather than to the Chiang Kai-shek government and the last vote in the General Assembly of the United Nations before the Cultural Revolution on the question of the PRC's representation there had produced a tie. (This was the first time that the United States had not won outright — but a two-thirds majority in favour of the PRC would have been necessary in order to win the day). Nevertheless from Mao's point of view such developments, while not unwelcome, did not go to the heart of the issue *vis à vis* the superpowers, especially given the American intervention in the Vietnam War from early 1965.

The American intervention in the Vietnam War ineluctably brought the Soviet Union to the aid of a socialist country under attack. And while it precipitated a complex strategic debate in Peking and exacerbated the leadership conflict on the eve of the Cultural Revolution, it was not without its compensations from Mao's perspective. It made it more difficult for Russo-American collusion against China. That was probably one of the reasons for his vehement opposition to any suggestion of a negotiated settlement to the war which he consistently regarded as a means by which the war would be settled to suit the interests of the two superpowers. Mao angrily rejected his colleagues' suggestions of a compromise with the Soviet Union. In his view the Soviets by this stage were no longer just revisionists, they were counter-revolutionaries. This was in the spring of 1966, by which time the issue had become linked with the impending Cultural Revolution and Mao's efforts to stop China from 'changing colour', going down the revisionist, or as he now called it, the 'capitalist road'. Meanwhile Zhou Enlai and the United States Secretary of State, Dean Rusk, had signalled to each other that neither government sought a war with the other; for one of the dominant fears in China from the end of 1964 was that the Americans might escalate the war into China itself.[33]

It was at this point that China was plunged into the turmoil of the Cultural Revolution. Until the end of the sixties China was turned inwards and presented an incomprehensible picture to the outside world as a kind of revolutionary bastion prepared to deal with very few governments indeed. At one point, for a few weeks in the early summer of 1967, the revolution spilt over into the Ministry of Foreign Affairs and it led to numerous diplomatic incidents of which the most serious was the burning down of the British mission. Within China there was a wave of xenophobia which affected especially those Chinese with any kind of foreign connections, including oversea Chinese. International trade continued but at a reduced rate, and there were no more new agreements signed for the importation of whole new plants such as had been arranged in 1963—66.

Alignment with the West

This period saw the PRC's full entry into the international community as symbolised by its taking over the China seat at the United Nations from the Chiang Kai-shek regime and the normalisation of China's relations with most countries in the world. However this last phase of Mao's foreign policy was born out of the harsh realities of international armed conflict and perceived changes of the balance of world forces. It was also the subject of acute factional struggles in the Chinese leadership.

The change of China's alignment is often presented as a product of the search by Mao and Zhou for countervailing power against the Soviet threat which had grown immensely in the late sixties by its military build-up to the north. By the end of 1968 the Soviet border troops had been augmented by some thirty highly modernised divisions which were soon to be increased by a further ten. At the same time, Soviet forces were stationed near Mongolia's China border. The highly publicised battles over an island in the Ussuri River border in March 1969 were accompanied by thinly veiled Soviet nuclear threats. Moreover, by its armed intervention in Czechoslovakia, the Soviet Union not only proved its readiness to suppress a dissenting ally by force, but it also articulated a doctrine of intervention in other socialist countries judged to be in danger of losing their socialist gains.

Important as the Soviet threat was, this explanation is too one-sided as it misses out Chinese perceptions of the other superpower. 1968 was indeed a turning point, but in the first instance for the position of the United States. In the wake of the Tet offensive (February–March) in Vietnam, President Johnson refused to escalate the war still further and announced his intention not to run again for the coming election – which was tantamount to a resignation. In Mao's view this signalled that America was now thrust on the defensive and that its expansionist behaviour since the Second World War had come to an end. Domestic opposition to the Vietnam War had become widespread and it was aggravating the other sources of conflict in American society; there was a growing international crisis regarding the dollar and America's trading position. Moreover, the importance of Western Europe in diplomatic terms as an independent centre constraining American international behaviour was also recognised in Peking. The balance between the superpowers had also changed. In a confidential briefing to his juniors in December 1971 to explain Nixon's impending visit Zhou Enlai asserted that one of the primary reasons was that:

> when the U.S. got stuck in Vietnam, the Soviet revisionists embraced the opportunity to extend vigorously their sphere of influence in Europe and the Middle East. The U.S. imperialists cannot but improve their relations with China to combat the Soviet revisionists.[34]

One of the main reasons which the Chinese leaders gave for the American need to withdraw from Vietnam was to meet the growing Soviet challenge, and they argued that as a result the collusive aspects of the relations between the superpowers were now less important than the contention. They also held that the focal points of their contention were Europe and the Middle East rather than East Asia.

The Chinese response to the events of 1968 culminating in the opening to the United States also drove a deep wedge into Sino-Vietnamese relations. The Vietnamese supported the Soviet invasion of Czechoslovakia and rejected Zhou Enlai's assertion that by this action the Soviet Union had become a 'social imperialist' power and had brought about the demise of the socialist camp. Later in 1972 Zhou openly told a Western diplomat that China was opposed to any one country (Vietnam) dominating the others in Indo-China. From a Vietnamese perspective, China's opening to the United States was nothing less than betrayal, and a betrayal made all the more bitter because it had been paid by the blood and suffering of the Vietnamese people. Clearly many of the seeds of the later Sino-Vietnamese conflict were sown at this time. It should also be noted that China's support for the Pol Pot regime in Kampuchea as a centre of resistance to both Soviet and Vietnamese influence in Indo-China was established from the moment it assumed power more than a year before Mao's death when his grasp of foreign affairs was still clear.

Mao's initial shift of alignment was accompanied by an acute struggle with his declared successor, Lin Biao, who according to Peking died in a plane crash in Mongolia en route to Russia on 11 September 1971. Although the available evidence is internally consistent and it was repeated and expanded at the major trial in Peking in the winter of 1980–81 of the 'Lin Biao Clique' and the 'Gang of Four', there is no independent confirmation. The official version of the Lin Biao affair has always excluded all reference to the foreign policy dispute. Contemporary Chinese publications suggest that Lin strenuously opposed the new directions in foreign policy, preferring instead to continue the Cultural Revolution line which sought unity with oppressed and revolutionary peoples. He objected to the way Zhou Enlai had used the formulation of the 'Five Principles of Peaceful Coexistence' to establish relations with a wide range of governments. But above all he and his associates objected to the opening of relations with the United States. The Lin group held that America should be the target of any internationalist united front, and by 1971 it was implied that if a choice had to be made between the superpowers it would be better to tilt to Russia.[35]

President Nixon duly arrived in China in February 1972. The Shanghai Communiqué, which spelt out the character of the new Sino-American relations, outlined their differences, but it also pledged both sides not to seek hegemony in the Asia—Pacific region and to oppose any country or group of countries which sought to do so. An intricate formula was worked out regarding Taiwan which satisfactorily stood the test of changing circumstances until the normalisation of Sino—American relations nearly 7 years later. The Sino—American relationship was one of peculiar paradoxes during the remainder of Mao's life. There were times, especially in 1974, when there were indications that Mao and his colleagues thought the Americans were conceding too much to the Russians in the name of détente. Occasionally there were signs of Chinese suspicion that they were being used by the Americans as a means of exercising leverage on the Soviet Union. There also seemed to be a difference regarding each side's interpretation of the terms of the Shanghai Communiqué. Unlike the Americans, the Chinese saw it as a self-fulfilling agreement by which the United States was committed to withdraw altogether from the island. Over and above this there was an ambivalence in official attitudes to America. On the one hand they were pleased to note the closeness of their relations, and on the other they would describe America as an imperialist superpower albeit less dangerous than the Soviet Union. Trade developed very rapidly; in 1973 it reached the value of $800 million and in the following year it passed the $1000 million mark, to reach about the same level as Soviet—American trade. The trade was badly out of balance since Chinese exports barely reached a tenth of that figure. Thus, for technical reasons, the trade was bound to decline somewhat in 1975. The alignment with the United States was very much identified with Mao personally. Yet from the outset certain tensions in the relationship were evident. These arose in part from their very different social systems, but they focused on the Taiwan issue, on aspects of American—Soviet relations and on Chinese misgivings about American policies in the Third World. In fact these three issues continued ever since (albeit in different ways) to dog their relations.

In Mao's last two years there was a sense in which the new theory of the three worlds (by which the first world consisted of the domineering superpowers contending for global power; the second consisted of the small and medium capitalist powers who had an interest in resisting the superpowers, but who had to shed their own imperialist traditions; and the third consisted of the less-developed countries with a history of colonialism and who were bound to be the main force of resistance to the superpowers) was indeed the framework and perhaps even the guiding principles which shaped China's actual foreign policy. The theory, however, did not of itself explain Mao's clear preference for the United States, nor the attempt to build up an anti-Soviet coalition. In Africa and Latin America China lost much prestige in radical and nationalistic circles because of the extent to which the preoccupation with the Soviet Union led it into strange associations in Angola and in Chile.

Of greater long-term significance perhaps was the way in which the factional conflict between the 'Gang of Four' on the one side and Zhou Enlai and Deng Xiaoping on the other, over policy and succession spilt over into foreign affairs, especially those of foreign trade. After 1972 it seemed as if China was about to embark on a new phase of industrial and foreign trade expansion similar to that of the Soviet period of the fifties. The cycle of interdependence/autarky seemed as if it might have turned full circle in the sense that the industrialisation achieved during the Soviet period had generated a feeling of dependency which resulted in a period of proud isolation and independence and now it was felt that the cost of falling behind the technological levels in the rest of the world was too high a price to pay. Therefore it was necessary once again to turn to the outside world, but this time to the Western world. However, trade problems arose from the inflation in the industrialised countries and the quadrupling of the price of oil after the Arab–Israeli war. Consequently, the price of China's imports rose sharply, while the demand for many of China's exports and potential exports declined without rising in price at the same rate as imports. This led to an unprecedented balance of payments deficit in 1974 of

$810 million followed by a deficit in 1975 of $455 million, which also exceeded the previous record.

These developments sparked off much criticism from the 'Gang of Four' and their supporters who attacked the policy of relying on trade as a means of developing modern industry and who accused the Zhou—Deng group of selling out China's resources. A continuation of these policies, it was argued, would return China to a semi-colonial status in which it would be a dumping-ground for imperialist goods, a source of raw materials, a centre to which international companies would export capital and develop the country as a repair and service shop. But the leftists were never able to dent the Zhou—Deng policy and such setbacks in trade as did occur were part of a policy to reduce the deficit. Moreover, during this period (1973—76) agreements were reached to import sixty whole plants to the value of $3500 million, of which twenty-four were contracted in 1973.[36] The general policy, if not every single contract, seems to have been tacitly endorsed by Mao. This was too great a departure from previous practice to have gone unnoticed. Had Mao voiced any disagreement the leftists would surely have cited that in their polemics on the issue. But their writings revealed no new pronouncements by the Chairman. Moreover it seems likely that Mao must have personally endorsed the agreement to import and build under licence the Spey jet engines of Rolls Royce, which, apart from its intrinsic technical value, was regarded at the time as a very important development in the complex web of Sino—Western—Soviet relations. Clearly, in this, as in other areas, Mao was no xenophobe or ultra-leftist. But at the same time, apart from when he was forced by Stalin to accept joint-stock companies (which reverted to whole Chinese ownership soon after Stalin's death), Mao never entertained the idea of joint enterprises with foreign countries, nor did he accept international credits. (Arguably the practice of deferred payments on various projects came close to this — but the Chinese insistence on the difference between the two suggested the sensitivity of the subject.) Still less is there evidence to suggest that Mao would have solicited for capitalist investment in China, or sought to open special economic zones where foreign capitalist companies could utilise cheap Chinese labour and special facilities for exporting the produce thereof.

There can be no doubt that Mao was the architect of China's foreign policy on the strategic plane. But while he was very much in favour of modernisation, there is doubt as to how far he agreed with the Zhou—Deng line as it emerged in 1975. Significantly, he did not attend the National People's Congress in January 1975 when Zhou announced that China would once again pursue the 'four modernisations' (which he originally outlined to a previous NPC in December 1964). Instead, as if to publicise his absence, Mao received the right wing German politician Franz Joseph Strauss in another part of China. Mao certainly seemed to have opposed Deng's proposals for professionalising the education system. But the evidence even on this is not conclusive.[37] In so far as it is possible to pin down Mao's own preferences as he physically decayed during his last 18 months, it would appear that such objections as he had to Deng Xiaoping centred on the latter's readiness to downplay the significance of class struggle. That went to the heart of Mao's Utopian vision (to use Stuart Schram's term[38]) of his last 10—20 years.

PART ONE
MAO'S LEGACY

2

Chinese Society and Foreign Relations

Few aspects of Mao's legacy are as ambiguous and as susceptible to varying interpretations as that concerned with the
relationship to be established between the Chinese people
with their socialist society and the outside world. Mao himself had coined the slogan 'Make foreign things serve China'.
In other words he had called upon his people to learn from
the good and socially serviceable things developed in the
outside world while eschewing the harmful and the undesirable.
How to distinguish between them was never made clear. Nor
did Mao address the issue of how advanced foreign experience
or technology could be absorbed without dragging in tow
undesirable consequences. For example, he seems to have
had little to say on the question as to whether technology
was socially neutral. That is to say, whether technology, for
instance, in the shape of a whole industrial plant with a
complete set of equipment necessarily carried with it the
imprint of the society in which it had been originally made.
He presided over the period of the First Five Year Plan
(1952—57) in which China's doors were open wider than
ever before or since to the influences of a foreign country —
the Soviet Union. But he was notionally the 'supreme helms-
man' of the Cultural Revolution when in 1966—68 China's
doors were closed to foreign influence in self-chosen revolutionary isolation.

Mao's successors have largely spurned the legacy of the last
20 years of his life. His theory of continuing the revolution
during the socialist period has been condemned by his survivors as incompatible with his systematic ideology known as

Mao Zedong Thought. The theory of continuous revolution which elevated the significance of carrying out extensive class struggle even after the establishment of a socialist system underlay the Cultural Revolution. One of its implications in practice (if not necessarily in theory) was that China as the most advanced socialist country had to be most careful of the corrosion which would be caused by contact with foreign ('bourgeois' or 'revisionist') influences. Thus Mao could be cited as the authority for legitimising both the open-door and the isolationist postures.

The question of Mao's position does not turn on whether one accepts his Party's verdict on him that his last 20 years were characterised by fundamental mistakes. The last 4 years of his life were years during which the value of his country's foreign trade trebled and complete industrial plants were imported to the value of nearly 3½ thousand million dollars. Unlike the Soviet period 20 years before, Mao seems to have played little part in initiating these developments. But there is no evidence to suggest that he opposed them. The old man continued to cast his immense prestige behind the larger strategic dimensions of foreign policy and he continued to lend support to the sustenance of his 'Utopian vision'. Had he perceived this as being undermined by the increased economic exchanges with the capitalist West, it is reasonable to suggest that he would have given some indication, but no such indication has been given.

Foreign relations for Mao and the other Communist leaders did not begin with their capture of state power and the establishment of the PRC in 1949. To be sure statehood transformed these relations. Up until then these leaders conducted their relations with foreign powers and assessed international developments mainly with regard to whether these would promote or retard the progress of the Communist-led revolution. But statehood immediately involved the additional issues of sovereignty, territorial integrity, borders, international recognition and the assertion of an international identity within a world of other states. Nevertheless many of the attitudes and approaches which these leaders brought with them to the new tasks of statehood had been formed during the long years of struggle before 1949.

In many respects, however, the Communist Party under Mao's leadership had experience of dealing with foreign-related issues long before the seizure of state power.[1] Mao's struggle for ascendancy in the Party from the late twenties until the early forties can be seen as a struggle against those inspired (and often nominated) by Moscow.[2] What Mao called the 'sinification of Marxism'[3] was in a sense a formal claim to a separate Chinese identity within the international Communist movement. Moreover it was in Yan'an in the early forties that Mao and his colleagues negotiated with representatives of a foreign government (the United States) for the first time. Indeed, to mark the occasion of the 'start of our diplomatic work' the Central Committee of the Party issued in August 1944 a directive 'On Diplomatic Work' which may be seen as the first attempt to establish a Chinese Communist diplomatic style.[4]

In a broader sense Mao's revolutionary strategy in the 22 years before the seizure of state power in 1949 was intimately concerned with the question of imperialism. As will be argued in the next chapter, much of his thinking about power and international politics was formulated in the course of dealing with the practical problems of revolutionary struggle in a semi-colonial society – i.e. in a society still dominated by foreign armies and foreign interests despite its nominal independence.

It is within that context that the Communist revolution can be placed within the larger framework of China's modern history in which the central theme has been the transformation of Chinese society under the impact of the West. The Western impact, though, was more than a question of superior military force based on advanced technology. It also involved dragging China into the world of the industrial revolution and ultimately into the world of Western ideas and social movements. Communism, of course, was derived from the West and *part* of its appeal was as a means by which China as a socialist country would be ahead of the historical process of the capitalist West while catching up in industrial and technological terms.[5] The alternative was the psychologically less satisfying role of trailing behind that which was acknowledged to be more advanced in every way. Ishwer Ojha

in the late sixties characterised the impulse to modernisation
in China, as in much of the Third World, as 'anti-Western
Westernisation'.[6] In other words, modernisation (or westernisation) was being pursued in order to stand up to the West
and to reassert a national pride and dignity which had been
bruised and shaken by the West. Much of this nationalist
sentiment, itself, was a product of the Western impact. In
the terms put forward in the Introduction, the societal
dimensions of foreign relations for Third World countries
like China raise issues which cannot be dealt with on the
strategic plane alone.

Like many nationalist leaders of new states, Mao looked
back on the period before liberation as one of darkness and
humiliation — all the more severe in the Chinese case because
of the greatness of the Chinese past. In his speech inaugurating
the PRC Mao spoke in a language common to all Third World
nationalist leaders on attaining independence:

> The Chinese have always been a great, courageous and
> industrious nation; it is only in modern times that they
> have fallen behind. And that was entirely due to oppression
> and exploitation by foreign imperialism and domestic
> reactionary governments.

He then went on to place China's liberation within a main-
stream of 'unyielding struggles' against these two oppressors
waged 'for over a century by our forefathers'. But with the
founding of the PRC, he declared, 'Ours will no longer be a
nation subject to insult and humiliation. We have stood up.'[7]

Mao was clearly wrong if he was implying that China, on
the eve of the Opium War in 1840, was as advanced in technology and industry as the West. But if by 'modern times' he
meant the last two or three centuries, the problem was less
that China had 'fallen behind' than that the West had leapt
ahead. Ten years earlier, in 1939, Mao had argued that China's
traditional society 'carried within itself the seeds of capitalism'
and that left to itself China 'would have developed slowly
into a capitalist society'. 'Penetration by foreign capitalism
accelerated this process.'[8] Mao in this case followed Marx,
but only to a certain extent. Marx certainly welcomed the

destruction of pre-capitalist modes of production in Asia. But he saw no signs of any budding sprouts of capitalism in the existing societies. On the contrary, the reason that he thought capitalism had a progressive role to play here was precisely because he saw it as shaking these societies out of what he regarded as their stagnancy. This is not the place to examine Marx's concept of the 'Asiatic mode of production' or why in the late Ming and early Q'ing periods China did not develop towards capitalism, but it is interesting that only after Mao's death have Chinese historians been able to debate the question independently of the framework (intellectual strait-jacket might be a better term) set down by Mao.[9] I have touched upon the issue only in order to discuss Mao's attitude towards the Western impact on China. It is, however, worth observing that, unlike many other nationalistic leaders of Third World countries, Mao did not see that impact in wholly negative terms. Later in the same 1939 essay Mao asserted that the introduction of capitalism had led to the undermining of the traditional, and the establishment of a modern industrial, sector which in turn led to the creation of a Chinese pro-letariat and a Chinese national bourgeoisie. These positive consequences, however, he contrasted with the 'obstructive aspect' of imperialist penetration, 'namely, the collusion of imperialism with the Chinese feudal forces to arrest the development of Chinese capitalism'. This was because in his view the imperialist powers sought to transform China to their own semi-colony. 'To this end', he argued, they 'have used and continue to use military, political, economic and cultural means of oppression . . .'.[10] Although Mao went on to list a whole litany of imperialist acts of aggression, oppression and exploitation, he nowhere joined that fashion-able chorus of Third World leaders and those writers in the West who assert that the economic development of the West was the result of having exploited the Third World or that the material backwardness of the Third World was wholly the result of Western capitalist exploitation.

To be sure Mao regarded imperialism as highly obstructive to the further development of Chinese society. But at the same time he recognised that it had brought modern industry, and that it had been the midwife of change in Chinese society.

Although he was a man of the interior who spoke no foreign language and who was imbued with a deep sense of national pride, Mao was not anti-foreign, nor did he blame imperialism alone for China's backwardness. Like all men of his generation Mao would have witnessed many scenes of the degradation of Chinese people at the hands of arrogant foreigners. The century of shame and humiliation was clearly no empty slogan for Mao. Yet from his early pre-Marxist days as a radical nationalist onwards, his focus was less on getting rid of the imperialist foreigner than on moblising and transforming Chinese society.

The development of the concept of self-reliance

Arguably, few revolutions have been more autonomous than that which Mao led to initial victory in China in 1949. It may seem strange therefore to consider this period as any other than self-reliant — at least once Mao established his leadership by the late thirties. But even in the formulation of the principles of self-reliance in this period Mao paid much attention to the question of foreign assistance and it is only after consideration of this period that we shall be able to examine the extent to which the new China's dependence on the Soviet Union in the fifties was in a sense an 'aberration'. This period will also be of significance in assessing the changes which have taken place after Mao's death.

The concept of self-reliance has been used to describe a variety of different policies from virtual autarky to the importing of a wide range of agricultural products and industrial plants. Literally translated from the Chinese, self-reliance means 'produce even more by one's own strength' (*zi li geng sheng*). It bespeaks more of an attitude of mind than a specific set of policies. It calls for an independent outlook, self-conscious creativity and, above all, the determination to avoid dependency. This means the retention of the capacity for self-initiative and independent decision-making even to the extent of isolationism, if that is the price which must be paid for keeping mastery of one's own fate. It is intimately linked with Mao's notion of what might be called national dignity. But in itself self-reliance does not imply isolation.[11]

Curiously, the first formulation of self-reliance in relation to foreign affairs was designed with the aim of securing foreign assistance.[12] It was issued in the form of a resolution by the Party's Central Committee in August 1944 from Maoist Yen'an to define the appropriate policy for the visiting American delegation known as the Dixie Mission.[13] The Resolution argued that co-operation with the United States and Great Britain would enable the liberated areas to attain 'even greater growth' and it foresaw the 'possibility' of continued co-operation after the war. Cadres were instructed to welcome foreign military, diplomatic, cultural and religious missions. They were told to look forward to foreign economic aid, capital investment and technical co-operation.

Such an attitude hardly accords with what is usually considered to be the hallmark of the 'Yenan spirit' or the 'Yenan Way'[14] associated with the rigorously independent new society established in the blockaded liberated area. Perhaps the passage of time and the complexities of running a highly bureaucratised state in the 1950s elevated memories of the allegedly halcyon days of Yenan into myth-like proportions so that the deliberate search for aid was forgotten. In any event the anticipated aid did not materialise. The Resolution, which was an inner Party document and which was not meant for circulation as propaganda, then went on to warn against repeating Chinese recent history of cringing passively before Westerners and of coming to rely upon foreigners. Liberated Chinese should demonstrate their vigour and determined spirit. Assistance was not to be requested, rather cadres had 'to arrange it so that foreigners would offer us help themselves'. The quest for aid should not be allowed to erode self-reliance. The Resolution then spelt out the classic attitudes of self-reliance for the first time:

We must intensify the feeling of national self-respect and faith in ourselves, but without boycotting foreigners; we must study the positive experience of others while improving co-operation with them, but without worshipping and flattering the foreigners. This is what constitutes the correct national platform, this is what constitutes the essence of the prototype of the new man in new democratic China.

These sentiments were reflected in Mao's talks with John Service later that month. For example: 'China must industrialise. This can be done — in China — only by free enterprise and with the aid of foreign capital. Chinese and American interests are correlated and similar. They fit together economically and politically. We can and must work together.'[15] In January 1945 Mao expressed a desire to visit Washington; a desire which Zhou Enlai repeated to Marshall a year later, saying that Mao would prefer Washington to Moscow 'because he thinks he can learn lots of things useful to China'.[16] These sentiments all belonged to a period in which Mao hoped for various forms of co-operation with the United States. But perhaps more importantly, they belonged to the period of 'new democracy' (rather than to that of socialism) in which the purpose was to struggle for the new democratic revolution rather than for the attainment of socialism. In Mao's Report to the Seventh Party Congress in April 1945, the international scene was also portrayed as the struggle of democrats and anti-fascists against anti-democrats and fascists. In passages excised from the current edition of Mao's *Selected Works*, he was most generous in his praise for England and the United States.[17] Interestingly in this period Mao attacked Chiang Kai-shek as a 'xenophobe' for his opposition to the appointment of the American General Stillwell as the Commander in Chief of China's armed forces.[18]

However, once it had become clear that the American Government under Truman's Presidency had turned its back on any co-operation with China's communists, Mao's attitude also changed. CPC commentaries interpreted the issue in terms of a 'factional' struggle between 'democratic and anti-democratic elements'. The turning point was the arrest in America of John Service in April 1946 for passing on for publication some of his interviews with Mao and others.[19] Nevertheless even as Mao proclaimed in July 1949 that the new China would lean to the Soviet side and that there was no third way, he declared in his well-known essay 'On the

People's Democratic Dictatorship' that his government would be ready to establish diplomatic relations on the basis of true equality with any foreign government. He also looked forward to 'doing business' with, and possibly obtaining credit, 'on terms of mutual benefit' in the future from Britain and the United States but only because their capitalists want to make money and their bankers want to earn interest to extricate themselves from their own crisis. Genuine and friendly help could only come from the side of the Soviet Union.

Earlier in the essay Mao summarised his view of China's experience in learning from other countries. He recounted how after China's defeat in the Opium War of 1840, Chinese progressives went through untold hardships in the quest for truth from the Western countries. He admitted:

In my youth, I too engaged in such studies. . . . They were called 'the new learning' in contrast to Chinese feudal culture which was called 'the old learning'. China's progressives for quite a long time were certain that the culture of western bourgeois democracy would save China. Only modernatization could save China, only learning from foreign countries could modernize China.

The trouble was that the Western countries continued with imperialist aggression — 'Why were the teachers always committing aggression against their pupil?' But perhaps more importantly, Mao also argued that the Western experience was inapplicable to China. He suggested that although the Chinese learned a good deal from the West, 'they could not make it work and were never able to realize their ideals' (emphasis added).[20] It might be noted that the British Foreign Office key advisers on China in the 1940s shared Mao's view. 'The idea that western ideas could be grafted onto Oriental roots and that China could become a western-style democracy struck them in the short run as palpable nonsense.'[21]

Mao then went on to describe the process by which the Chinese people found 'the universally applicable truth' and began to change their country:

World War I shook the whole globe. The Russians made

the October Revolution and created the world's first socialist state. Under the leadership of Lenin and Stalin, the revolutionary energy of the great proletariat and labouring people of Russia, *hitherto latent and unseen by foreigners, suddenly erupted like a volcano*, and the Chinese and all mankind began to see the Russians in an extremely new light. Then and only then, did the Chinese enter an entirely new era in their thinking and their life. They found Marxism-Leninism, the universally applicable truth, and the face of China began to change. [Emphasis added.]

The reference to the limited perceptions of foreigners and the volcanic eruption are typical of Mao's views of the latent creativity in people (the 'poor and blank') which can be unleashed once the historical social shackles binding them are removed. Interestingly, the idea that foreigners did not understand Russia was considered by Mao to apply to China also. Mao had held both before and after 1949 that not even the Russian revolutionaries understood China.[22] But this revolutionary populism was also tempered by the reference to 'the universally applicable truth' — which of course came to China literally from the West. Those British diplomatic advisers referred to earlier may have disagreed as to whether 'the distinguishing features of Soviet Marxism—Leninism were of Occidental or Oriental origin'[23] but regardless of the view from London, Mao and his colleagues in China clearly perceived Russia as more occidental than Asiatic. The original Bolshevik revolutionaries, however, saw their revolution in internationalist terms and at first thought it could only survive if it sparked off socialist revolutions in the more advanced West European countries. Mao and his colleagues, however, may be said to have conceived of their revolutionary struggles as having more of the character of a national liberational movement than of international class war.

As is well known, Mao's struggle for ascendancy in the CPC for himself and his revolutionary strategy in the thirties was also a struggle against leaders who had been approved by the Soviet-dominated Comintern articulating Soviet-derived doctrine and strategy. From 1938 to 1943 Mao was heavily engaged in undermining the legitimacy and ideological credibility of such people. He called for the sinification of Marxism and for abandoning 'dogmatism' derived from the prolonged study of Marxist–Leninist books in Moscow in favour of deepening one's activities among China's peasants.[24] Likewise it is easy to catalogue Mao's assertions of the independent creativity of the Chinese Revolution or what the Russians have regarded as his heretical deviations. Indeed as an example of Mao's alleged sino-centricity and Chinese chauvinism Russian writers have claimed that Mao's strategy in the later 1930s involving Mongolia and Xinjiang was designed to draw the Soviet Union in the war against Japan. The unstated assumption was (and perhaps still is) that any true proletarian internationalist would obviously put the interests of the Soviet Union before any other.[25] Supposing these Soviet writers to be correct about Mao, are they claiming any more than that he looked upon the world as a Chinese revolutionary? It was not necessarily incumbent upon Mao to subordinate the interests of the Chinese revolution and its people to the Soviet Union, particularly after his experiences of Comintern errors and of struggle against Soviet nominees. As Schram has suggested, Mao was uniquely qualified to lead the revolution precisely because of his 'Chineseness'.[26] But in itself, that cannot be regarded as testimony to chauvinism and xenophobia on Mao's part.

In principle, however, Mao never repudiated the affinity with the Soviet Union and he always deferred in principle to Stalin's leadership of the Communist world. There have been many instances of Mao's proclaimed recognition of Stalin's leadership,[27] but these were always cast in highly generalised terms. For example, in the late thirties he compared Stalin's leadership of the international Communist movement to what he regarded as Chamberlain's leadership of the imperialist world. This did not mean, however, that he accepted Soviet direction or control of the Chinese revolution. Indeed Mao never clarified precisely what he understood by recognising Stalin's leadership. If Chinese Communist decision-making was autonomous, if the pattern and direction by which universalist Marxist–Leninist principles should be applied to China was to be decided exclusively by the Chinese, and if the Chinese revolution was to be held up as the model (super-seding the Soviet one) for the colonial and semi-colonial world, it is difficult to see the claimed leadership of Stalin as anything more than rhetorical or some declaration of fealty. On the eve of nationwide victory, in his essay on the People's Democratic Dictatorship, Mao suggested two ways in which the Soviet Union had provided leadership. First, as a source of inspiration. As we have seen, he noted that 'the salvoes of the October Revolution brought us Marxism—Leninism' and that 'progressives' in China and elsewhere decided 'to adopt the proletarian world outlook as the instru-ment for studying a nation's destiny and considering anew their own problems. Follow the path of the Russians – that was their conclusion'. In other words, the Soviets were depicted as path-breakers and teachers who were to be followed – but presumably not to be aped blindly. Second, arising out of Mao's view of the Soviet Union as a bastion against imperialism, he rejected the view that the liberation of China had been achieved unaided. It was not so much a question of direct material aid (in fact no mention was made of that[28]); rather it was the very existence of the Soviet Union as a socialist state and, for good measure Mao added, the struggles of the popular masses throughout the world that was decisive: 'If not for all of these in combination, the international reactionary forces bearing down upon us would certainly be many times greater now.' In this sense the Soviet socialist state could be depicted in the imagery of the Chinese revolution as the massive rear base area in front of which China's revolutionaries were able to struggle for the liberation of their country.

There is then an ambiguity in Mao's acknowledgement of Soviet or Stalin's leadership. The Soviets were the bearers of 'the universal truth' to China's progressives, but it was for the latter to distinguish between the universal and the particu-laristic aspects of the truth so that they could apply these to Chinese conditions which, unlike any foreigner, they alone could know. The Russians, then, were teachers and not instructors training Chinese apprentices. Likewise the Russian model was not a blueprint, but rather an example. Similarly the most important aspect of Soviet international assistance was not direct material aid, but rather its function as a reliable rear base area whose triumph in the war and whose parallel — but not identical — struggle against imperialism after 1945 was a major factor in the victory of the Chinese revolutionaries. The very real differences between Mao and some of his associates on the one hand and the Soviet Union on the other in the 1945—49 period may be likened to the distinction which Mao was to draw in 1957 (applied to domestic Chinese politics) between contradictions among the people which were soluble by peaceful means and the contradictions within the enemy which were irreconcilable although temporary compromises could be made in the short run.

Mao's attitude towards the United States during this period was much more ambiguous. While regarding it as the leading imperialist power he nonetheless claimed to detect a 'democratic faction' in Washington with whom co-operation was possible in 1944—46, and as late as the summer of 1949 he certainly looked forward to a trading relationship with America. Indeed the leading interpreter of his thought and life in the West, Stuart Schram, has suggested that since his early days Mao was an admirer of the American War of Independence and of certain aspects of the American achievement which co-existed uneasily with his consistently trenchant criticism of American imperialism.

To return, however, to the theme of self-reliance, it is clear from this brief account that Mao recognised the importance of external assistance. Even during the period before the establishment of the PRC when all scholars are agreed, whether on the left or on the right (except for certain writers in Taiwan who have a vested interest in asserting otherwise) that the Chinese revolution under Mao's leadership was, in the genuine meaning of the word, autonomous, yet Mao was prepared to seek foreign aid. It would be better perhaps to turn the argument around and suggest that in Mao's view it was only a genuinely independent movement or country that could accept foreign assistance without becoming the client of the donor. But there were ambiguities in this too.

Mao's position may be seen more clearly if it is compared with that of some of his colleagues. The extensive studies of Mao's rise to power within the Party and the development of the Chinese road to revolution bring out very clearly how at every turning point in the Party's internal struggles and debates Mao was never linked with those who argued for a closer Soviet link or, on the other hand, for an association with the KMT (Kuomintang) which would have forfeited the independent military command of the Communist armed forces.[29] The period from 1945 to 1949 has received less critical attention. Throughout 1946 and 1947 there were pessimistic viewpoints among the Party leaders about the prospects for launching a civil war in China. According to the editorial note to a document of Mao's of April 1946 in the official *Selected Works*[30] there were those who

> over-estimated the strength of imperialism, underestimated the strength of the people, feared U.S. imperialism and feared the outbreak of a new world war; they showed weakness in the face of armed attacks of the U.S.—Chiang Kai-shek reactionary gang and dared not resolutely oppose counter-revolutionary war with revolutionary war.

Mao's document was designed to refute these views; but as the note indicates it was not until December 1947 that Mao won the approval of all his colleagues. Even then the note implies a qualification by referring to the agreement of the 'comrades present' at the December meeting, implying that this was not necessarily true of those who were absent from the Central Committee meeting. These 'pessimistic' views paralleled those of the Soviet leaders. Contemporary evidence is also available for this. In early 1946 Liu Shaoqi published an article in the main Communist journal of the time which reflected much more the Soviet point of view than that adumbrated by Mao both in the aforesaid document and in his talk with Anna Louise Strong of August that year.[31] In fact as late as 1949 Zhou Enlai confided to the Americans that there was a majority faction in the Party leadership which favoured a close association with the Soviet Union and which opposed his initiative in seeking contacts with the American government.[32] These inner Party differences were reflected in Manchuria where Chinese Communist forces made contact with the Soviet Red Army.

Peng Zhen and Ling Feng were accused of anti-Soviet activities first in 1946 and then again in 1949.[33] Gao Gang, the leader of the communist region in Manchuria, on the other hand was closely associated with the Soviet Union and was regarded as Stalin's man in the Chinese Political Bureau.[34] During this time Mao was not directly associated with Zhou's diplomatic efforts to open a dialogue with the Americans — but he must surely have known of them and not vetoed them. Yet he was not associated with the pro-Soviet elements either.

As the prospect of victory in the Civil War grew unexpectedly nearer, Mao, ever alert to changes in his social and international environment, reported to the second Plenary Session of the Seventh CC on 5 March 1949 that 'the centre of gravity of the Party's work has shifted from the village to the city' and that the period of 'from the village to the city' was henceforth to be replaced by 'the city leading the village'. The Party would have to learn how to run cities and 'how to wage political, economic and cultural struggles against the imperialists, the Kuomintang and the bourgeoisie and also how to wage diplomatic struggles against the imperialists'. At the end of his report, like other modern populists, Mao warned against the corrupting influences of the city. He depicted his simplistic war heroes who, having withstood enemy gunfire, might now succumb to the 'sugar-coated bullets' of the unctuous city bourgeoisie. Mao's suspicion of the city and the intellectual, both of which were associated with a suspect cosmopolitanism and elitism, is a theme which will be discussed in greater detail later in this chapter. It is mentioned at this juncture to point up an aspect of the well-known difference between the Chinese and Soviet revolutionary experience in which the latter, unlike the former, had always been city-orientated. In this same report Mao surveyed China's 'backward economy' and drawing on the Leninist tradition he argued for the necessity of strengthening state power against domestic class enemies and the external imperialist threat; he also asserted the need to establish tight control over capital at home and over foreign trade. He looked forward to the establishment of 'an independent and integrated industrial system' once the country had been 'greatly developed economically'. Typically, he was optimistic about the prospects for 'fairly fast' economic development because of the 'bravery' and 'industry' of the Chinese people, the Party's leadership and the support of other communist countries, 'chiefly' the Soviet Union. These positive factors were listed in that order, implying that external assistance was necessarily secondary.

A few months later, in July, Mao spelt out in greater detail how much would have to be learnt from others:

> We shall soon put aside some of the things we know well and be compelled to do things we don't know well. . . . We must overcome difficulties, we must learn what we do not know. We must learn to do economic work from all who know how, no matter who they are.

This was a reference to former Kuomintang people and capitalists who had stayed at their posts. Mao later pointed to the Soviet success in revolution and in the work of economic construction. 'The Communist Party of the Soviet Union [CPSU] is our best teacher and we must learn from it.'

Thus on the eve of nationwide victory, Mao, perhaps daunted at the magnitude of the tasks which lay ahead and for which the revolution in the countryside had ill prepared him, nevertheless still combined the duality of the concept of self-reliance. The Chinese revolutionaries must learn from others including foreigners and especially their 'best teacher', the CPSU; yet the purpose of the exercise was to build an 'independent' industrial system and the most important factor which would lead to rapid success was the bravery and industry of the Chinese people as led by the CPC. Yet it was not explained precisely how the Chinese people were 'to learn' these things while still relying on their own efforts. For his part, Mao was to admit later that he had in effect allowed the Chinese people to follow the Soviet model blindly — or as he put it, 'dogmatically'. Following the disasters of the Great Leap Forward and its aftermath Mao confessed that he had never learnt how to run industrial affairs. At the same time it is clear that Mao's aim in 'leaning to one side' was not to make China dependent upon the Soviet Union, but rather to enable the Chinese to build up an *independent* industrial system.[35] The period of the formation of the Sino-Soviet alliance was also one in which efforts were made to advance Mao's claims to ideological originality and to assert the special significance of the Chinese revolution in Asia — both of which were in effect an affirmation of the independence of the CPC and a qualification to the all-embracing authority of Moscow in the communist world. But they were also an assertion of the internationalism of the Chinese revolution. These claims were only grudgingly and partially conceded by the Russians at the time.

If Mao had identified the spirit of self-reliance, the evidence suggests that, as articulated by him, there were inherent ambiguities in the concept. It fell somewhere between the two extremes of autarky and dependence. But nowhere did he suggest how this could be translated into specific policy guidelines or what criteria should be applied in deciding when to lean towards the one or the other of the two extremes.

Self-reliance and external assistance* after the establishment of the new state

It is important to note at the outset that at no point during Mao's lifetime was the PRC truly autarkic in the sense of having no foreign trade at all. In 1959 the value of foreign trade registered the highest level it was to reach in the first 20 years of the PRC. It will be recalled that 1959 was the year immediately after the high tide of the Great Leap Forward which supposedly epitomised the spirit of self-reliance. The value of imports, principally from the Soviet bloc, reached US$2060 million. The next high point (in terms of the value of imports) was reached in 1966 ($2035 million) which was the first year of the Cultural Revolution — generally regarded in its early stage as a period of isolation and autarky. Yet although the value of imports did fall in 1967 and 1968, it did not drop more than 10 per cent below

---

* For the purposes of this analysis foreign trade and foreign credits are considered as external assistance. During Mao's lifetime the PRC did not receive foreign aid *gratis*, although China's leaders clearly thought that Soviet military aid during the Korean War should have been given free.

the 1966 figure.[36] From 1969 the value of foreign trade climbed steadily to reach a new peak in 1975 of $14,320 million, of which $7385 million were imports. Nevertheless at no point during Mao's lifetime did the total value of foreign trade in any one year exceed 5 per cent of China's GNP.[37] Five years after his death it was to reach 18 per cent.

The organisation of foreign trade was highly centralised along Soviet lines with a special ministry under the highest administrative and political authorities. The Ministry incorporated foreign trade corporations which specialised in particular commodities, e.g. cereals, machinery, etc. Subordinate to the Ministry was the China Council for the Promotion of International Trade which functioned as 'the socialist equivalent of a Chamber of International Commerce'.[38] The financial side of China's trade was conducted by the Bank of China.

Both the scope and the pattern of China's foreign trade was to be changed markedly by Mao's successors. However, even during Mao's lifetime China's foreign trade exhibited important variations and it would be misleading to suggest that Mao's application of self-reliance restricted this trade by the deliberate pursuit of import substitution and import minimisation as the overriding goals. Christopher Howe divided the period 1952–75 (the years 1949–52 were concerned with the consolidation of communist rule and the rehabilitation of the economy) into four stages:

> In the first, between 1952 and 1960, there was an expansion of 12.42% per annum, which reflected the Soviet link. Trade then fell, and did not approach the 1959 level again (even in money terms) until 1966. During the Cultural Revolution trade stood still, but after 1970, trade again grew very rapidly. Between 1970 and 1975 the growth was 27.26% p.a. in money terms – about 9% in real terms.

Howe then noted that in the expansionary periods of the fifties and seventies trade grew more rapidly than the domestic economy.[39]

There is a tendency to associate Mao's true position on economic affairs with a rather narrow view of the principles of self-reliance. This arises from the identification of Mao with the promotion of mass-mobilisation politics and the related values of the selfless communal socialist man. While it is true that Mao was at the forefront of the martial barn-storming socialist approach to economic affairs which down-played the significance of the expert and advanced (foreign) technology, he also presided over the pursuit of very different kinds of policies and economic strategies. In any case the nar-rowest view of self-reliance was articulated in the early 1960s when Mao was playing very much a back-seat role in the management of the Chinese economy. Among those in the front seat was Deng Xiaoping who has since introduced very different policies. In the early 1960s self-reliance was explained as follows: 'A country should manufacture by itself all the products it needs whenever and wherever possible . . . [self-reliance] also means that a country should carry on its general economic construction on the basis of its own human, material and financial resources.'[40]

As on other issues Mao's position was complex and it varied over time. Mao certainly leant his weight in the early fifties to learning from the Soviet Union, just as in the late fifties he was the prime mover in departing from the Soviet model. The drop in trade in the early sixties was due to the depressed state of the Chinese economy rather than to political decisions to restrict trade. During this time Mao was not engaged in the day-to-day affairs of running the state. But he played an active part in seeking to establish closer relations with the West European countries and praised French businessmen as more reliable trade partners than the Russians.[41] Mao also lent his considerable prestige to the cultivation of relations with Japan and Japanese businessmen at this time. In the seventies Mao associated himself still less with foreign trade issues, but he supported the rehabilitation of those who did. Given the international and defence im-plications of the 1973/74 $200 million agreement to import Rolls Royce Spey jet engines and build a factory for their production in China, it is inconceivable that even the ageing Mao would not have been aware of the deal and at least tacitly endorsed it. In 1975 the trade policies of Deng Xiaoping were attacked by those associated with the 'Gang of Four' as endangering the socialist quality of China's economic system.[42] As has been noted in the previous chapter, this campaign, unlike others launched by the Gang of Four against Deng and Zhou Enlai, did not cite any alleged comments by the Chairman. If Mao had objected to the expansion of foreign trade in the early seventies, surely the 1975 detractors would have publicised his objection with much fanfare. The extent of this new trade in the seventies can be gauged not only from the rise in the value of trade from $4720 million in 1971 to $14,320 million in 1975, but also from the scale of the import into the Chinese economy of whole plants utilising technology. Between December 1972 and September 1974 the revived Technical Export—Import Corporation signed 41 contracts for the construction of a total of 95 plants valued at between $4100 and $2500 million. The last such orders had been placed with Western Europe and Japan in 1963—66 to the value of $200 million.[43] Some of these plants, such as the 13 ammonia and the 13 urea factories and those manufacturing synthetic fibres, were to make significant contributions to Chinese agriculture and textile industries, but others, such as the giant Wuhan steel complex, were to prove very costly white elephants as they demanded more energy and resource inputs than the Chinese economy could bear. The Rolls Royce jet engine factory near Xian was duly completed, but in the absence of a suitable air frame, it too is operating — if at all — at only a minimal level of its full capacity.

It would be wrong to assign the ageing Mao specific responsibility for these developments. He clearly took no active part in foreign trade decision-making. Indeed he deliberately absented himself from the National People's Congress in January 1975 when Zhou Enlai recommitted the country to the goal of the four modernisations, first advanced with Mao's blessing in December 1964. It was not that Mao openly opposed Zhou on this (although certain of Deng's proposed policy guidelines later that year went against many of the principles advocated by Mao on the eve of the Cultural Revolution and Mao indicated disapproval of the suggested reforms of education); it was rather that he withheld approval in an ostentatious manner. Similarly, Mao did not associate himself with the foreign trade policy positions of the Gang of

Four, although they owed their political prominence to their association with him. Perhaps the ageing Mao's position is best considered less in terms of policy preferences than in an attempt to determine the complex issues concerned with the imminent succession.

If Mao cannot be held fully accountable for the foreign trade developments of his last 4 years, he cannot be completely freed of responsibility either. By not opposing these developments (and by taking an active part in the formulation and execution of a foreign policy in which foreign trade played an important role, Mao had in effect at least tacitly approved them. Indeed the policy of rapidly expanding foreign trade and the importing of turnkey projects had been carried out with his approval before in the history of the PRC. In sum the trading practices of 1970–75 were not a major departure in principle from policies endorsed by Mao in earlier periods, and there is no evidence that he opposed the new policies – on the contrary they were an important aspect of his foreign policy at the time.

There were, however, limits to the trade practices associated with self-reliance in Mao's lifetime: Foreign investment was precluded, as were joint enterprises with foreign companies; foreign loans were eschewed although in the seventies deferred payments became an accepted practice; Chinese labour was not for hire to foreigners; and generally 'the worship of foreign things' was decried. As will be seen in a later chapter all these limits have been removed by Mao's successors.

At this point, however, it is useful to look more closely at the 'Soviet period' in China's economic relations. Many, if not all, of these limits were not applied in the fifties either. For example, in 1950 Mao was compelled by Stalin to accept joint ventures with the Soviet Union in Xinjiang and Manchuria as well as a continued involvement in the running of the old Chinese Eastern Railway in Manchuria and a Soviet naval presence in Dairen and Port Arthur. However, the relevant treaties and agreements also set a time limit to the Soviet 'rights' in China. This meant that in principle at least the Soviet Union was not laying claims to absorbing these Chinese border regions into the Soviet sphere. By calling these areas Soviet 'colonies' Mao showed how much the Soviet demands were resented, by him at least. Nevertheless Soviet withdrawal finally took place in 1955 on what were generous terms. For example, all the naval and shipbuilding facilities in Port Arthur and Dairen were passed on to the Chinese free of charge despite a 1950 agreement that had provided for Chinese payment for those installations which had been built after 1945. This, however, was not typical of Sino-Soviet economic relations. On the whole the Chinese paid for all the material aid they received and they paid interest (albeit at the low rates of 1–2 per cent) on the loans.

Total Soviet credits have been estimated at \$1370–\$2240 million.[44] Between 1950 and 1955 they were reflected in a surplus of Chinese imports over exports. Thereafter Chinese exports exceeded imports until the loans were paid off in 1965. A considerable proportion of Soviet credits, and indeed of Soviet imports, will have been of military and related goods about which little information has been revealed in public. Indeed the only aspect of the economic relationship with the Soviet Union about which the Chinese were to complain specifically was the requirement to pay for the military equipment they received in order to prosecute the Korean War. The impact of Soviet aid on the Chinese economy was considerable. By 1960, when the break occurred, 130 major industrial projects had been completed (and a further 27 by East European countries). Soviet economic support was responsible for half of the growth of China's National Product during the First Five-Year Plan – a period which Chinese economists in the early eighties looked back on as the halcyon years compared with the economic performance of the next 20. In the mid-fifties about 50 per cent of China's trade was with the Soviet Union while China accounted for only 20 per cent of Russia's total trade. The underdeveloped state of the Chinese economy and China's greater economic dependence on Russia gave the Soviet Union greater bargaining power in the economic sphere; however, according to Eckstein, 'there is no evidence to suggest that this power resulted in economic exploitation of the Chinese'. Nor did the Soviets use their bargaining edge to impose their views on the Chinese.[45] Indeed in 1958 and 1959 the Chinese were able to alter at very short notice the pattern of their exports to the Soviet Union to the inconvenience of Soviet economic planners; and the Russians consistently failed to persuade their Chinese colleagues to arrange the Chinese side of the trade on a long-term basis. Moreover, the Chinese refused to join the Council for Mutual Economic Assistance (CMEA or Comecon) because of its emphasis on the international joint division of labour. They held observer status only, and they withdrew altogether in 1961. It should also be noted that more than 12,000 Soviet and East European specialists and technicians were sent to China between 1950 and 1960 and 15,000 Chinese students and engineers were trained in the Soviet Union. In addition up to 23,000 blueprints, licenses, technical documents, etc. were given to the Chinese without charge.

It is quite clear in retrospect that far from tying in the Chinese economy to that of the Soviet Union, Soviet aid helped to establish a relatively independent industrial system. A further indication of the independent quality of China's economy and economic decision-making may be seen from the developments in China from the mid-fifties onwards: the socialisation of agriculture, commerce and industry was carried out in 1955–56 along lines different from the Soviet Union. The debates and the sets of decisions taken in 1956–57 which took China away from the Soviet model were totally free from any Soviet pressure. Finally, Khrushchev's opposition to the Great Leap Forward of 1958 arose out of the claims that implied that China might reach Communism before the Soviet Union rather than because of any principled insistence that the Soviet model had to be followed by all members of the socialist camp. Subsequent Chinese claims that he had interfered in Chinese domestic affairs by conspiring with the Peng Dehuai (the Minister of Defence and major critic of the Great Leap Forward who was purged by Mao in 1959) are not supported by the available evidence.[46]

Looking back on Sino-Soviet economic relations of the fifties, the evidence strongly suggests that it was their relative political bargaining power rather than the Soviet economic predominance which was decisive in determining the terms and extent of Soviet aid. During Stalin's lifetime the PRC was hemmed in and received far less in aid than had been hoped. The 50 industrial plants which the Russians had agreed to deliver by the 1950 agreements turned out to be the rehabilitation of the Japanese heavy industry plants which the Russian armies had stripped from Manchuria in 1945. A Chinese delegation was held up in Moscow from August 1952 to May 1953 before agreement was reached on Russian aid for the First Five-Year Plan which began on 1 January 1953. Indeed it was only after Stalin's death when Moscow was politically relatively weak that China attained the return of assets on Chinese soil and considerably enhanced offers of aid. The end of the Korean War saw China an acknowledged great power with a rehabilitated economy. The scales of relative political weight had changed markedly between Mao's low-key visit to Moscow in the winter of 1949—50 and between the visit to Peking by Khrushchev and Bulganin in October 1954. It was not until Khrushchev had settled the upheavals in Eastern Europe and purged his rivals in 1957 that the political scales began to tilt back to Moscow. But by that stage China was a fully fledged independent power. It is quite clear in retrospect that far from tying the Chinese economy to that of the Soviet Union, Soviet aid had helped establish a relatively independent industrial system.

Given the great economic benefits to China which did not prevent China's leaders from pursuing independent strategies in domestic or foreign affairs, it may be wondered what Mao found objectionable in the relationship from the point of view of self-reliance. One obvious aspect was China's vulnerability to Soviet sanctions as was made apparent by the unheralded Soviet withdrawal of all the specialist and technical personnel together with their blueprints in July 1960. This was at the height of China's deepest economic crisis. It caused the abandonment of 161 planned or partially built projects and the economic impact of the withdrawal was very severe. The lesson which Mao and his colleagues drew from this was never again to become dependent upon one source for the import of either raw materials or advanced technology.

There was, however, a more profound objection, and one that was typical of Mao and his deeply felt revolutionary Chinese nationalism. His objection was to the blind emulation of the Soviet model in which fellow Chinese reverted to a cringing passivity in face of the superior know-how and achievement of the foreigner. Ever conscious of the independence and particular socialistic values associated with the revolution under his leadership as summed up in the evocative terms of the 'Yan'an Spirit', Mao was anxious to inculcate once again a Chinese creativity and a pace of economic development even faster than that of the Soviet Union. Perhaps the more fascinating and truly revealing of Mao's thoughts on these questions emerge from his talks and speeches which were not published at the time and which have become available either through publications released unofficially during the Cultural Revolution or in volume V of his *Selected Works* published under the overall editorship of Hua Guofeng in March 1977 (the editorial policy of which reflected very much the mood and interests of the leadership in the immediate aftermath of Mao's death and the overthrow of the 'Gang of Four').[47]

Right from the outset of the policy to follow the Soviet model at the beginning of the First Five-Year Plan there was a qualitative difference between the way Mao and some of his colleagues approached the issue. Bo Yibo, the influential Finance Minister, in a report on the national budget declared quite simply on 17 February 1953: 'The Soviet Union of today will be the new China of tomorrow.' Although Mao also called for initiating a nationwide 'tidal wave' in learning from the Soviet Union 10 days earlier in an address to the Political Consultative Conference (which also included non-CPC members) he confined himself to the need to study the advanced experience of the Soviet Union in national construction because the Chinese lack sufficient experience in these matters. Mao never once suggested that China would simply replicate the experience of others as implied by Bo.

Well before the time from which he later pinpointed the beginnings of the Sino-Soviet dispute (i.e., the February 1956 Twentieth CPSU Congress) Mao drew comparisons between China and the Soviet Union which favoured his country. In this speech of 6 December 1955 he asserted even further

The Chinese peasant is even better than the English or American worker, and that is why he can advance more, better and faster towards socialism. Let us not always

make comparisons with the Soviet Union. If we can produce twenty-four million tons of steel a year by the end of
three Five Year Plans, that will be faster than the Soviet
Union.

In many respects this is typical of Mao's populist belief in the
inherent capacity of Chinese peasants. The context of the
speech was the high tide of rural collectivisation in China
initiated largely by him and opposed by some leaders who
cited the Soviet experience as a reason for adopting a slower
and more gradual approach. Nevertheless in his final sentence
Mao displayed his essential nationalistic qualities.

By this stage the emulation of the Soviet Union was not
confined to the establishment of great industrial complexes.
The state administration, and especially the institutions of
economic planning, were almost carbon copies of their Soviet
models. Tertiary, secondary and much of primary education,
as well as research institutes, replicated their Soviet equivalents. Whole ministries, the organisation of health, cultural
matters, legal institutions, trade unions, aspects of factory
management etc. were either wholly or largely copied from
the Soviet Union. In March 1958, when Mao had begun to
initiate moves towards a Chinese way to socialism, he looked
back critically at the period of the First Five-Year Plan:

In the period following the liberation of the whole country,
dogmatism made its appearance both in economic and in
cultural and educational work. A certain amount of dogmatism was imported in military work, but basic principles
were upheld, and you still could not say that our military
work was dogmatic. In economic work dogmatism primarily
manifested itself in heavy industry, planning, banking and
statistics, especially in heavy industry and planning. Since
we did not understand these things and had absolutely no
experience, all we could do in our ignorance was to import
foreign methods. Our statistical work was practically a
copy of Soviet work; in the educational field copying was
also pretty bad, for example, the system of a maximum
mark of five in the schools, the uniform five years of
primary school, etc. We did not even study our own experience of education in the liberated areas.[48]

Two years earlier, in his address of 25 April 1956 on the Ten Great Relationships, Mao had still argued for learning from the Soviet Union, but on the basis that the strong and weak points of both countries should be recognised, and he returned to the theme he had first advanced in the late thirties of the need to combine the 'universal truth of Marxism—Leninism with the concrete reality of China'. He added significantly, 'We must be able to think independently.' As for China itself he identified two weak points which were also strong points:

(1) China's backwardness: arising from its past colonial and semi-colonial status and the lack of industrial development we 'felt inferior to others in every respect', so that it is necessary 'to raise the self confidence of our people' and at the same time study 'all the good points of foreign countries, their politics, their economics, their science and technology and their literature and art.

(2) The relative lateness of the Chinese revolution. But arising out of these weaknesses he made the point he was to make famous 2 years later, that the Chinese people were poor and blank. Therefore they want change and revolution and they have unlimited potential. Here he hastened to add that he was not saying we have no knowledge at all. Two years later at the height of the Great Leap Forward this qualification was omitted.

Mao's general position is clear, however, in that like radical nationalists elsewhere in the Third World, he recognised the need to 'learn' from abroad, while at the same time asserting the independence and creativity of his people. The success of the Soviet transfer of heavy industrial technology in the fifties was in part achieved because China also transferred much of the administrative and managerial infrastructure of which it was a product. Yet it was precisely the stifling effect of this copying on China's capacity for independent creativity and initiative which Mao found offensive. By the Eighth Party Congress of September 1956, although few of Mao's colleagues found favour with the leap forward approach which Mao had pushed through in the latter part of 1955 and the early part of 1956, they had also recognised real difficulties in following the Soviet model and various economic strategies were mooted at the Congress. But few if any shared Mao's 'revolutionary romanticism'. His propagandists defined it as 'an attitude consisting in . . . trying to see the new things in life, trying to be good at reflecting the new things and helping them develop'.[49] For Mao in particular what was objectionable about the Sino-Soviet economic relationship was less its economic aspects than the uncritical copying of Soviet institutions and the passivity of psychological dependence which it engendered.

In some ways it could be argued that Mao was less uneasy with acquiring advanced technology and 'learning' from the West than he was with learning from the Soviet Union. China and the CPC had much more in common organisationally and ideologically with the Soviet Union and with the CPSU, and therefore they were much more in danger of being 'taken over' or subordinated to the advanced position of the Soviets. The Capitalist West, however, by virtue of its capitalism could perhaps be more easily kept at arm's length and Chinese society could be more readily closed off from its influences. At least this was arguable for the sixties and early seventies. At the same time it should be recognised that nothing that Mao has said or written suggests that he would have countenanced what his successors call their 'open-door' policy of economic relations with the West.

Socialist values and foreign influence

Few leaders have been as concerned with the transformation of their society as Mao. Moreover his concern has been as much with the inculcation of a revolutionary socialist consciousness as it has been with changing social structures. Indeed his preoccupation with the question of socialist values deepened in the late fifties and came to dominate much of his thinking during the last 20 years of his life. The issues acquired shape and coherence in his approach to politics in the context of the conflict with the Soviet Union and his attempt to learn from the 'negative' example of what he considered to be revisionism in the Soviet Union and Eastern

Europe. From there it was but a short step to arguing that the spectre of revisionism existed in China too and that there was a real danger of China 'changing colour'. These concerns played a major part in the unleashing of the Cultural Revolution. Although Mao was not xenophobic it is easy to see how the idea that a China which was undergoing a kind of self-purification, and which was endangered from 'revisionist' influences from the Soviet Union and its associates on the one hand and from bourgeois attitudes associated with the West, headed by the United States on the other, would seek to close its doors to all foreign societal influences. Thus for Mao the question of China's socialist development was by no means only an economic one. The relationship between the pursuit of socialist values within China and the cultivation of relations with other countries is clearly an important element of Mao's legacy.

As we have seen in his articles and speeches in 1949 Mao touched upon the theme of cultural imperialism as well as other aspects of imperialist penetration of China. Moreover he was also engaged in the exercise of persuading the Chinese people to re-think their attitude towards the Soviet Union. An important feature of the first 3 years of rehabilitation and consolidation after the 1949 victory was a campaign to denigrate American cultural influence in the cities, especially among the Western-educated intellectuals. The campaign was accentuated during the Korean War – known in China as Resist America, Aid Korea.[50] At the same time great efforts were made to project a positive image of the Soviet Union. Both because of Chinese traditions and communist organisational methods it was possible to keep a tight rein on Chinese contacts with foreigners and to control the extent of direct foreign influence upon Chinese society. This was especially true of the urban areas where the main problem lay. Western influence was associated with bourgeois attitudes and was linked especially with two social groups: the national bourgeoisie and the intelligentsia. Although the national bourgeoisie tended to have links with the Overseas Chinese (including those in Hong Kong) it was perhaps the intelligentsia, and particularly the higher intellectuals, who were seen as posing most problems for the CPC and for the inculcation of a social-

ist consciousness. If Chinese tradition and communist organisational know-how facilitated the maintenance of tight social
controls over the intelligentsia, these two factors also ensured
that the intelligentsia had an importance out of proportion to
their numbers of capacity to wield political power. Chinese
tradition, of course, accorded the highly educated high status
as the purveyors of true social value and as the people from
whom officials were recruited, while the Leninist Party, in
basing its legitimacy on its self-appointed role as the bearer
of true proletarian consciousness, has always paid importance
to intellectual themes and cultural challenges to its 'correct
line'. No Communist Party in power has enjoyed good relations with the intellectual community of its country; and, as
many have pointed out, there has always been an antipathy
in Mao towards intellectuals. As a Third World country China
was short of a trained intelligentsia for economic development. The overwhelming majority of Communist cadres who
ran the urban sector in the early fifties were ill-educated men
from the countryside who had proved themselves in the civil
war and in the Land Reform Campaigns. In the long term it
was hoped that a new intelligentsia would be trained who
would be both 'red' and 'expert'. In the event the Cultural
Revolution decade of 1966—76 destroped that hope. But no-
one could have known that in the fifties, and meanwhile it
was necessary to make do with the available talent. The problem in the early fifties, however, was Communist mistrust of
the largely Western-educated intellectuals who therefore were
compelled to undergo a process of remoulding.[51]

By 1956 it was thought that a sufficient number of China's
intelligentsia had been remoulded so that 80 per cent of their
number either actively or passively supported the CPC.
Moreover, now that the economy had been socialised, their
services were needed even more to prime the pumps of economic construction. In his report on the question of January
1956, Zhou called on the Party to treat the intellectuals better
in order to get the best out of them. Mao endorsed the new
policy, putting most emphasis on the need to attain rapidly
the advanced scientific levels of the outside world. Following
this, intellectuals were given better conditions with higher
salaries. The more relaxed conditions, followed by Mao's reac-

tion to the upheavals in Poland and Hungary later that year, led to the Hundred Flowers movement in which intellectuals in particular were encouraged to identify problems in the Party's behaviour towards them. The assumption was that they accepted the general socialist programme and the political system. Instead, by a combination of opposition in the Party to the movement itself and the extremism of the criticism of some of the intellectuals, the campaign came to an abrupt halt in June 1957, to be replaced by an anti-rightist campaign. Hundreds of thousands of intellectuals were condemned as bourgeois rightists. As Roderick MacFarquhar has pointed out, Mao had sought to improve relations with students and intellectuals against the wishes of his senior colleagues by inviting the former to air their problems with the Party. But Mao had underestimated the bitterness of the intellectuals. He was able to minimise the Party's revenge to a certain extent — but his own prestige had been badly damaged. Thereafter Mao paid more attention to the need for the proletariat and the peasantry to train their own intelligentsia.[52] It should be noted that the leading 'bourgeois rightists' singled out for most criticism were all non-communist older intellectuals who were leaders of the small powerless so-called democratic Parties.

The Great Leap Forward as a time of high mobilisation politics which was self-consciously asserting a Chinese way to socialism was necessarily anti-expert and therefore also against the foreign expert. The Russians were later to complain that their technicians and experts were subject to unacceptable pressures and that this was an important reason for the decision to withdraw them. Although Mao had called for people to be both red and expert there was a sense, as has been pointed out in the first chapter, in which redness was associated with nativism and the guerrilla style, and the expert with foreignness and an elitist style. Both aspects, of course, combined negative and positive connotations.

The early sixties of the economic depression and the recovery from that saw something of a rehabilitation of the role of the expert. But in the context of the deepening rift with the Soviet Union and the struggle with imperialism against a backdrop of a weakened economy, the opportunities for foreign links were minimal. The contracts for the importation of turnkey projects from Western Europe and Japan between 1963 and 1966 were only worth some $200 million compared with more than ten times as much in the early fifties and the early seventies. Meanwhile Mao was manoeuvring towards the Cultural Revolution which entailed the closing of the doors to foreign influences and the attack on the intelligentsia and Party officials at all levels in a mood of acute xenophobia.

However, as on other issues, Mao's position on the relationship between domestic socialist values and foreign influence is not free of ambiguities. As Stuart Schram has pointed out:

> while Mao [was] a deeply convinced Leninist revolutionary, and while the categories in which he reason[ed] [were] Marxist categories, the deepest springs of his personality [were], to a large extent, to be found in the Chinese tradition; and China's glory [was] at least as important to him as world revolution.[53]

Such a man would clearly not wish to pave the way for his country to become wide open to foreign penetration. Yet at the same time he recognised the need for the importation of foreign technology. In 1956 Mao dismissed the nineteenth-century slogan of 'Chinese learning for substance (*ti*) and western learning for practical application (*yong*)' on the grounds that Marxism is a universal theory which came from the West and therefore it was not possible to distinguish between what was Chinese and Western in that regard. On the other hand, 'complete Westernisation' was unacceptable to the Chinese people and the reason for learning from abroad was 'to develop Chinese things'. By 1965, after Mao had come to regard China as the true source of Marxism—Leninism because of the revisionism of the Russians, he changed his position on the *ti-yong* slogan. He now argued:

> The substance (*ti*) was like our General Line, which cannot be changed. We cannot adopt western learning as the substance, nor can we use the substance of the democratic republic. We cannot use 'the natural rights of man' nor 'the

theory of revolution'. We can only use western technology.[54]

This was said on the eve of the Cultural Revolution, but in its attitude to Western technology it reflects the position which he endorsed in the early seventies. Whether or not by then he was as confident about the General Line as he was in 1965 cannot be known. While Mao certainly had directed China's foreign policy along the new lines of the seventies and may be said to have approved 'the use of Western technology' employed then, Chinese politics during these last 5 years of his life were marked by factional strife and the absence of an agreed or recognisable 'General Line'. To be sure foreign influences in Chinese social life were subject to tight controls and they were kept to a minimum. But unlike the fifties when his credibility and that of the Party were still high, especially in the enthusiasm for the new China in the early years, the seventies were marked by disillusionment with both Mao and the Party and especially by disillusionment with the Cultural Revolution and the dislocations it had created. The Tian An Men demonstration of 5 April 1976 — which was the first truly large-scale spontaneous mass demonstration since 1949 — was to a large extent a popular outcry and protest against the arbitrary tyranny for which Mao had been largely responsible by his launching of the Cultural Revolution. He had, perhaps unwittingly, bequeathed to his successors not a China that would not change colour, but a disillusioned populace with social and economic problems of gargantuan proportions. Yet such was his mark on the Chinese Revolution and on the PRC that he could not be repudiated by his successors without undermining the political system itself. Thus the question would be as to how his successors would choose to identify his legacy. It was to Mao's credit that whatever course they might choose, xenophobic isolationism was not part of his thought. Beyond that his 'true position' on relating Chinese society to the outside world remained elusive and shot through with ambiguities.

At times Mao has presided over policies which entailed significant degrees of dependence on other countries to import advanced technology and techniques of management,

etc., as in the early fifties when he called upon his countrymen to set up a 'tidal wave of learning from the Soviet Union',
or in 1963—65 and still more, in the early seventies when he
allowed the importation from the west of large-scale industrial plants employing advanced technology. At other times
Mao presided over policies of virtual autarky in which he
claimed that once their energies were unleashed the Chinese
masses could storm the economic heights by their own unaided efforts. Yet both sets of policies were justified by
reference to the slogan of 'self-reliance'. Mao's other related
slogan to use foreign things selectively to serve China was
equally ambiguous as the basis for the selection was never
made clear, nor in practice was it ever consistent.

3

Mao's Legacy of Geopolitical Thought

Mao's legacy in the strategic domain of what might be called
geopolitical thought or power politics is less ambiguous even
though it has never been formally articulated. By geopolitical
thought I refer to the broader use of the term. As used here
the term refers not only to the significance of geographical
factors in international politics, but it also relates to the
larger view as to the nature of power and its place in international affairs. In other words, I shall argue that Mao had a
coherent and distinctive view of the character of international
politics in which considerations of balance of power played a
large part. It will be argued that it was this vision which
effectively guided the Chinese ship of state in its position of
relative weakness in the face of challenges to its independence
by countries militarily stronger than itself.

Mao's thinking on these questions, as on many others, has
not been synthesised into a coherent analytical whole. Rather
it has to be deduced from his writings and speeches on related
aspects of the subject spanning many years. These must then
be considered in the light of Chinese actions. Nevertheless it
is possible to identify a consistent viewpoint on questions
relating to political power in Mao's writings and actions spanning his 40 years' leadership of the CPC from 1935 until his
death in 1976. Indeed in certain respects it is possible to trace
this consistency back to the beginnings of his leadership of
the guerrilla base established in 1927—28. Throughout this
entire period Mao and the forces which he led were weaker
than the enemy. Thus until virtually the very end the opposing
armies of first Chiang Kai-shek, then the Japanese, and finally

Chiang Kai-shek again were superior on paper to those of the Communists before they won nationwide victory in 1949. Since 1949 the PRC has been under the constant threat of attack by one or other of the militarily superior superpowers. Mao's 'text' therefore may be described in one of his deceptively simple slogans to the effect that the weak can defeat the strong; or as he once put it towards the end of his life:

> Innumerable facts prove that a just cause enjoys abundant support while an unjust cause finds little support. A weak nation can defeat a strong, a small nation can defeat a big. The people of a small country can certainly defeat aggression by a big country, *if only they dare to rise in struggle, dare to take up arms and grasp in their own hands the destiny of their country*. This is a law of history. [Emphasis added.][1]

As the italicised passage makes clear, the key lies in daring to struggle and daring to determine one's own fate independently. Mao's writings and actions throughout the various stages of the Chinese revolution and the different phases of the PRC testify to an unshaken belief in the invincibility of a people aroused to revolution under a leadership which is in continuous direct interactions with it. The task of that leadership is to articulate the demands and aspirations of the people in accordance with Marxist–Leninist principles as they apply to the conditions of that country.

This may be regarded as a view as to what constitutes political legitimacy and indeed Mao evolved the doctrine of the 'mass line' to give it substance as a political process. One might add that it was a process that worked relatively well in the revolutionary base of Yan'an, but one that raised acute problems under the conditions of the bureaucratised state power of the PRC. Yet this was more than a view of political legitimacy; it also lay at the heart of Mao's geopolitical theories as to how national liberation could be won in Third World countries and as to how an apparently militarily inferior developing country can hold out for true independence against the superpowers.

Strangely, despite the vast corpus of scholarly writing on

Mao and on Chinese foreign policy, there is not a great deal devoted to specific analysis of his thinking and conduct of foreign policy. Various aspects of the subject have been extensively analysed and debated by Western writers, but a general study of his approach to, and conduct of, China's relations with the outside world has yet to be written. As a result this chapter will not attempt to provide what might be regarded as a synoptic overview of Mao's legacy in foreign policy. Instead it will focus on what I have called Mao's geopolitical thought. That is to say it will examine the thinking about international politics which has underlain the strategic dimensions of China's foreign policy.

First, however, a few caveats are in order. For convenience of analysis the following account will attribute much of the thinking and attitudes underlying China's foreign policy to Mao personally. Although there can be little doubt that Mao's was the dominant voice in the making of Peking's foreign policy, it was by no means the only one. Zhou Enlai, for example, is generally considered to have been the main architect of the policy of cultivating better relations with other Asian governments in the mid-fifties and as the main implementor of China's foreign policy, he was much more than a mere mouthpiece for Mao.[2] Nevertheless, it is not unreasonable to suggest that he operated within a framework of a general design which emanated largely from Mao. Moreover, unlike the domestic arena, there are no recorded instances of other voices prevailing over Mao's objections on a major foreign policy issue. Liu Shaoqi in 1966 and Lin Biao in 1968–71 tried to promote alternative foreign policy lines to those favoured by Mao and they both lost.[3] It is also true that on those occasions when the initial idea for a foreign policy initiative did not emanate from him (for example, when Foreign Minister Chen Yi suggested in the early sixties that the PRC might cultivate better relations with the Western Europeans) it required Mao's ultimate approval before it could become an important component of China's foreign policy position. Thus no significant distortion will arise from using the convenient shorthand of attributing so much to Mao.

A graver objection to this 'shorthand convenience' is that to personalise China's foreign policy in this way is to ignore important characteristics about the making of foreign policy which are as true for China as they are elsewhere. Namely, that much of foreign policy is the result of contingency adjustments to unexpected developments in the external environment coupled with the different 'pulling and hauling' of interested domestic groups and bureaucracies. Nevertheless the personalised approach to be followed here can be justified in the sense that it is not directed towards explaining China's foreign policy process; but it is instead concerned with identifying the general themes which provide the guidelines and priorities within which these processes take place. Indeed it is possible to go further and claim that it was Mao's strategic vision which shaped China's general foreign policy and which determined its main turning points. Whenever this was challenged — for example, on Sino—Soviet relations in the sixties, or on the opening to the United States in 1968—71 — Mao always exerted himself to prevail over his domestic opponents.

Mao's geopolitical perspectives

Although Mao did not specifically address himself to this theme, a very strong and insistent geopolitical strand is clearly visible in his writings. Much of Mao's writings on imperialism, for example, is concerned with its political and military aspects rather than with discourses on such orthodox Leninist themes as the political economy of advanced capitalism and its impact on the rest of the world. Similarly, one can look in vain in his writings for analyses of the impact of imperialism on class relations in colonies. To be sure he had much to say about class relations in China, especially during the period of revolutionary and civil wars before 1949; but if his writings on these themes are examined more closely it will be seen that he was less concerned with the analysis of the political economy in question than he was with the political and revolutionary consequences of China's class divisions.[4]

Mao analysed at some length, and at different stages in his career, the peculiarities of China's status as a semi-colony and the consequences of that for class alignments. But despite his avowed interest in revolution in what is now called the Third World and in the importance of the newly emerged Third World in international politics, Mao did not choose to inform himself closely about these countries.[5] Unlike Zhou Enlai, he never once visited any of the countries of Asia, Africa or Latin America. The only country he is known to have visited is the Soviet Union. The bulk of his writing and discourses on foreign affairs dealt with the Soviet Union and the United States. In fact Mao had far more to say about the medium capitalist powers such as Britain, France and Japan than about the countries of the Third World.

Mao was not a geopolitical theorist as such, but like Lenin — especially when he became leader of Russia — considerations of power and balances of forces in international affairs were an important component of his political vision. Indeed it was unavoidable that this should be so, as both leaders were confronted by an implacably hostile international environment in which their fledgling new régimes were under constant threat from overwhelmingly more powerful countries. It was also true that in their different ways both the Bolshevik and Chinese Revolutions challenged the existing international order. Nevertheless in the immediate situation (and as things turned out, for the indefinite future) the new revolutionary régimes had to devise strategies which would enable them to survive amid external threats while at the same time building socialism at home and developing their economies. These sets of goals all required the establishment of a strong state able to marshall the country's resources for external defence and domestic construction. These imperatives have given rise to the apparent paradox by which both China and the Soviet Union in their different ways have carried out revolution at home and relatively conservative balance of power politics abroad.

Mao's approach must also be understood within the context of China's modern history and the experience of revolutionary armed struggle which ultimately brought him to power in 1949. Modern Chinese history in the century before the establishment of the PRC is regarded by most Chinese as one of shame and national humiliation. Beginning with the Opium War of 1840 China fell into decay under the impact of foreign intervention. Imperial China crumbled; its traditional values were shown to be unequal to the tasks of meeting the new challenges; and it eventually fell, leaving the country as prey to warlord armies. Meanwhile China had become the object of great power competition as various powers divided the country into respective spheres of influence, and its major cities had sections where foreigners claimed extraterritorial rights. Those of the generation of Mao and Deng Xiaoping who were born before the First World War had all experienced directly this sense of national shame and humiliation. Whatever their political persuasion, Chinese who have been marked by this experience have all been committed to the goal of establishing a strong and united Chinese state. No Chinese, especially of this generation, needed to be taught Bismark's lesson that the great issues of the day are not settled by resolutions or by majorities, but by iron and blood. However, these national revolutionaries also knew that if China's international position were to be transformed there would first have to be a domestic social and political transformation.

Mao's leadership of the Chinese revolution under conditions of armed struggle in the countryside may be seen as the triumph over adversity in which the revolutionary forces moved from abject weakness to absolute power. His speeches and writings during this period may be seen as concerned with charting the appropriate strategies and tactics of gradually shifting the adverse balance of forces in favour of the CPC while maintaining and developing its revolutionary identity. These balances of forces include not only domestic factors but the external forces of imperialism as well. It was the geopolitical thought developed in those years which largely shaped Mao's approach to international politics after the establishment of the PRC.

Contradictions

One of the most significant elements in Mao's thought generally, and in his strategic thinking in particular, concerns the question of contradictions or the conflicts within and between all social phenomena. For Mao, contradictions were the stuff of life. At one point he even asserted, 'If there were no contradictions and no struggle, there would be no progress, there would be nothing at all, no life.'[6] Contradictions, dialectics and the unity of opposites were so crucial to his epistemology that he once suggested that it was possible to do without Hegel's and Marx's negation of the negation (which in their view alone ensured progress in the dialectical cycle of thesis and antithesis).[7] This however is not the place to examine Mao's epistemology.[8] Suffice it to say that Mao's universe was one of constant change in which balance and harmony were by definition temporary and relative whereas imbalance and struggle were enduring and absolute.[9] More than once he addressed his colleagues as follows:

> One thing destroys another, things emerge, develop, and are destroyed, everywhere is like this. If things are not destroyed by others, then they destroy themselves. . . . Socialism, too, will be eliminated, it wouldn't do if it were not eliminated, for then there would be no Communism. Communism will last for thousands and thousands of years. I don't believe that there will be no qualitative changes under Communism. . . . The life of dialectics is the continuous movement towards opposites. Mankind will also meet its doom. When the theologians talk about doomsday they are pessimistic and terrify people. We say the end of mankind will produce something more advanced than mankind. Mankind is still in its infancy. . . . [10]

> There is hardly a matter which is not transformable. The urgent becomes relaxed and the relaxed becomes urgent. Labour becomes leisure and leisure becomes labour. . . .

> Matter always has a beginning and an end. Only two things are limitless, time and space. . . . Everything develops gradually and changes gradually.[11]

As Michel Oksenberg has pointed out, Mao viewed power in dynamic rather than static terms; he had a different sense of time and history from that typically possessed by Western leaders. Being so concerned with motion he focused less upon immediate power balances than upon trends.[12] In a world of flux determined by contradictions — the struggle between opposites — the political leader must be ever sensitive to identifying which of the many changes are truly significant so that he can seize the initiative and try to determine their outcome.

Applied to politics and strategy, from an early stage Mao's insistent approach was that it was necessary at any given time to identify among the many contradictions confronting the Chinese revolution which was the primary or the principal one. Once identified all the other contradictions should be subordinated to it. In this way the principal contradiction, or major enemy, depended on the particular stage of the Marxist historical process and on the relative strengths of the opposing forces. Thus during the War of Resistance to Japan Mao sought to unite all those who could be united in the struggle against Japan. Once the war was over the target shifted to Chiang Kai-shek with the corollary that the potential partners in the united front changed to all those groups and classes who had a stake in opposing Chiang and his Western backers. Thus landlords, providing they were patriotic, were potential allies against Japan, but were enemies in the second united front. This perhaps helps to account for the fluidity of Mao's alignments and indeed for his view of international politics as being in constant flux. In 1971, when China's propagandists tried to explain why Mao was prepared to open his doors to President Nixon (hitherto regarded as the chieftain of American imperialism), they re-issued a long-forgotten essay by Mao from 1940 which dealt with the formation of united fronts.[13] Still later in the seventies, when it was necessary to explain how uniting with apparently reactionary leaders of Third World countries could be described as revolutionary, the propagandists referred to a little-known passage in Mao's celebrated article 'On New Democracy' (also of 1940) which goes right to the heart of his strategy of united fronts:

No matter what classes, parties or individuals in an oppressed nation join the revolution, and no matter whether they themselves are conscious of the point or understand it, so long as they oppose imperialism, their revolution becomes part of the proletarian—socialist world revolution and become its allies.

As Mao explained it:

> The contradictions and struggles among the cliques of war-
> lords in China reflect the contradictions and struggles
> among the imperialist powers. Hence as long as China is
> divided among the imperialist powers, the various cliques
> of warlords cannot under any circumstances come to terms,
> and whatever compromises they may make will only be
> temporary. A temporary compromise today engenders a
> bigger war tomorrow.[14]

A good example of the application of Mao's application of
his thinking on contradictions in his early writings is what
John Gittings has called 'Mao's theory of semi-colonialism'.[15]
In the 1920s it was commonplace among Chinese revolutionaries to compare unfavourably China's position with India,
because the latter had only one colonial oppressor and the
former had to contend with all the great powers. When small
red rural bases were being established in the hinterland of
southeast China after the Communists had been virtually
wiped out in the cities, Mao rallied his pitifully few forces
against the threat of extinction by the more numerous and
better armed forces of warlords and Chiang Kai-shek backed
by the Western powers. He argued that it was precisely because
there were several warlord cliques and various imperial
powers all vying for control and influence in China, that they
would have difficulty in uniting against the red bases. The
revolutionaries could survive and prosper if they held fast to
their political line and if they were good at exploiting the
contradictions among the enemy. India, by inference, was
less favoured by having only the one colonial overlord which
would have little difficulty in mustering its forces to suppress
an armed uprising or a red base area.

Mao's understanding of contradictions and his practice of
united fronts also had the corollary of making him (and as
long as he led them) the CPC and the PRC the most unpredictable and unreliable of allies. Given Mao's position that the
CPC should at all times be careful not to lose its identity in

any united front and that it should be ever ready to change its policies in accordance with changes in the direction of the principal contradiction, the CPC could only ever be a temporary and uneasy ally. The list of Parties and groups within China and of countries outside who have been allies and friends only to be discarded with the march of the dialectic is a long one.

The assessment of strengths and weaknesses

In a world of flux in which the underlying trends of the weak-becoming-strong or the strong-becoming-weak were considered by Mao as more significant in the long run than any temporary balances of military strength it is important to ask what, for Mao, was true strength or weakness? What, for him, were the main sources of power? Oksenberg has argued persuasively that while acknowledging the potency of wealth and material abundance, Mao preferred to rely on other types of power. Wealth facilitates corruption, and abundance can lead to decay. Mao certainly recognised the efficacy of military power but, as is well known, he always argued that although weapons were important in war, people and their morale were ultimately decisive. While he was not averse to using physical coercion, Mao recognised the need for popular support. As he once said, 'The army must become one with the people so that they see it as their own army. Such an army will be invincible.' Yet Mao also 'felt that those who controlled the thoughts of the Chinese people thereby determined their destiny'. This in turn required contact with popular opinion, knowledge of their social conditions and proper organisation to mobilize an 'aroused people' so that the leader could seize and hold the initiative with the appropriate strategy.[16]

This is especially relevant to revolutionary forces struggling for material liberation against militarily more powerful reactionary and imperialist armies and, by extension, to countries subject to threats of external dominance by militarily superior powers. As noted in the beginning of this chapter, implicit in this approach is the doctrine that legitimate political power is held only by revolutionaries who truly represent the aspirations of the people and who are fully integrated with them.

On this point Mao had a highly elaborate set of doctrines
about the correct relationship between the leaders and the
led which are generally subsumed under the headings of the
'mass line' and 'democratic centralism'.[17] Perhaps the most
widely known of Mao's writings on how to overcome a superior and modern force are those on people's war — principally
his celebrated essays on the war of resistance to Japan.[18] Of
greatest interest to us is less the doctrine of people's war itself
(with its elaboration of the three modes of warfare — guerrilla,
mobile and positional — and when to move from one phase
to the other) than how to calculate the relative strengths and
weaknesses of aggressive Japan and defensive China. In sum-
marising a long and complex argument Mao concluded:

> . . . Japan has great military, economic and political—
> organizational power, but . . . her war is reactionary and
> barbarous, her manpower and material resources are in-
> adequate, and she is in an unfavourable position internation-
> ally. China, on the contrary, has less military, economic
> and political—organizational power, but she is in her era of
> progress, her war is progressive and just, she is moreover a
> big country, a factor which enables her to sustain a pro-
> tracted war, and she will be supported by most countries.[19]

Mao went on to claim that the above factors would determine
the policies and strategies of the conflict and that they would
ensure that the war would be protracted and that China would
inevitably win in the end. Interestingly Mao had specific
meanings for the much-abused and often empty terms 'reactionary' and 'progressive'. Japan's war was reactionary because,
unlike the British during their subjugation of India, imperialism
was now on the wane, the fascist countries were engaged in
desperate last struggles while many of the other countries
were either embroiled in war or were about to be so. China
was progressive because much had changed since the nineteenth century. China was no longer completely feudal, there
now was some capitalism and there was a bourgeoisie and a
proletariat too. Moreover vast numbers of people had been
'awakened'; there was a Communist Party which led a red
army and a people which had been schooled by the decades

of revolution and political struggle. Hence it was possible to achieve popular unity against Japan.

In the light of this it is worth considering Mao's explanation for the subjugation of Abyssinia (Ethiopia) by Italy:

> Why was Abyssinia vanquished? First she was not only weak but also small. Second, she was not as progressive as China; she was an old country passing from the slave to the serf system, a country without any capitalism or bourgeois political parties, let alone a Communist Party, and with no army such as the Chinese army, let alone one like the Eighth Route Army. Third, she was unable to hold out and wait for international assistance and had to fight her war in isolation. Fourth and most important of all, there were mistakes in the direction of her war against Italy. Therefore Abyssinia was subjugated. But there is still quite extensive guerrilla warfare in Abyssinia, which, if persisted in, will enable the Abyssinians to recover their country when the world situation changes.[20]

These brief extracts from Mao's essay 'On Protracted War' of May 1938 bring out very well some of his enduring thinking on geopolitics. Far from ignoring what might be regarded as the hard facts of military capabilities Mao accorded them a high priority in his analysis. But he qualified their significance in ways different from those of conventional Western strategists. Like them Mao has paid attention to military capabilities and to the size of the country, except that we should also note that he is heir to traditional Chinese concerns for the importance of geographical space and of the significance of time. But Mao was also concerned with the capacity of the society to organise itself for conflict, which he analysed within a Leninist framework. He additionally placed the conflict within a larger international context — a point which will be enlarged upon later. There is also the implication in his analysis that a drawn-out war favours the defensive side, especially if it is also morally correct. Mao attached considerable significance to the quality of leadership. Although set-backs were unavoidable, ultimate victory would still belong to the defender against imperialist aggression provided that he continued to maintain a principled armed struggle. He could then hope for a combination of deepening domestic problems for the aggressor and for changes in the international situation which would put growing pressure on the aggressor so as to deliver ultimate victory to the defender of national integrity. Even though Mao may not have had much to say about the political economy of imperialism, as a self-conscious Marxist–Leninist he accepted implicitly that imperialist aggression was undertaken by a government which was necessarily divorced from its people; so that prolonged conflict would ultimately bring this underlying tension to the surface. But the primary factor is that the people should 'dare to rise in struggle, dare to take up arms and grasp in their own hands the destiny of their country'.

Imperialist strategy and the significance of the Third World

One consequence of Mao's position as sketched out above is that unlike the Soviet leaders he did not go in for what I have called elsewhere 'bloc thinking'.[21] In other words, the logic of Mao's position is that the world does not divide itself into objectively definable camps or blocs. Although Marx's classic slogan of proletarian internationalism, 'workers of the world unite', has always been prominently displayed in Peking's Tian An Men Square from 1949 onwards, that has never formed an important part of Mao's thinking. Unlike some of his colleagues, Mao was never closely involved with the Comintern and his independent course from Moscow is too well known to require elaboration here. In many respects Mao might be thought of as more of a Third World Marxist revolutionary than as a figure within the European or Soviet Marxist traditions. Perhaps the most significant indication of this in the realm of geopolitics as developed by Mao before 1949 is his analysis of the world situation in the aftermath of the Second World War. Not only did his analysis differ considerably from that of Stalin, but it accorded a significant independent role to the 'intermediate zone' — or what is now called the Third World — in determining the issue of peace or war in the world at large. At the same time it also brought his struggles in China to the heart of the issue.

The Soviet Union at that time was moving towards the 'two-camp' thesis which held that the world was divided into two antagonistic blocs and that the purpose of the imperialist bloc headed by the United States was to attack the Soviet Union, the head of the camp of socialism and peace. It followed therefore that every Communist movement should prudently avoid provocative acts against the United States lest this might lead to an attack on the Soviet Union, which would spark off World War III. This was undoubtedly one of the reasons which led Stalin to advise the CPC not to take up arms against Chiang Kai-shek in 1945–46. Mao, however, argued very differently and advanced a view about the targets of imperialism and, by implication, about the characteristics of the conflict between Russia and America which was to have a most profound influence on subsequent Chinese assessments of world politics and on China's actions in the strategic–political arena. He suggested that, despite the anti-Communist declaratory statements by American 'reactionaries' their immediate target was not the Soviet Union:

> The United States and the Soviet Union are separated by a vast zone which includes many capitalist, colonial and semi-colonial countries in Europe, Asia and Africa. Before the US reactionaries have subjugated these countries, an attack on the Soviet Union is out of the question.

Mao went on to argue that the supposedly anti-Soviet military bases which were located in various countries had as their first targets the places where they were based. These he claimed, were being transformed into American dependencies. In characteristic language Mao declared:

> I think the American people and peoples of all countries menaced by US aggression should unite and struggle against the attacks of the US reactionaries and their running dogs in these countries. Only by victory in this struggle can a third world war be avoided; otherwise it is unavoidable.[22]

This analysis not only provided a rationale for carrying out armed struggle against the forces of Chiang Kai-shek, allied as they were to the United States, but in fact it made that the internationalist duty of the CPC. The analysis, however, was to have a wider significance as it made out the case for arguing later that the basic struggle between the two superpowers was to be fought out not in direct conflict between them, but rather in attempts to gain control of what might be called their periphery — principally the countries of the Third World. It also prepared the ground work for the later argument that the issue of peace or war in the world would be decided by the degree of effective resistance by Third World countries to superpower attempts to dominate them.

Mao's geopolitics and Chinese foreign policy

As was suggested in Chapter 1, the 27 years of Mao's leadership of the PRC can be divided into three roughly equal periods: for most of the fifties China was allied with the Soviet Union and under threat from the United States; from the late fifties until the late sixties China was in dispute with the Soviet Union while seeking alignment with the Third World and still under threat from the United States; and from the early seventies China was under threat from the Soviet Union and in alignment with the United States. As this oversimplified account suggests, the one common theme throughout these years is the sense of threat from one or other of the two superpowers. It is also true that China too loomed very large in the strategic calculations of the two super-powers. Throughout the fifties and the sixties America strove to maintain the capability to fight 'two and a half wars' — that is, against Russia, China and a half war elsewhere. During the same period the United States fought two major wars in Asia (the only wars, as opposed to brief military interventions, which American forces have fought singe 1945) with the declared aim of 'containing' China. In the seventies China has been regarded by successive American administrations as an essential factor in managing the relationship with the Soviet Union. As for the Soviet perspective, China has been transformed from an uneasy ally to a seemingly implacable enemy so that since the late sixties a quarter of the Soviet armed forces have been deployed in the Soviet Far East and in Mongolia near the borders with China. The old Soviet fear of possibly having to face two fronts simultaneously in the East and in the West would appear to have been realised.

A case can be made for the proposition that both the super-powers in their different ways have exaggerated the importance of China in their strategic perspectives. As was argued in the first chapter, China's military capabilities, combined with its limited transport and communication systems and its relatively technologically backward economy, have limited China to being a military power of only regional significance. Even within its region China's capacity to project its military power has been limited. To be sure the PRC has shown itself prepared to use armed force to uphold what its leaders have regarded as major security interests, and all these occasions have witnessed Chinese armies engaged in warfare outside Chinese territory. But these incursions have always been adjacent to China's borders and they have been limited in duration and in the extent of penetration of neighbouring territory. The one exception was the Korean War, but that exception is highly suggestive of the limitations of China's war-fighting machine. In one sense Korea can be represented as a major Chinese success; it was the first occasion in modern history when Chinese forces successfully held out against Western armies, and indeed they claimed victory by virtue of having driven these modernized armies back from the Chinese border to the 38th Parallel. But a closer examination reveals a more complex situation. China's initial success was due very largely to surprise. Even so Chinese casualties were high against the more modern firepower of the enemy. Once the war had settled during its last 2 years into a war of attrition roughly along the 38th Parallel which still divides North and South Korea, Chinese casualties rose even more alarmingly. Moreover, despite the comparative advantages of operating near to home and having longer flight-times over battle areas, the Chinese airforce was greatly outperformed by that of America: ten Chinese planes were shot down for every American. Interestingly, the Chinese have never officially released their casualty figures for the Korean War and, despite the almost uninterrupted flow of memoirs and reminiscences of Chinese generals and soldiers about the revolutionary wars and the war against Japan, the Chinese have had remarkably little to say in this respect about their fighting in Korea. Yet these reminiscences are supposedly designed to guide the young in the principles of warfare. American sources suggest that Chinese casualties in the Korean War numbered in the hundreds of thousands.[23] Whatever Mao's true feelings about China's performance in Korea (where he lost a son) he never again engaged modern Western armies, and the fear of that may have been one of the factors which led to the withdrawal of China's forces from Korea after the end of the war. The only other occasion on which China's airforce engaged American planes in prolonged combat was during the offshore island crisis of 1958 when once again it suffered badly, but that time by planes flown by Chiang Kai-shek's pilots.

This hardly suggests that China was a country of global military strategic significance. It should also be noted that China has always lacked an ocean-going navy. Yet first America and then the Soviet Union have devoted considerable resources over many years to the containment of a supposedly expansionist China which the Russians allege is seeking world hegemony. Obviously a country of China's size, population and geographical location was bound to play an important part in world affairs once it had been united under an effective government. Yet it is difficult to explain the great, almost obsessive, attention which both the superpowers have paid to China. To be sure Mao was a thorn in the side of Khrushchev as he strove from the late 'fifties to reach a superpower accommodation with the Americans, but in the end Mao was powerless to stop him as he signed the Test Ban Treaty in 1963. Thereafter it is highly debatable as to how important the China factor really was in affecting the dialogue between the two super-powers. To be sure, the Sino-American realignment of the seventies has given the Americans additional leverage in their dealings with the Russians. But it has hardly been the decisive factor in either propelling or retarding understandings between the two. For example the problems that arose in concluding the Second Strategic Arms Limitations Treaty (SALT 2) agreement had very little to do with China.

Perhaps the high priorities accorded to China by both American and Soviet leaders over the past three decades should be explained in terms of misperceptions and the emotionalism which has been applied to China in both countries. The Russians appear to have deep-seated anxieties about the Chinese as latter-day Mongol hordes;[24] whereas the American myth of a China which they had always encouraged towards modernisation, and to which they were closely tied by bonds of friendship, was rudely shattered by Mao's victory in 1949, particularly as this took place at the height of the Cold War. During the next two decades this was replaced by another myth of the implacably hostile, expansionist and irrational China, only to be succeeded in the seventies by a variant of the older myth. In a sense it could be argued that if China is a vital factor in global strategic alignments it is largely because the two superpowers have made it so.

There is room clearly for much argument about the significance of China to the two superpowers, but there can be little disagreement about their significance to China. Labouring under conditions of perpetual strategic inferiority the PRC has been the target of continual active or implied threats of nuclear or other forms of attack by first the Americans and then the Russians. It is not surprising that the bulk of Mao's speeches and writings on foreign affairs since 1949 have been concerned with the two superpowers. Moreover, because of China's relative weakness it has been cast essentially into a reactive position. This does not mean that China has simply responded passively to American or Soviet moves. But it does mean that China's room for manoeuvre was severely limited by the great disparities between itself and the two superpowers. It was their relationship which determined the global strategic balance, and their capacity to alter China's strategic environment was always greater than China's very limited capacity to reciprocate. To be sure China could affect the balance between them, but only as a reactive power. Similarly with regard to economic questions: at different times and in different ways both the United States and the Soviet Union have had a considerable impact on the development of the Chinese economy, whereas China's impact on them has been negligible. As we have seen in the previous chapter, the modernisation of the Chinese economy has depended to a large extent on access to advanced technology and know-how from abroad. Mao's geopolitical legacy, therefore, may be seen as concerned with the question as to how a large Third World country can preserve its independence in conditions of strategic adversity and inferiority.

Mao's view of China's place in international politics

Mao's attitude to world politics, like most of his colleagues, reflected many of the problems and aspirations of other Third World countries which had won, or were to win, national independence after 100 years or more of colonial or semi-colonial domination. But perhaps like India, China as a huge country with ancient traditions aspired also to great power status, and even more than India, China was ranked very high in global strategic significance by the two super-powers. As a consequence Mao and his colleagues tended to think in global terms even though China's actual capabilities were only of regional significance. Nevertheless, Mao's peculiar emphasis on the domineering aspects of imperialism, rather than the orthodox Leninist emphasis on its special capitalist roots, testifies to his Third World perspective as a leader of a country which had been the victim of imperialist aggression and which was under the continual threat of imperialist attack. Thus many of Mao's statements on imperialism were designed to foster a psychological readiness not to be cowed by its apparent overwhelming power as much as they were designed to suggest strategies for overcoming it. Even though Mao wrote little about what might be called the political economy of imperialism, he was alert to the problems of economic dependency. His outlook was tempered essentially by China's experiences of the ill effects of imperialist economic penetration in the first few decades of this century, coupled with the 'lessons' he drew from the independent path to revolution and to power of the CPC under his leadership. His approach to the problems of economic dependency, consequently, was an adjunct to his approach to politics and to the assertion of independence. The latter was interpreted for China as the capacity to construct a revolutionary socialist society at home free of foreign influence. Few other leaders of Third World countries either aspired to, or indeed could have pursued, such an autarkic approach to independence. Mao very much endorsed China's programme of aid and trade with Third World countries which began in the middle 1950s and which was expanded considerably in the 1960s despite China's own severe economic difficulties at home. From 1954 until Mao's death in 1976 China's economic aid came to about US$5 billion.[25] There was opposition to this within China and in fact, since Mao's death, that aid has been cut back and China itself has sought and accepted aid from the international community. China's aid under Mao was not simply philanthropic or even mainly designed to emphasise solidarity with other Third World countries. It was also designed to serve larger political purposes relating partly to China's national interests of supporting friends and allies and partly to Mao's concerns of building international united fronts. However, the aid also implied that China was claiming a leading role among Third World countries and that it was challenging the Soviet Union as well as the Western powers. Although China's economic aid has been less tied and more disinterested than most, the idealism which inspired it was linked to Chinese aspirations to 'greatness'. This found expression in Mao's call on the Chinese people to 'contribute more to humanity'.

Perhaps the clearest statements of China's aspirations to great power status came in the wake of the 1954 Geneva Conference on Korea and Indo-China. The *People's Daily* editorial of 22 July 1954 proudly declared:

For the first time as one of the Big Powers, the People's Republic of China joined the other major powers in negotiations on vital international problems and made a contribution of its own that won the acclaim of wide sections of world opinion. The international status of the People's Republic of China as one of the big powers has gained universal recognition. Its international prestige has been greatly enhanced. The Chinese people take the greatest joy and pride in the efforts and achievements of their delegation at Geneva.

But it was to be another 17 years before the PRC was finally accepted by the international community as symbolised by its taking up of the China seat at the United Nations in 1971. Not surprisingly, in the intervening period the PRC lent its weight to attempts to transform the existing international order in a revolutionary way, whereas beginning in the seventies China's leaders have so moderated that position that many consider China to be playing the role of a *status quo* power in the international system.

Statehood and independence

If Mao can be described as a leader who sought to revolutionise the international order he did so only in certain limited ways. Indeed it can be argued that in at least one fundamental respect Mao and his colleagues fully endorsed the key element of the contemporary international system — the modern state. China's leaders also accepted the basic ground rules of the system to the extent that they regarded states 'as bound by certain rules in their dealings with one another, such as that they should respect one another's claims to independence, that they should honour agreements into which they enter, and that they should be subject to certain limitations in exercising force against one another'. Nor did China's leaders oppose other aspects of the inter-state system and they were prepared to 'co-operate in the working of institutions such as the forms and procedures of international law, the machinery of diplomacy and general international organisation, and the customs and conventions of war'.[26]

Indeed one of the important ways in which modern China differs from its imperial past concerns the transformation of the Chinese state. In the past China was separated from the outside world by frontier areas which were ill-defined. These were pushed out far into Central Asia when the empire was relatively strong and came close to the heartland of China when the empire was relatively weak. In the modern period these 'frontiers' have been replaced by borders which are supposed to demarcate precisely where the 'sacred soil of the motherland' ends and foreign territory begins. One of the major unresolved problems of the PRC is that it has inherited the approach to borders and statehood as developed by Chinese nationalists in the 1890s if not before. This tended to identify

the modern state borders with the limits of the areas adminis-
tered by the Manchu Qing Dynasty. These included, as well
as the Chinese core, the periphery provinces peopled by non-
Han Chinese nationalities of Manchuria, the two Mongolian
provinces, Xinjiang (or what used to be called Chinese Turkes-
tan) and Tibet. It raised question marks as to what precisely
the 'modern' Chinese claimed had been unjustly snatched
away by imperialism from their imperial predecessors which
they would now seek to reclaim. It also left ambiguities as to
the attitudes which a 'modern' China would take towards the
former tributaries of the empire.[27]

The basis for this assertion of statehood was not self-
determination which might be regarded as the linchpin of
modern states which base their legitimacy on popular sovereignty. Rather, as with most Third World countries, the
definition of statehood is expressed as independence from
colonial rule and great power interference. China, however,
had not been under direct colonial rule; but it entered the
modern international system as a victim of imperialism which
claimed special rights within China, which reduced Chinese
control over its periphery and even detached large territories
away from China completely. Chinese nationalism began
partly as an attempt to restore these losses and the PRC has
largely inherited the notions of territorial integrity and the
concept of sovereignty implicit in those early claims.

The independence which had been won in 1949 was described as liberation. The Chinese people, it was claimed, under
the leadership of the Communist Party had liberated themselves from the feudalism of landlord and tenancy farming,
from the bureaucratic capitalism of those who were in effect
agents of foreign companies and who monopolised state
power, as well as freeing the country from imperialism. In
other words the liberation of the PRC was perceived as a
more profound assertion of independence and self-renewal
than was true for the overwhelming majority of other Third
World countries who had done no more than remove alien
rule without really changing their domestic societies or the
domestic elites which had in many cases been groomed by
the old colonial power.

The independence and sovereignty claimed by Mao was

frequently synonymous with total autonomy or autarky within virtually hermetically sealed borders. Perhaps the clearest expression of this was during the first two years of the Cultural Revolution in 1966—68 when behind a barrage of ineffective radical rhetoric China turned inwards to consume itself in revolutionary political struggle. Precisely because China's liberation was essentially a form of national renewal which stressed the significance of statehood, it did not challenge the basis of the inter-state system. It helped to transform the distribution of power within that system and it challenged the existing order in a number of ways, but despite the rhetoric of Mao and others the Chinese Revolution (or liberation) never threatened the international system in the way that it was threatened by the French and the Bolshevik Revolutions. The Chinese Revolution, in this view, should be seen as part of the general trend begun after the Second World War which heralded the end of the pre-war imperial/colonial structure. The new China therefore was not really challenging the basis of the inter-state system. It sought rather a special role for itself within that system.[28]

It is true that Mao and various Chinese Communist leaders have always asserted that 'in the final analysis national struggle is class struggle', but in fact international class alignments were always of minor significance in the conduct of China's foreign policy. Even during the high tide of what many consider to be the revolutionary phase of Chinese foreign policy from the late fifties to the early sixties, the touchstone of Chinese policy towards other governments and revolutionary movements was their attitudes towards the United States and the Soviet Union. At that time the thrust of China's foreign policy was to establish an international united front against the United States to the exclusion of the Soviet Union.

Like all Communist countries the PRC formally distinguishes between state and party relations. But it is doubtful whether the distinction mattered much to Mao, except in so far as it was useful in the prosecution of his policy and ideological concerns. During the early stages of the Sino-Soviet dispute when he complained of the patriarchal attitude of the Soviet Union and suggested that the socialist camp should embody unity and diversity, he was unable to come up with any suggestions as to how the camp might be reformed along new organisational lines. Nor did he later move towards establishing a new Communist international after the full break with the Soviet Party. Interestingly, it was Liu Shaoqi, at this stage in the middle sixties, who sought to develop a special relationship with Asian Communist Parties. As befitted a man who took a more orthodox Leninist view than Mao to questions of party organisation and to the administration of the economy, Liu tended to pay higher regard to keeping China within the orthodox Communist movement. Indeed Liu's last officially published statement in July 1966 implied that whatever their differences China and the Soviet Union were still members of the socialist world and it called for co-ordination between China and Vietnam to deal 'joint blows' at the American forces in that country.[29] Mao, by contrast (having failed to get the kind of anti-American united front in the Third World which he had wanted, and having long written off the Soviet leadership as counter-revolutionaries), was already deeply engaged in the early stages of the Cultural Revolution and he took an entirely different view of the international situation. From the early sixties Mao had argued that the two superpowers were in collusion against China, hence any realignment with the Soviet Union could only lead to a new dependency and double-cross. As he put it to Edgar Snow a few years later: 'compromising with either of the superpowers could then only lead to a split on the home front . . . ', whereas 'a resolutely independent and united China could weather any storm'.[30]

Mao and the two superpowers

In a sense Mao's deepest imprint on China's foreign policy concerns the relations with the Soviet Union and the United States. All the other dimensions of foreign policy were dependent upon the changing character of that double relationship. Only these two powers had the capacity to challenge China's independence and from its inception the PRC has lived under the shadow of their overwhelming threats. The PRC is the only country in the world to have been threatened by nuclear attack by both the USA and the USSR.[31] Yet

China has been all along a Third World country which has
lacked the industrial and technical base to develop a military
capability equivalent to that of its two superpower adversaries.
How then did Mao envisage that the PRC could develop a
socialist society and build its economy without becoming
dependent on one or the other of them?

It was not until the late 1950s that the problem presented
itself in this way. It was only when Mao had decided that the
Soviet Union was not a dependable ally and that Khruschev
was wrong in both his strategy and his ideology that Mao
began to develop an autonomous path for China, separate
from both the superpowers. This entailed domestic and external policies which were notionally distinctly separate, but
which were in fact closely interlinked. In order to pursue an
independent way that rightly or wrongly was perceived by
one or by both of the superpowers as a challenge to their
interests Mao sought to demonstrate that China could be
neither successfully invaded nor overawed by superior power.
To these ends he stressed China's capacity to defend itself
through people's war and he developed nuclear weapons to
deter nuclear attack or nuclear blackmail. The doctrine of
people's war also brought into play the distinctive experiences
of the revolutionary and civil wars period when the army and
the people and the Communist Party were closely integrated.
It put a premium upon mass movements, class politics and
'correct' ideology. The emphasis on autonomy and independence in international affairs was designed to thwart attempts
at control or dominance by the superpowers separately or
collectively. Only that could ensure that China could develop
along the revolutionary socialist lines favoured by Mao. If
that was the primary goal, it followed that any foreign policy
which would protect the homeland and insulate its socialist
order from alien influence or superpower dominance would
be acceptable in principle. As we have seen in the previous
chapter, this still left considerable leeway for disagreement
among the leadership. Moreover we have also seen that Mao
himself was not always consistent on how to weigh the priorities of the goals of revolution and modernisation. Nevertheless
there was no incongruity, as far as Mao was concerned,
between the various foreign policy roles which China played

between say 1965 and 1971. In this relatively short period China moved from the pursuit of a Third World united front against the United States, through a time of revolutionary isolation and to a *rapprochement* with the United States against the Soviet Union. The essential purpose remained to build an international coalition against the more globally assertive of the superpowers, while retaining sufficient autonomy to choose the domestic priorities without foreign interference.

China's independence after the break with the Soviet Union ultimately rested on its capacity to defend itself by people's war and by the development of a minimal nuclear deterrent force. But Mao's strategy in dealing with the two superpowers depended partly on his capacity to manipulate the main trends in world politics as he saw them, and partly on China's capacity to seize the initiative tactically on its periphery under conditions of general military inferiority. However, as the 'third power' China also had a certain advantage compared with Russia or America. China could hope to manoeuvre within the relative central balance which has obtained between the two superpowers and indeed at different times it has sought and obtained military and technological assistance from both. As the weaker third party, China has not developed extensive global commitments and it has both contributed to, and benefited from, the emergence of multi-polarity in world affairs. China's emphasis on the politics of independence fitted in well with a significant trend in world politics, namely the rise of the Third World. The example of Gaullist France in the mid-sixties suggested to Mao that the concern with national independence and irritation with superpower controls was shared by the middle-ranking powers too.

Mao's view of the superpowers was first developed with regard to 'American imperialism' and was then applied later to 'Soviet social imperialism'. Drawing on his pre-1949 experience Mao held that American imperialism carried with it the seeds of its own destruction. Though technologically powerful it was a paper tiger because it lacked popular support. Imperialism, according to Mao, was driven by an inner logic to try and expand. Interestingly, he never sought to explain the nature of this logic; he simply accepted Lenin's assertion. But,

as we have seen, unlike Lenin, Mao did not pay much attention to the political economy of imperialism which after all
lay at the heart of Lenin's theory. Mao focused more on the
military strategy of imperialism and he asserted that the more
military bases that were established throughout the world the
more extensive would be the resistance to American controls.
On 14 August 1949 Mao put it as follows: 'Make trouble, fail,
make trouble again, fail again . . . till their doom; that is the
logic of the imperialists. . . . This is a Marxist Law.' Whereas,
'fight, fail, fight again, fail again, fight again . . . till their
victory; that is the logic of the people. . . . This is another
Marxist Law.'[32] In Mao's view the establishment of foreign
military bases by the United States was a source of weakness
as well as a sign of strength. This tied America down and it
led to over-commitment of resources. It also provided targets
for popular resistance and opportunities for China to exert
pressure on the United States at times of its choosing. Thus
Mao argued at the height of the second Taiwan crisis in 1958
when America and China seemingly stood on the brink of
war that, as the result of having established a base there,
Taiwan had become 'a noose around the American necks'.[33]
Two years earlier in 1956 Mao claimed that the Americans
'put their bases everywhere, just like an ox with its tail tied
to a post, what good can that do?'[34] In 1958 Mao also reintro-
duced the theme which he had last raised 12 years before, to
the effect that the real immediate target of American imperialist aggression was the nationalism of the Third World rather
than the socialist bulwarks of China and the Soviet Union.

> We too have done a bit of crisis handling, and we made the
> West ask us not to go on doing it. It's a good thing for us
> when the West gets afraid about making a crisis. . . . All the
> evidence proved that imperialism has adopted a defensive
> position and that it no longer has an ounce of offensiveness
> [that is, against China and the Soviet Union].[35]

It was this kind of reasoning which led to a growing rift with
the Soviet Union whose leaders, beginning with Stalin, have
continually asserted that the advance of socialism and the
opportunity for progress of the nationalist independence of

Third World countries depend in the first instance on the Soviet Union and on its relations with the United States. In their view progress elsewhere depends in the final analysis upon the Soviet Union and upon being linked to it. All other struggles were in effect subordinate to the struggle between the socialist camp headed by the Soviet Union and the imperialist camp headed by the United States. Therefore if the security of the Soviet Union in the nuclear age demanded the reaching of an understanding with the United States and the prevention of local conflicts escalating into a major East—West clash, then it was incumbent upon all other socialist countries and movements for national liberation to operate within that framework. Mao's approach totally denied the validity of this Soviet-centric analysis. As we have seen, Mao argued that the socialist camp was not the immediate target of the United States. Being inherently expansionist the United States would seek to bring the Third World and the entire capitalist world under its tight control. This was the focal point of the struggle against it, and moreover that struggle should take precedence for the immediate future over the East—West confrontation. One should not allow oneself to be cowed or blackmailed by nuclear threats. Generally speaking, according to Mao it was essential to stand up to imperialist threats for imperialism would be defeated only as the result of determined resistance. This meant that Mao had to answer the obvious question, 'what if the imperialists actually resorted to nuclear weapons in a crisis?'. Already in 1954, Mao had told Nehru 'if the worst came to the worst and half mankind died the other half would remain while imperialism would be razed to the ground and the whole world would become socialist.'[36] This chilling prospect, however, was being advanced by a leader who had already faced the threat of nuclear attack more than once in the previous 5 years and who was to face them several more times in the future. Mao had proved his capacity to handle crises under a nuclear threat, and he was no nuclear warmonger as his Soviet critics alleged. His point was that one had to be prepared for the worst case and one could not rely on imperialists not to use nuclear weapons. Mao further argued that nuclear weapons were irrational even for imperialists:

Exploitation means exploiting people; one has to exploit people before one can exploit the earth. There's no land without people, no wealth without land. If you kill all the people and seize the land, what can you do with it? I don't see any reason for using nuclear weapons, conventional weapons are better.[37]

At the same time Mao appreciated the deterrent value of nuclear weapons since it was around that time that he issued his first public instruction to start on a programme of manufacturing nuclear weapons.

Mao's position at the end of the fifties was that China and the Soviet Union were not the immediate target for American aggression. But the deepening Sino-Soviet rift had reached the point by the summer of 1963 when the Soviet Union and the United States demonstrated a common interest in colluding together against China — or at least that was how Mao perceived the significance of the Test Ban Treaty. *The People's Daily* editorialised:

It is most obvious that the tripartite treaty is aimed at tying China's hands. The U.S. representative to the Moscow talks has said publicly that the United States, Britain and the Soviet Union were able to arrive at an agreement, because 'we could work together to prevent China getting a nuclear capability'. . . . This is a U.S.–Soviet alliance against China pure and simple.[38]

How had Mao allowed this situation to arise? Surely China's independence rested on its capacity to manoeuvre between the two superpowers rather than on having them both in collusion against it before it had acquired even the most elementary nuclear deterrent against either? Indeed there were those in the Chinese hierarchy who argued that Mao had carried his opposition to Soviet revisionism too far.[39] But Mao's point was that China could only have remained a close Soviet ally by sacrificing its independence and by following the wrong road in both domestic and foreign affairs. In other words if China were to assert its independence and struggle against superpower dominance this was the price that would have to be paid. By being organised to fight a defensive people's war China could still claim the ability ultimately to defeat an invasion by either of the superpowers. In 1962 it had already demonstrated the capacity to deal successfully with threats on its borders.[40] Meanwhile the break with the Soviet Union was not yet complete: it was not until 1966 that Mao finally ended Party to Party relations with Moscow. At the same time the Kennedy and Johnson Administrations had begun what was seen in China as a new wave of attack on the Third World which culminated in the Vietnam War whose original goal was to check China and to show the world that America had the answer to insurgency warfare. Mao initially tried to build relations with the medium powers, as epitomised by De Gaulle's France which recognised China in 1964 much to the chagrin of the Americans. But when that failed to develop as a united front China's leaders turned to the Third World and tried to establish a united front without the Russians against American imperialism. But by the end of 1965 that too failed to materialise.

In retrospect the PRC was saved from a burgeoning anti-China front of both the superpowers by the American escalation of the war in Indo-China. The Soviet Union had little option except to intervene on Hanoi's side. Their common anti-China concerns became lost in their adversorial relations over Vietnam. Moreover Peking's vital security interests required the continuation of the war and the prevention of negotiated compromises.

The turning point for China was 1968 when, following the Tet Offensive, Lyndon Johnson finally acknowledged that America had to scale down its commitment to the war and he sought and obtained Hanoi's agreement to negotiate. Peking had been vehemently against this. Indeed Zhou Enlai reportedly told the head of the Vietnamese delegation en route to Paris that 'in Mao Zedong's opinion the talks were a mistake'.[41] The talks were regarded as a product of Russo-American collusion. There was the fear that the United States might soon facilitate Soviet activities against China. The gulf with Hanoi widened after its approval of the Soviet conquest of Czechoslovakia. Le Duan rejected Zhou's speech to his delegation in which he repeated an earlier assertion that the Soviet Union had demonstrated by the invasion that it was now a social imperialist country (that is, a country whose leaders practise imperialist policies while engaging in the rhetoric of socialism). Zhou also went on to add that as a result 'the socialist camp had ceased to exist'.[42] Hanoi was unimpressed and it still held on to its special relations with Moscow. Meanwhile the Russians began to move significant military forces to the Soviet Far East adjacent to the borders with China and there was the suspicion that the same doctrine by which the Soviet leaders claimed the right to intervene in Czechoslovakia might also be used for intervention against China. By the end of 1968 the Chinese Foreign Ministry sought to reopen talks with the United States on the basis of the five principles of peaceful coexistence.

Peking then became divided between the nativists headed by Lin Biao who opposed the opening to the United States and preferred instead to continue with the revolutionary isolation of the Cultural Revolution and to sustain China's defences by vastly increased military spending, especially on missiles and aircraft. This line was linked with Lin's position in the domestic political struggles. Mao Zedong and Zhou Enlai opposed this trend and won. They chose instead to seek the broadest possible international diplomatic united front against the Soviet Union. In Mao's view 1968 was not only a crisis year for China, but it also marked a major turning point in international politics. The American retreat from escalation in Vietnam, coupled with the Soviet invasion of Czechoslovakia, were perceived by Mao as the beginning of a new stage in which American imperialism was to be thrown on the defensive and Soviet imperialism was to embark on an expansionist phase. It also meant that the main danger to China was to be posed by the Soviet Union and not by the United States. Although there were many problems to be overcome before Henry Kissinger made his dramatic visit to Peking in July 1971, it was these broad strategic calculations which underlay Mao's decision to open the door to the United States.

In many respects Mao's geopolitical analysis of imperialism could be said to have been vindicated by these events. The reason for 1968 being considered the high-water-mark in American post Second World War expansionism, rather than say a temporary setback, was less because of what had happened in the fields and cities of South Vietnam than because of the growing contradictions or problems which the American Administration was confronting in prosecuting the war. It was as if Mao's analysis of 30 years earlier, on how to defeat the Japanese by protracted war, had come true with regard to the United States. Thus the United States, being unable to win the war by decisive battles, was continually escalating the war by pouring in ever more troops and national treasure. It was becoming isolated from its allies; the costs of the war were damaging its economy and weakening its international standing; the unpopularity of the war was exacerbating domestic social divisions and weakening the political order at home. In short it proved the paper tiger character of imperialism. Even the vast military and economic strength of the United States had been proved unable to impose a *pax Americana* on an awakened Third World determined to resist. Mao was to argue that the same in time would apply to the new rising imperialism of the Soviet Union.

This readiness to perceive and react to the new trends of international politics may be seen as the hallmark of Mao's approach to the fluidity of power relations. But at the same time it also brought sharply into focus the limits of Mao's commitment to proletarian internationalism or, more precisely, the commitment to support revolutionary movements in other countries. By viewing the question of imperialism in global strategic terms Mao necessarily subordinated his commitment to revolutionary struggles elsewhere to these global issues. Like the Soviet Union in the 1920s, China under his leadership was now open to the charge that it put its own state security interests above any kind of revolutionary internationalism.

It was not until 1974 that Mao reportedly chose to identify the general patterns and forces which shaped this new stage in world history.[43] He held that there were now three worlds: The two imperialist superpowers, the medium industrialised powers and the countries of the Third World. The United States and the Soviet Union were seen as contending for global dominion; except that the former was generally on the defensive and could be aligned with against the latter. The

Third World, to which China was said to belong, having but recently emerged from colonialism (and where some residual colonial outposts still existed) was therefore the most determined to resist the new imperialism, and its countries were striving to develop their economies which in turn required the construction of a more equitable New International Economic Order. The second world was described as lying uneasily between the other two with its true interests being defined as in alignment with the Third World against the first. It is almost as if an analogy was drawn between this second world and the national and petit bourgeoisie of the Chinese Revolution who wavered in their support for the revolutionary peasant and working classes in their struggle against the big reactionaries.

It is debatable how far this framework of analysis influenced the operations of Chinese foreign policy over the following 2½ years before Mao's death in September 1976. The factional struggles and the conflict for succession at this time had a profound effect on foreign relations as well as on more strictly domestic issues. In addition to which, specific foreign policy developments depend on many factors, of which the perceptions and guidelines of the Chinese leadership are only one. Moreover it is one whose influence is more likely to be observed over a long period. Nevertheless the Third World theory was not arrived at lightly, and it reflected a distinctly Maoist interpretation of the history of the world since 1945. It argued that for a period after the Second World War a socialist camp had come into existence which served as a reliable revolutionary base area for the nationalistic struggles against American imperialism in the intermediate zone. The struggles were complicated by the fact that America was trying to replace the old declining imperial countries such as France and Britain whose colonies were simultaneously striving for independence. However, in the 1950s, as the Third World was winning its independence and beginning to confront the new and more dangerous imperialism of the United States, the Soviet Union began to abdicate its proper role as its leadership embraced a 'revisionist' position. There then transpired a period of chaos and turbulence in world affairs as these new processes unfolded. In Mao's view it was not until the early seventies that a new pattern emerged with sufficient clarity.

Once again it will be seen that Mao's preoccupations in identifying these developments were less the orthodox Marxist concerns of the development of capitalist economies or the international division of labour. They were rather concerned with the relative power of imperialism and the significance of the struggle for national independence and liberation. The analysis of the dangers of the Soviet Union as an imperialist power was remarkably similar to those allegedly posed by the United States in earlier decades. Despite certain differences of style, geography and capabilities, like the United States before it, the Soviet Union, it was argued, did not intend to attack China as an immediate priority. China, it was claimed, was well prepared to fight a popular war of defence, in addition to which the superpowers were more directly engaged in their bilateral conflict, and that because of geography and Russia's economic and technological inferiority, the Soviet leaders' primary target was Western Europe. However, as that was relatively well defended the Soviet Union became engaged in a massive outflanking strategy to control vital areas of the Third World. That was the real purpose, Chinese spokesmen argued, for the Russian intervention in Africa through the use of Cuban proxies which began in 1974–75. Until he became too weak and ill to receive them in July 1976, Mao used to tell his visiting Western statesmen of his belief that, like the United States before it, the Soviet Union would try to expand its military control until it too would be limited by its internal contradictions. Meanwhile, he argued that the danger of world war existed and that it could be postponed only by determined resistance to Soviet expansionism.

The use of force despite strategic adversity

Mao's readiness to use force in defence of perceived threats to China's borders and to its national security interests under conditions of overall strategic superiority by hostile super-powers is an important part of his geopolitical legacy. Indeed one of the reasons for China's significance as a great power is China's record in the use of force and the handling of crises.

These include the war in Korea (1950–53), the two offshore islands crises (1954 and 1958), the border war with India (1962), the border battle with the Soviet Union (1969) and the battle with South Vietnam for the Paracel Islands (1974). The Chinese incursion into Vietnam in 1979 took place well after Mao's death and, as I shall argue in chapter 5, there were dimensions to that war which distinguish it from these earlier wars when Mao was at the helm. Nevertheless like the earlier military engagements, this too was not fought on Chinese soil.

China's general military strategy has all along been concerned with defence. The doctrine of people's war can be flexibly applied to use a greater or lesser modernised army as its main force, but its main point is defensive in the normal use of the word. Namely, it is designed to defend the country within its borders following an invasion. The development by China of a minimal nuclear deterrent dovetails neatly with the people's war doctrine because it offers deterrence from nuclear attack to which China would be otherwise vulnerable. Yet all of China's wars since 1949 have been fought either on the borders or on adjacent foreign territory. Chinese official explanations have always explained these wars and incidents as responses to unprovoked challenges by others to Chinese-claimed territory or national security. Moreover it has also been asserted that others have tried to take advantage of times when China was weak or apparently internally divided, but especially when superpower pressure on China was deemed to be strong. Whatever the truth of such explanations, they do not really explain the political and military doctrines employed in these military conflicts. Nor have the Chinese leaders ever explained their tactical calculations in resorting to limited warfare under conditions of strategic adversity. It will be seen that several of these conflicts involved the United States directly and at least one directly engaged Soviet forces in battle.

In order to identify what might be regarded as the main tenets of Mao on the handling of these military crises it will be necessary to examine at least one. I shall choose the border battles with the Soviet Union of 1969, principally because they brought China to the brink of war with a superpower, thereby illustrating a certain brinkmanship in Mao. Analysis of this should reveal most clearly Mao's approach to the larger problem of how a weaker power can engage in tactical or limited warfare under conditions of strategic inferiority.

Before doing so, it may be best to highlight more particularly the character of the problem which the PRC endeavoured to encounter. Mao's defence doctrines were concerned with fighting against an invasion; people's war called for drawing the enemy in deep, which meant surrendering territory over time before the tables could be turned on an over-extended invading army. These doctrines did not explain how to defend China's state borders against attacks that fell short of all-out invasion. Nor did they explain how a superpower adversary could be deterred at times of tension from applying discrete military pressures on China's periphery in an attempt to gain advantages from its overall strategic superiority. How could the PRC ensure that it did not lose the initiative while it waited for the massive invasion that might not in the end take place? Or to put the question more positively, how could the PRC translate its claimed defensive invincibility into practical advantage against challenges on or near its borders? These questions were further complicated by the fact that many of China's borders were unsettled and in dispute. Moreover, Taiwan during Mao's lifetime was still ruled by the rival régime of Chiang Kai-shek which was allied to the United States. Challenges on China's borders, therefore, involved both considerations of Chinese sovereignty and independence on the one hand, and the handling of superpower pressures on the other. The issue is further complicated by the fact that Chinese behaviour as a military power necessarily affected China's relations with its neighbours and with other countries in its Asian region.

Mao's response to these sets of problems has to be deduced from his handling of the various crises for, unlike issues concerning the domestic political arena, he has not explained his tactics on these matters. Recent studies by Western scholars, however, have suggested a certain consistency in Mao's responses.[44] In the event of specific threats on China's borders Mao advocated the limited use of force as a kind of 'tit for tat' retaliation designed to deter the aggressor. Mao's concern was to demonstrate that, despite its weakness, the PRC could not

be bullied or deflected from its self-chosen domestic programmes by external coercion. Obviously, he was most concerned
to demonstrate this at times of domestic crises or disorder;
yet it appears that, contrary to the claim of certain observers,
these crises were not used to mobilise society against the
external threat in order to diffuse domestic discontent or
disunity. Indeed it would have weakened Mao's tactical exercises to have done so. For the purpose of the limited use of
force was to deter the aggressor, by leaving open to him the
option of de-escalation and a diplomatic settlement or the
option of so enlarging the conflict as to transform it into a
major war with incalculable consequences. On all six occasions
listed above the PRC used force in a *pre-emptive* manner for
deterrent purposes. With the exception of the 1974 battle for
the Paracels (which will be discussed further in chapter 5) the
pre-emptive attacks were soon followed by a pause and an
implied invitation for the enemy to take stock and try for a
political solution to diffuse the crisis, at least for the time
being. The initial Korean intervention was followed by a 3-
week disengagement; the first attack on Indian positions was
also accompanied by a pause, and after its victory the Chinese
army withdrew as if to suggest that a lesson had been taught
and that China had no greater aims than those declared all
along, but that now that the initiative had been gained, it
was up to the Indians as to whether or not they would negotiate; the artillery bombardment of the offshore islands in
1958 was followed by a call for talks with the United States;
and the attacks on Soviet troops on the border in 1969 were
followed several months later by a temporary diplomatic
settlement between Kosygin and Zhou.

The border battles with the Soviet Union of 1969[45]

The clashes on the border beginning in March 1969 may be
regarded as a typical example of Mao's approach of using a
limited force in a pre-emptive strike to diffuse a larger strategic threat. The rapid build-up of Soviet forces near the
Chinese border, and a growing number of border incidents
and Soviet subversive activities accompanied by implied threats
of war or intervention in China, built up a new sense of crisis

in Peking in early 1969 on top of the acute uncertainties already felt from the previous year. The Soviet military build-up had begun with the conclusion of a new defence treaty with Mongolia in January 1966. Within a year Moscow had moved in about 100,000 troops and the forces on Russian soil had been substantially increased. Military manoeuvres by these forces were accompanied by intensive border patrolling which often penetrated Chinese-claimed territory. Subversion was a particular problem in Xinjiang. But the main challenge was presented along the Amur and Ussuri Rivers in the northeast. The Russians had long claimed that the border ran on the bank on the Chinese side of the rivers and that their entire waterways and the 700 or more islands which they contained belonged exclusively to Russia. The Chinese disputed the Russian claim and held that the border, following the standard Thalweg principle, ran along the centre of the main channel and that therefore about 600 of the islands belonged to China. The rivers had local strategic importance and they were of significance for transport and local fishing. The winter of 1968/69 saw heavy Soviet vehicles being used on the ice-bound islands to expel or otherwise interfere with Chinese occupants and Chinese patrols. These incidents took place against an international background which was perceived in Peking as increasingly threatening. Chinese sensitivity to Soviet–American collusion against China was reinforced by the beginnings of American–Vietnamese negotiations in Paris and by the Soviet invasion of Czechoslovakia. The first was seen as something long desired by Moscow. It was also suggested that the Vietnamese were being asked in effect to make concessions to the Americans in return for the latters' acquiescence in the Soviet conquest of Czechoslovakia.[46]

In Mao's view China had to act on the Soviet border despite Russia's military superiority and the fear of a larger war. Not to have responded would have given the impression of a China that was cowed and that could be bullied. That would only increase the dangers. Chen Bao (or Demansky Island) was chosen as the site on which the Chinese forces would make their stand as the local topography was most advantageous. In a sense the Chinese side only had to establish a presence there against Soviet opposition in order to make its point on the riverine border issue as a whole. Accordingly, the Chinese deliberately initiated the clashes with the vigorous Soviet patrols. The Chinese claim to have won occupation of the island and a few years later they were able to arrange for a visit there by a Western observer.[47]

In April, a month after the armed clashes on Chen Bao, Mao addressed his Central Committee on the general issues of the conflict:

> Others may come and attack us but we shall not fight outside our borders. We do not fight outside our borders. I say we will not be provoked. Even if you invite us to come out we will not come out, but if you should come and attack us we will deal with you. It depends on whether you attack on a small scale. If it is on a small scale we will fight on the border. If it is on a large scale then I am in favour of yielding some ground. China is no small country. If there is nothing in it for them I don't think they will come. . . . If they invade our territory . . . they would be easy to fight since they would fall into people's encirclement.[48]

His distinction between a small-scale war which could be fought on the border and a large-scale one which would be fought deep within Chinese territory is critical. It is in a sense an exercise in brinkmanship, for Mao is in effect challenging his apparently superior adversary either to settle for the small-scale war in which the tactical initiative might very well be taken by China, or to risk a large-scale war on Chinese territory. The Russians toyed with the possibility of using nuclear weapons against China and its nuclear installations in particular, but in the end desisted. Indeed that high crisis paved the way ultimately for the Sino-American *rapprochement*. Following a Soviet armoured limited incursion into Xinjiang in August, the crisis was eventually diffused by a diplomatic agreement between the two respective Premiers, Kosygin and Zhou, in September of that year. Mao presumably was content that by having displayed a readiness to fight a small-scale border war he had stood up for Chinese sovereignty; he had refused to be coerced by superior firepower and he had perhaps averted a larger war later.

Problems of Mao's geopolitical heritage

If Mao's geopolitical heritage is concerned with how a relatively weak but socially mobilised large Third World country can maintain its independence and autonomy against the threats of the military superior superpowers, it necessarily contains inescapable particular paradoxes and problems. For convenience of analysis these may be regarded as the paradoxes of independence, alliance and power.

The PRC leaders have sought independence as the framework within which to modernise the economy and to develop a socialist society (even though they have had severe political conflicts as to what this entails and how it may be achieved). Moreover economic development has been sought not only for its own sake and to improve the living conditions of the Chinese people, but also to ensure that China could continuously improve its defences lest it should once again be humiliated by foreign powers as in the past. This in turn requires that China should open its doors to import advanced technology and to absorb the latest advances in the sciences. Otherwise a relatively backward country like China would inevitably fall further and further behind its great adversaries until its hard-won independence would eventually be in jeopardy. Notionally Mao's doctrine of self-reliance allowed for combining the right mix of independent development and foreign imports. In practice, however, Mao swung from an over-dependency on the Soviet Union in the fifties to almost complete autarky in the sixties (especially during the early years of the Cultural Revolution) only to prevaricate uneasily in the seventies on the side of the closed-door nativists headed by his wife Jiang Qing and her 'Gang of Four' against the open-door modernisers headed by Zhou Enlai and Deng Xiaoping.

Mao's approach to international politics placed a high priority on the establishment of alliances or, more properly, united fronts against whichever happened to be the more dangerous of the superpowers. But not a single one of China's alliances can be said to have held, and its attempts at building international united fronts have not been crowned with success. Thus alliances with the Soviet Union, Vietnam (from 1971 to 1972), North Korea (for the Cultural Revolution years 1966–69) and Albania (in effect from the early seventies even though the formal break was delayed until Tito's Peking visit in 1977) have all broken down at one stage or another. The Chinese attempts to establish an anti-American united front which excluded the Soviet Union broke down in a rather unsavoury way at the second Afro-Asian Conference at Algiers in November 1965. One of the reasons for this catalogue of failures arises from Mao's political thought itself as well as from Chinese behaviour. Mao's thought as applied to international affairs calls for an independent self-reliant China whose leaders perceive the world from the prism of China's revolutionary experiences as being in continual flux. Their task is to identify the principal contradiction to which all other conflicts must be subordinated until that primary contradiction might change. Implicit in this view is that the Chinese viewpoint alone is correct. It follows that all international associations are by definition temporary and conditional. Furthermore, as Mao's China tended to insulate itself from the outside world and because Mao tended to identify the changing currents in world affairs in terms of their impact on China, the Chinese position has not always been shared or understood. This, combined with the startling and often mystifying changes in China's domestic politics, have caused the PRC to be regarded as a less than reliable partner.

Mao's geopolitical legacy also includes several paradoxes regarding the central question of power. Although Mao was ever alert to changes in power relations affecting the superpowers, and he was always conscious of the threats of dominance which they posed to smaller or weaker countries, he was curiously unaware or dismissive of China's impact as a major power in its Asian region. From the perspective of the PRC it is possible to argue that China's policy in the region has been consistent. In this view the Chinese people having 'stood up' themselves understand full well the significance of independence and they have therefore deliberately eschewed any policy of 'reaching out'. They have confined their regional policy to attempting to deny access and control to whichever has been the most dangerous of the superpowers. In the first two decades after 1949 this was the United States, but since then it has been the Soviet Union. China's strategy, then, has been one of denial rather than acquisition. But as seen from within the region, because China's regional policy is decided in the light of developments outside the region, the PRC has tended to be regarded as dangerously unpredictable. Most of the countries concerned have historical experience with China stretching back over many centuries, during which they were in a subordinate capacity. Many of them have disputes with China which arise out of that history. In Southeast Asia in particular the Overseas Chinese minorities are a further complication. Moreover, by continuing to extend moral and at times material support to Communist insurgencies in some of these countries, the PRC is perceived by the host governments to be challenging their legitimacy and to be 'throwing its weight' about in the region in ways that are bound to be increasingly uncomfortable as China's proportionate strength grows. As a result some governments in the region are prepared to contemplate a long-term presence there by the external great powers as an extended insurance against the emergence of a Chinese preponderance. By having made China's policy within its region dependent upon its global policy *vis-à-vis* the superpowers, Mao has paradoxically led to a situation in which countries within the region might, as a result, encourage the kind of superpower presence which China's policy was designed to deny.

In sum Mao's approach may be said to have ensured China's survival and emergence as a great power, but in so doing the support for the revolutionary struggles of others has been marginal and largely conditional on China's relations with the two superpowers. Indeed Mao's geopolitics may be said to have constantly focused on the conflictual elements of superpower politics at the global level. This clearly led to difficulties in establishing policies based on a co-operative pattern, such as alliances of various sorts, or managing relations with suspicious smaller neighbours. Perhaps this is the result of China's peculiar paradox of being strong enough to thwart the superpowers and too weak to establish common ground with others on a consistent basis.

PART TWO

FOREIGN POLICY
AFTER MAO

4

Chinese Society and Foreign Relations After Mao

No aspect of China's foreign relations has changed as much since the passing of Mao as China's societal relations with the outside world. The policy of the 'open door' has become an integral part of the programme for the modernisation of the country. The 'open door' policy has gone beyond simply extending still further the trends begun in the early seventies of expanding foreign trade and importing turnkey industrial plants. It has paved the way for a wide range of societal interactions with the outside (largely) capitalist world. Many of these interactions have challenged long-standing social conventions and political practices in ways that have not always been welcome to the régime, or rather to particular political groups. Although much of the closer association with the Western world has been officially welcomed as necessary for modernisation purposes and for raising Chinese scientific and technological standards, other aspects have been condemned from time to time as inculcating corrupt and so-called 'liberal bourgeois' values.

The new association with the outside world is occurring at a time when public confidence in the Communist Party, its leaders and the other main institutions of state is low. China's intellectuals had lost much of their faith by the wilting of the Hundred Flowers movement in 1957 when hundreds of thousands of their number were disgraced as rightists. A similar crisis of faith took place in the countryside in the near-famine conditions that prevailed in many areas in 1960–61 after the failure of the Great Leap Forward. Inner Party confidence had been badly scarred by Mao's purge of Peng

Dehuai in 1959 for opposition to the Great Leap which Mao chose to interpret as a personal attack. That purge offended against the established Party norms on internal debate.[1] However, the final blows were delivered by the Cultural Revolution when the bulk of the older generation of Party leaders were rusticated, or worse, and the remaining intellectual and managerial strata were mercilessly cast aside. The blind faith of the youthful Red Guards in Mao was rudely shattered by the factional strife of 1967–68, culminating in their dispersal to the countryside. The Lin Biao affair of 1969–71 was a shattering blow to both the Party and the People's Liberation Army – the two great institutions which had liberated China in 1949. The conflict until Mao's death between, on the one hand, the modernisers as led by Zhou Enlai and Deng Xiaoping, and on the other, the nativist ultra-leftists of the Gang of Four which culminated in the strife of 1976, left a badly bruised factionalised Party, Army and country. The society that was being opened to external influence was not only one that had to recover from the bitter divisions of the Cultural Revolution, but it was also one whose leaders had progressively destroyed the deep reservoir of support and trust with which it had begun in the fifties. Such trust, once destroyed, is not easily rebuilt. For example, nearly 5 years after the fall of the Gang of Four and the beginning of the new order, *People's Daily* 'commentator' on 2 August 1981 (the day following Army Day) complained about the attitudes of the 'broad masses of youth both inside and outside the army':

> Having never experienced oppression in the old society and in the old army, the young do not understand the glorious traditions of unity between the army and the government and between the army and the people, nor do they grasp the truth that without a people's army the people have nothing; they do not have a deep comprehension of the close relations that existed between the army and the people during the years of war that made them as inseparable as fish and water and as close as flesh and blood.[2]

As Deng Xiaoping gradually established his ascendancy, a

determined attempt has been made to establish a new domestic political and economic order. This may be seen as involving three important elements. The first centred on the attempt to resolve the long-standing political and economic problems arising out of the Cultural Revolution. At the ideological level this has meant moving beyond the vilification of the Gang of Four, which had occupied much of the first year after the death of Mao, and preparing the ground for the larger issue of extirpating the influence of long-standing leftist currents in Chinese politics. This inevitably affected different political institutions and social groups in different ways. The victims of the Cultural Revolution, expecially the older Party Cadres, the educated (or intellectual) groups and the old-style bourgeoisie with their Overseas Chinese connections, had been rehabilitated in a context in which their impulse towards vengeance has had to be tempered by the need to promote 'stability and unity'. This led to the uneasy situation in which all the various organisations and units throughout the land have continued to be staffed by both victims and beneficiaries of the Cultural Revolution. About half the membership of the 39 million strong Communist Party were admitted during the Cultural Revolution decade, and that is necessarily a source of great tension. Furthermore, important elements in the armed forces appear to have become the principal upholders of the remnant leftist viewpoints. Interestingly, their advocacy of this viewpoint appears to be derived from the *conservative* impulse to protect their institutional interests rather than from the radical urge to transform society. Still other elements in the PLA welcome the new path of modernisation and professionalism.[3] To a large extent many of these issues centred on the question as to how to judge Mao Zedong and his legacy. It took the reconstituted Party almost 4 years to deliver its verdict.

The second element has focused on the need to establish greater institutional regularity and legality. Few countries had experienced as much organisational change and uncertainty within two decades as China underwent in the last 20 years of Mao's life. The period of the Great Leap Forward in the late fifties witnessed the replacement of many aspects of the authority of state institutions by those of the Party. In the Cultural Revolution the Party was virtually destroyed as a coherent organisational structure and many of its functions were taken over by the armed forces. This was also the period when the previous patterns of legitimate authority were superseded by the elevation of Mao Zedong as the ultimate, and at times the only, source for legitimate action. During the 20 years after the Great Leap Forward the minimal aspects of legality which had been built up in the first half of the fifties were cast aside. This was especially true of the Cultural Revolution. All this did not mean, however, that in their daily lives the Chinese people were free of the tight bureaucratic controls that determine nearly all facets of social intercourse. In a sense they were worse off because these controls came to be exercised in more brutal and arbitrary ways. Moreover the turmoil of mass movements only increased the pressures on daily social life. Thus one of the important promises of the post-Mao leaders is never again to allow such mass movements to unfold.

The changing fortunes of the great national organisations during the two decades of turmoil did not in fact remove the power of the localised organisations which hold the Chinese people in thrall. Everyone in China belongs to what is called a 'unit' (*danwei*) — usually the organisation of the work-place, such as a school, factory or office in the urban areas. These units, to which a person usually belongs for life, dominate nearly all aspects of personal life. They issue work and residence permits, ration coupons (for certain foods, clothing and other daily necessities). They allocate housing and in most cases their permission is needed for the purchase of scarce commodities or for travel to other areas. Most aspects of social life take place within these units and their leaders wield great power. The political changes during the two decades of turmoil may have caused variations from time to time concerning who or which faction may lead a unit, but at no point did this lead to the breakdown of the powers of the unit. In the countryside the production team or brigade performs similar functions.

The reforms enacted since the death of Mao have not been designed to curtail the powers of the unit as such. But in so far as they restore and extend the legal norms of the fifites, they will undoubtedly minimise the abuse of power by local leaders. The main administrative reforms, however, are primarily designed to restore institutional order among the major national organisations. The new political leadership is dominated by those who were victims or battered survivors of the Cultural Revolution. Under the aegis of the double victim Deng Xiaoping they have edged out the main group of the Political Bureau beneficiaries of the Cultural Revolution and they look back with nostalgia to what they have perceived as the halcyon days of the mid-fifties when proper organisational norms prevailed. Their immediate aim is to separate more clearly the functions of the Party, Army and State institutions as well as to ensure that the Public Security and judicial organisations should operate within a publicly defined legal framework.

At the same time the reforms are wedded to the perceived needs of modernisation. Greater organisational specialisation and more specific lines of responsibility, it is hoped, will lead to more rational patterns of decision-making. The idea is that officials and managers of enterprises will respond more effectively to administrative and economic incentives. It is recognised that China's bloated bureaucracy is itself a major hindrance to the carrying out of economic reforms. Steps have been taken to cut back and streamline the central state bureaucracy, but it remains to be seen whether a similar exercise can be carried out at the middle administrative levels where most of the inertia is said to lie.

Another purpose of the reforms is to try to ensure that the new emerging political and economic order will be sustained after the passing of its makers, i.e., Deng and his fellow remaining first-generation revolutionary leaders. The key to changing much of the inert bureaucratic behavioural patterns of middle-order officials is to give confidence to the population at large and to the significant political groupings in China that the leftist fundamentalist current will not return. This can only be achieved if legality and institutional rationality should take root as the framework within which modernisation can be realised and if people's living standards continue to rise.

There is, however an ironic contradiction in the fact that the means by which Deng and his associates have sought to institutionalise the new order have been based on the time-honoured Chinese practice of using personal connections (*guanxi*), patron–client relations and at one point, even a popular movement – practices which hardly accord with the professed norms of the new order. It was by those practices that Deng eased out his opponents in the Political Bureau at and around the Third Plenary Session of the 11th Central Committee of December 1978 when the movement of 'democracy wall' in Peking was used effectively by Deng in combination with inner Party manoeuvring to demote the proto-Maoist group.[4] Moreover, as in other Communist countries, the Party leaders have reserved the right to subordinate the application of the law to what they regard as the overriding interests of socialism.

The third element, and perhaps the most important, has centred upon the drive for economic modernisation itself. It is this which commands widespread appeal for the nationalistic purpose of transforming China into a wealthy and strong (*fu qiang*) country. This ancient slogan has been one of the few aspects of traditional political thought to have been embraced by all Chinese nationalists since the end of the nineteenth century. Moreover, given the decline of the appeal of ideology in post-Mao China, the significance given to modernisation as a means of increasing people's income and their standard of living should not be underestimated as a legitimating factor for the post-Mao leadership and its programmes. But despite some progress, major problems have arisen. The heady and vainglorious plan to leap into modernisation as adumbrated by the March 1978 Seven-Year Plan to achieve significant modernisation by 1985 soon gave way at the end of the year to a realistic appreciation of the economic weaknesses and imbalances of China. Since then China has adopted a programme of structural reforms known as economic readjustment. Initially conceived as a temporary measure of 3 years' duration, this has recently been extended to 1986.

Despite the uneven and gradual way in which the new political and economic order has developed since the death of Mao and the downfall of the Gang of Four, the societal interactions with the outside world have been significant in all dimensions of these developments. The disillusionment of much of China's youth with Marxism and with much of the political experience of the PRC has been intensified by the growing external contacts. It is also realised how far China has fallen behind the enormous economic and technological advancements of the last 20 years, achieved not only in the United States and Japan, but also in countries nearer to home such as South Korea, Taiwan, Hong Kong and Singapore (known collectively in China as the 'four little tigers'). 'Democracy Wall' and 'Peking Spring' of 1979 demonstrated that articulate representatives of the younger generation looked to Western representative democracy for inspiration.[5]

From the perspective of the post-Mao leadership, the impetus to develop its legal programme has also been fuelled by the need for effective laws to meet the requirements of foreign companies operating in China. Moreover it is fully recognised that if the process of modernisation is to be at all successful, China has no alternative but to open its door to the modern world outside. China needs access to advanced science and technology and it needs to learn from foreign patterns of economic management if it is to improve its very low levels of economic efficiency. To be sure the foreign inputs can only be subsidiary to the efforts made within China. Nevertheless that subsidiary input is a necessary, if not a sufficient, condition for significant progress in modernisation. Whether or not the new association with the west (including Japan) will be perceived in time as threatening China's separate identity and the values of the régime remains to be seen. Meanwhile the emerging new order has already been marked by this association in several important ways.

The most visible and measurable external influence has been in the economic fields. The post-Mao leadership has sought foreign investment, foreign loans, a variety of joint ventures with foreign companies and it has opened several special economic zones designed to attract foreign enterprise. Moreover the trebling of the value of Chinese exports in the 4 years between 1977 and 1981 has involved a growing number of Chinese enterprises in production geared exclusively for foreign markets and it has also seen the spawning of a wide variety of compensatory trade deals. In particular close economic relations have been formed with Overseas Chinese, notably the 'compatriots' from Hong Kong and Macao.

Many of these developments have led China towards fundamentally new institutional policies, notably in seeking to improve the organisation of foreign economic relations and in developing appropriate new laws and legal practices. Nowhere is this more evident than in the reforms carried out in its banking and financial operations in order to be able to cope with the new international economic challenges. Over and beyond this the post-Mao leadership, in considering how to combine central economic planning with degrees of decentralisation and market forces, has encouraged the study of foreign models — notably those of Hungary and Yugoslavia. The reform of management of enterprises has led to close study of the managerial systems of foreign capitalist companies and to the search for training in business management in the west. Poland's experience in 1980 and 1981 has been followed closely in China and many observers consider that the projected reform of China's trade union movement in 1981 was abandoned in the light of China's leaders' dismay at the way the independent Polish Solidarity trade union movement challenged the power of the established Communist Party and set itself up as an alternative source of authority.

Chinese social interactions with the world outside have been greatly expanded in other ways. In a move of potentially considerable, long-term significance, thousands of students have been sent abroad to study, and a wide variety of scholarly and cultural exchanges have taken place so that Chinese should no longer be cut off from the intellectual, cultural and scientific developments taking place in the Western world.

Structural and political restraints

Before examining China's 'open door' policies and their implications in greater detail it is first necessary to consider the structural and political factors which will inevitably limit China's absorption into the international economic system. China's size, resource endowment, technological and economic levels of development will continue to ensure for a long time ahead that the primary cause of change in China will continue to be domestic. Considerations of size alone will prevent China from becoming dependent on international trade for its domestic economic development like Japan, let alone like city 'states' such as Hong Kong or Singapore. China's continental size suggests that, unlike those countries and indeed unlike nearly all the other less developed countries (LDCs), China in the long term is likely to find all the resources required by its economy within its own borders. Although the opening of the country to greater influence from the international economy has already had an important impact on China, its significance should not be exaggerated. The main determinant of the performance of the Chinese economy is still domestic. In its report on China the World Bank suggested that China could achieve a more rapid rate of growth by international borrowing. Indeed it projected two different growth rates dependent upon the scale of borrowing.[6] But there is no sign as yet of a Chinese readiness to engage in large-scale borrowing of this kind. Moreover, as will be shown later in this chapter, the Chinese authorities doubt their capacity to absorb successfully industrial plants with whole sets of equipment. Therefore what may be more significant may be the way in which the processes of domestic change within China affect the ways in which China's participation in the international economy will evolve.[7]

China's structural characteristics as an LDC are not amenable to rapid change. Although its size ensures that its GNP ranks as seventh or eighth largest in the world, it is nevertheless a poor country. Per capita GNP per annum is only $250—400.[8] That disguises significant inequalities between the prosperous Shanghai region with a per capita equivalent of about $1600 and poorer areas of the countryside where one-tenth of the population was said in 1978 still to be living on the margins of subsistence which obtained at the time of the establishment of the PRC in 1949.[9] Eighty per cent of the 1 billion population is engaged in largely unmechanised labour in the countryside. The expansion of agricultural productivity is extremely difficult. For example, the growth of agricultural production in the 20 years between 1957 and 1977 matched the natural increase in rural labour power. The management of this vast rural, technically backward and low-income sector poses problems familiar to all LDCs. Although China has a better record than most, the provision of education, health, electricity and other services to the countryside is well below that available in the urban areas. Moreover, the rural—urban exchange of food for industrial and consumer products requires careful handling both for economic and political reasons. Too great a rural—urban imbalance depresses rural production and stimulates migration to the cities; but an exchange which is generous to the countryside in the short run militates against the rapid expansion of heavy industry and it causes an increase in urban sale prices which may lead to unwelcome repercussions from the politicised urban population. In 1979 the Chinese government greatly increased the purchase prices of agricultural products and it allowed urban prices to rise. This was linked to a rise in the incomes of most workers and it led to an increase in the cost of the subsidy to urban consumers. The result was inflation and although most of the urban population was more than compensated by rises in income, some were not. This led to a degree of resentment. For example, reportedly, posters appeared in Tianjin and other cities in 1981 saying: 'We prefer Mao Zedong's low salaries to Deng Xiaoping's high prices.'[10]

The size and growth of China's vast population also pose immense problems which do not lend themselves to easy or rapid solutions. With a population of about 1000 million, 60 per cent of whom are under 26 years of age, China has undertaken an energetic programme to limit the growth of the population. After relatively unrestrained growth in the 1960s, China succeeded in reducing the population growth rate in the 1970s to a remarkable 1.2 per cent. The mix of economic inducements and penalties, combined with closer administrative controls, may enable the authorities to limit the urban population to just one child per family, but the prospects in the countryside seem less promising. Apart from the demographic factor by which a significant proportion of the population is reaching marriageable age, the latest agricultural policies are weighted to induce peasant households to focus on the need for more labour power. This, combined with the traditional preference for male children (who are also seen as insurance for old age) does not augur well for continued success in limiting population growth. Indeed already in 1981 the population growth rate began to rise to reach 14 in 1000.[11]

As in other LDCs, transport facilities are poor and inadequate for China's needs. Although the railway network has more than doubled since the establishment of the PRC, it is only 51,000 kilometres in length (less than the rail networks of Germany or France — countries which are only a fraction of China's size and which have been progressively cutting back in favour of road transport — and it is only about half of that in India). Yet rail is China's major means of transport, conveying 72 per cent of the nation's total freight volume and nearly 50 per cent of the passengers. According to a Chinese specialist even this existing network is backward and inefficient. Billions of yuan are lost every year in railway and port congestion. For example, each year more than 1 billion yuan is lost through spoilage of fruits, meat, eggs and other agricultural products because of traffic congestion. Moreover, the limited transport facilities also prevent the full exploitation of many of China's abundant natural resources and raw materials. Even if no account is taken of resource-rich Xinjiang Province in China's far west, it is still not possible to develop fully the coal fields of central north China's Shanxi Province (thought to be one of the world's largest reserves) nor the various ores in the southwestern province of Guizhou. Almost every passenger train in China is overloaded by 50 per cent and some even by 100 per cent, yet the average Chinese takes only one trip by train a year compared with five in India.[12]

Largely because of the Cultural Revolution China also suffers from an acute shortage of trained engineers, technicians and other specialists. Moreover, China's leaders have also highlighted the need to raise the educational and skills levels of ordinary workers. The 10-year period 1966—76 was one in which the educated and professional groups — the intellectuals — were condemned as the 'stinking ninth' (i.e. they were added to the list of eight categories of counter-revolutionaries and other undesirables). Basically anyone who undertook secondary or tertiary education or began work in factories during that decade is regarded as under-educated. In 1976 Zhang Nanxiang (a former President of Qinghua University who had been purged earlier in the Cultural Revolution and was later to be reinstated as Minister of Higher Education) reported to Mao on the then educational system: 'College students study the textbooks of middle schools. Their academic level is equal to that of primary school students.'[13] That whole generation of some 100 million people was freely regarded in 1977 as the 'lost generation'. The denigration of intellectuals and the isolation of the Cultural Revolution (and indeed of the previous 4 years) meant that the overwhelming majority of China's scientists, technologists, engineers, academics, etc. had been effectively cut off from their own professional work and, of course, they had little or no knowledge of the developments and advances made in their subjects in the rest of the world. Unlike India, which is comparatively well endowed with such trained people and whose skills have been used from Southeast Asia to the Middle East, China experiences acute shortages and an uneven distribution among different age groups of such skilled personnel. The economic, social and political ramifications of this are immense and they are not susceptible to rapid change.[14]

There are also important political and institutional constraints which have restrained, and will continue to restrain, China's absorption into the international economic system. China's dictatorial political system in which political power is centralised through the Communist Party is paralleled in the economic sphere by a command economy and centralised planning system. Economic decentralisation, especially to the enterprise level, can lead to political diversity if not to pluralism. That would necessarily challenge the Communist Party's vanguard role. Since the 1950s proposals for economic reform in Russia have foundered on this problem and the Eastern countries which have carried out reforms have not resolved the dilemma. The parallel with Russia and East

Europe is instructive in another way. Part of the reason for the success of the Soviet economic aid and technology transfer programmes to China in the 1950s was the political and institutional congruity of the two countries. China largely copied Soviet institutions and models; indeed to this day much of China's educational, commercial, industrial and governmental organisations still bear the Soviet imprint. Sino-Soviet ideological symmetry and the complementarity of their social and economic policies for most of the fifties facilitated the absorption by China of Soviet technology, economic goals and patterns of economic management. Opening China's doors to the West necessarily raised problems related to the systemic incompatibility between China's political and economic values and norms of organisation and those of the Western world.

The problems of reform

One way in which China could reduce the incompatibilities between its domestic systems and those of the Western world, in order to facilitate the rapid modernisation of its economy, would be to carry out many of the reforms advocated by its leading economists and endorsed by Deng Xiaoping and other like-minded senior leaders. Two particular sets of projected reforms are important in this context. The first is administrative and is concerned with establishing a clearer delineation of the roles of the Party, the government and enterprise management. The second is economic and it is aimed at following what Chinese economists call the law of value, by which they claim that it is possible to determine prices that reflect actual costs of production and that correspond more closely to those which can be balanced by supply and demand. It was hoped that these reforms would pave the way to economic decision-making that would not be ad-ministratively determined or carried out by incompetent Party committees. It would lead to the adoption of economic criteria that could be recognised by the international (capitalist) economic community as rational. The problems of establishing closer economic external relations and the absorption of foreign technology would be considerably eased.

However, there is no clear evidence available that the

separation of Party and government roles has been effected. Indeed even the proposal to do so declared that this should be done 'under the centralised leadership of the Party' and is therefore in itself an illustration of the problem.[15] The draft state constitution issued on 21 April 1982 further illustrates the studied vagueness regarding the role of the Party.[16] The draft declares in its preamble that the Chinese people are 'led by the Communist Party of China and guided by Marxism—Leninism and Mao Zedong Thought'. Nowhere else is the Party specifically mentioned by name except to stipulate that *inter alia* 'all political parties . . . must make the Constitution their basic norm of conduct and have the duty to uphold the sanctity of and ensure the implementation of the Constitution'. Thereafter, stipulations about the rights and duties of organisations and individuals are heavily qualified by injunctions such as in Article 1 which states ' . . . Disruption of the socialist system by any individual and in any form is prohibited', or Article 27 which *inter alia* declares that 'the state penalises actions . . . that wreck the socialist economy and other criminal activities'. The problem is that socialism is nowhere defined in the constitution and that its interpretation and the question as to which acts 'disrupt' it or 'wreck' its economy will presumably be left to the Party. The Party leadership presumably, as in the past, will decide upon this in accordance with the perspectives of whoever happens to occupy the leading positions and their prudential judgement of the political needs of the time. To be sure the draft constitution is an advance in restricting the arbitrary exercise of power which had been so pervasive in earlier years. But it does not really clarify any further the distinction to be drawn between the roles of Party and Government. The restoration of a governmental Central Military Commission and a Chairman to lead the armed forces seemingly tidies up the anomaly by which the Chairman of the Communist Party was automatically the Chairman of the Party's Military Affairs Commissions and hence overall leader of the armed forces. But the constitution says nothing about the relations between the two commissions. Although the constitution delineates different functions for the representatives' legislative organisation of the National People's Congress and for the executive

State Council and ministries and a separation of personnel, it does not really deal with the nub of the issue concerning the Party. Both Chinese and Russian past experience suggests that Party dominance will continue and that the blurring of the roles of Party Committees and State functionaries will not be resolved. Similarly, despite high-sounding words to the contrary the levels of responsibility as between national, provincial and enterprise have not been clarified. There remains a confusion of overlapping functions and duties. Meanwhile managers of enterprises are still restricted by 'a lingering fear' of taking decisions: previous experience has shown only too well how great the penalties can be for those found to be on the wrong side of changes in China's recent turbulent past.[17] Meanwhile the 1979 reform of allowing provinces and some 6600 enterprises independent leeway in investment policies and authority for the disposal of some 10 per cent of their profits led to over-investment, thereby defeating the national government's aim of curtailing the rate of public accumulation. The success in cutting back the domestic rate of accumulation from over 35 to about 30 per cent in 1981 could only have been achieved by once again curbing the part of the limited autonomy extended in the 1979 reforms.

Similarly, problems arise with regard to price flexibility. The granting to the 6600 enterprises of the right to administer roughly 10 per cent of their profits was less equitable than it might have seemed. Existing prices were derived from earlier historical conditions designed to meet socio-economic priorities determined by economic planning. These prices in turn permeated the economic system and without careful consideration any alteration in price ratios would inevitably lead to confusion. The profitablity of enterprises depended upon the existing pattern of pricing finished products relative to the costs of their production. Therefore of itself the profitability of an enterprise was not necessarily an indication of economic efficiency. In Chinese conditions petroleum, relative to other costs, for example, was notoriously over-priced, whereas coal was so under-priced that it was impossible to produce at a profit. Yet, according to the World Bank, the price of oil in China is one-sixth, and that of coal is one-half, of prevailing world prices. Moreover, even within a single industry profit ratios could vary between those advantageously located in a major coastal city and those located inland, or between labour-intensive plants and those using large amounts of (costless) capital. Rather than adjust prices or adopt a uniform incentive system, the authorities adopted a variety of schemes and subsidies to reduce the predetermined income inequalities. The reforms increased the inflationary pressures resulting from the rise of prices of agricultural products and the increase in urban wages. Firstly, local investment went up; secondly, new plants reduced the revenue of the central government and diverted raw material supplies from the more efficient and profitable larger enterprises to the less efficient localised ones. For example, tobacco was used by local commune-run, comparatively inefficient, small factories instead of being supplied to the major cigarette factories in Shanghai. Finally, the decentralisation of control over foreign trade helped to provide a large trade deficit alongside the inflationary budget deficit. In early 1981 strict price controls were brought back and the Chairman of the State Planning Commission, Yao Yilin, confirmed the reintroduction of a 'high degree of centralisation' and listed in particular capital construction funds, taxation, materials allocations, prices and foreign trade.[18]

Bruce Reynolds argues convincingly that the reform programme hinges on introducing sufficient price flexibility to move prices to market-clearing levels. Without that, administrative intervention and rationing is inevitable. Even if an efficient firm could successfully accumulate investment funds, possession of that capital would not necessarily guarantee access to the resources needed for expansion. The acquisition of those resources would still require application to the Market Supply Bureau and the allocation would be based on criteria other than efficiency.[19]

It is possible that the reform of the state bureaucracy — begun at the highest level of the State Council in early 1982 — and the economic readjustment policies now extended from 1982 to 1986 will make a substantive difference in inducing greater economic efficiency, but the problems are formidable. Established institutions have their own interests to protect. Enterprises may be shackled by the lack of independency in the existing system, but it does offer them security and minimal risks. Neither ministries nor provinces would deliberately seek to lose control of their enterprises or to operate in a challenging but possibly hostile new environment. It is hardly surprising that operating under these uncertainties and in competing for scarce resources there should be an upsurge in the cultivation of 'special relationships' or 'related household' by which personnel of different units exchange favours to obtain their needs outside the norms of the system. A 'contributing commentator' of the *People's Daily* of 28 September 1981 called for the 'doing away with the "study of relationships"' which 'block the normal channels of commodity circulation'. 'Anyone who does not invite people to dinner, send gifts and offer bribes is held up, with the result that no raw materials will be sent to the enterprises concerned and their products will be unmarketable. . . . ' Revealingly, the commentator noted that 'some comrades hold that it is hard to avoid indulging in the "study of relationships" in a situation in which materials are in short supply'. He also claimed that this problem was also 'most evident' with regard to 'recruiting workers, entering universities and colleges, going abroad to study, joining the Party, promoting cadres, transferring people to another post, advancing to a higher position, adjusting wages and positions and allocating houses'. The problem had reached such proportions that the State Council and the Party's Central Discipline Inspection Commission had promulgated separate circulars to 'end the unhealthy tendencies in commodity circulation' and with regard to 'related households'.

The reforms improving the balance between heavy industry, light industry and agriculture coupled with the focus on expanding energy production and transport may well improve China's long term prospects in the international economy. But such infrastructural changes will take a long time to put into effect. Much of these can only be achieved piecemeal. Take, for example, the expansion of the railway network. Although since 1949 China's 21,800 km of railways have been extended to 51,000 km, 75 per cent of the new lines have been built (for defence reasons) to the west of the north—south Beijing—Guangzhou (Peking—Canton) artery that roughly divides China in half. But most of the industries and mines are located to the east of that line with the result that the system in the east is heavily over-burdened. Coal accounts for some two-thirds of rail freight. One of the major current goals is to increase the capacity to move coal from the mines to the ports for export. As most of the coal is expected to be exported to Japan, low-interest long-term loans from Japan will be used for three railway projects and two port projects. In addition a total of fifteen trunk lines are to be double-tracked and electrified.[20] These developments will obviously improve aspects of the existing network and raise efficiency. But they do not amount to the provision of an integrated transport system even for China's more relatively developed eastern region. The development of such a system is certainly not in prospect for the eighties.

Likewise, the attempt to establish a leaner but fitter heavy industrial sector in which the most wasteful and loss-making enterprises have been closed down, restructured or amalgamated with others will stand China in good stead in the years ahead. But here too the reform of China's heavy industrial enterprises is a long-term process and difficulties in introducing genuine pricing according to the 'law of value' caution against undue optimism for rapid change. Indeed in 1981 it was decided not to extend the number of enterprises allowed to retain some 10 per cent of their profits beyond the original 6600 (which actually accounts for 60 per cent of the value of industrial production) to any of the remaining 75,000 state and provincial-run enterprises. Yet without these reforms to improve the efficiency of the economy China will be constrained from opening itself, except only marginally, to the fiercer winds of international competition.

The expansion of foreign trade

China's foreign trade has expanded at a tremendous rate since the beginnings of the seventies. During Mao's last years, discounting inflation, the total value of trade trebled from $4810 million in 1971 to $14,575 in 1975.[21] Between 1977 and 1981 it has trebled again from ¥27,250 million (or

$14,670 million)[22] to ¥73,530 million.[23] These figures must be treated with a degree of caution partly because it is not known how the Chinese figures are compiled; partly because China's trade accounting procedures value imports on a c.i.f. basis and exports on an f.o.b. basis (which tend to exaggerate the value of imports over exports according to conventional accounting methods);[24] and partly because of the effects of inflation and changes in relative currency exchanges. For example, the 1981 figure is 29 per cent higher than that of the previous year, but according to the report of Vice-Premier Yao Yilin the actual increase was only 11 per cent after discounting the effects of inflation and changing currency rates.[25] Nevertheless the expansion of foreign trade has been very rapid and extensive. It has certainly grown faster than the domestic economy. One indication of that is that the proportion of the value of foreign trade to that of China's Gross Domestic Product (GDP) has risen from around 8 per cent in 1977 to over 16 per cent in 1981. Again caution is required in interpreting these percentages because foreign trade largely reflects the prices of the international economy, whereas domestic prices in China are considerably lower so that the value of GDP is greatly understated in this ratio. Nevertheless the general trend is clear. During the fifties, sixties and early seventies, the total value of foreign trade varied between 3 and 6 per cent of GDP.[26] Does the rapid expansion of foreign trade mean that China has become locked into the international economy in some interdependent way? Does this mean, for example, that China has sacrificed a good deal of its autonomous decision-making on economic matters? Or that the costs of reverting to a more closed-door policy are unacceptably high because of the dislocations that may arise? Or, in radical terms, has the Chinese economy been permeated by external capitalism?

The answer to these questions would appear to be a cautious 'No'. It is true that the high ratio of foreign trade to GDP is beginning to approximate that of the United States (11–15 per cent) and to creep close to that of Japan (20 per cent).[27] But, as we have seen, the real figure for China should be considerably lower. Moreover, unlike the United States or Japan, China is not integrated into the world economy in the sense that the functioning of its domestic economy is dependent on international economic developments. Japan, of course, unlike either China or the United States, is a resource-poor country and is dependent upon the importing of raw materials and 90 per cent of its energy. China and the United States are continental economies with the capacity for self-sufficiency. But the United States is pivotal to the functioning of the international economy; its exports alone account for about 11 per cent of the world's trade. As the late seventies and early eighties have shown, its domestic fiscal policies affect those of the international economy as a whole, including such major economic powers as the EEC and Japan. China's exports, by contrast, account for only 1 per cent of the world's trade. Its impact on the international economy as a whole is negligible, while its own economic performance is determined largely by domestic factors. For example, the inflation which China experienced in 1980 and 1981 was the product of the raising of the prices of agricultural produce (and hence rural incomes) coupled with urban wage increases and the undue expansion of the national accumulation funds in the previous two years. External factors (which in any case arose out of balance of payments deficits) played only a marginal role.[28] In this sense China is still relatively unique among countries of the Third World in that its domestic economy is not dependent on the vagaries of the international economy.

As against this, however, the expansion of China's foreign trade has drawn sectors and regions of its economy into a close relationship with the international economy. For example, certain parts of the country play a disproportionate role in China's foreign economic relations, notably Guangdong Province and the Shanghai Muncipality. The former has long been the main provider of food exports to Hong Kong and since the adoption of the 'open-door' policy, its economic links with the colony have greatly increased. In 1980 Hong Kong accounted for 15.1 per cent of China's total foreign trade value and, even more importantly, it was the market for $4401 million or 24 per cent of China's exports. A great deal of that was accounted by food stuffs provided by Guandong. Shanghai in 1980 accounted for $3800 million, or one-seventh of the value of China's exports. This was equivalent to 10 per cent of the total value of Shanghai's industrial output which in itself was one-eighth of the national industrial output.[29]

At another level the imports of grain have grown substantially in the late seventies. In the period since the early sixties China's grain imports varied between 2 and 6 million tons, but in 1978 they reached an unprecedented 9.4 million and as part of the new policy of improving living standards they have continued to grow to reach an estimated 14.7 million tons in 1981. Although this amounts to less than 5 per cent of China's harvest of 325 million tons, it is a significant factor in the feeding of the northern coastal cities and is a very costly item of China's imports. In 1979 grain accounted for 10 per cent of $16.2 billion imports. But if imported grain has become a significant factor in the Chinese economy, China's grain imports have also made it an important element in the international trade of grain. China has become the world's largest importer of wheat and the third largest importer of grain after Japan and the Soviet Union. Australia, Canada, Argentina and increasingly, the United States, are China's main long-term suppliers of grain. In the 1980s the United States is expected to supply about half of all China's grain imports.[30]

China's current (as opposed to potential) significance in the international economy is not confined to its importance as a growing market for grain. China is well endowed with most minerals and metals. It is thought to have the world's largest resources of about 17 minerals including tungsten, molybdenum, titanium and a variety of rare metals vital for such high-technology industries as aerospace and electronics.[31] Indeed, China's post-Mao leaders have often spoken of utilising the exports of these resources (with the help of modern technology supplied by the industrialised countries) to pay for other imports as a component of the modernisation programme. This was one of the points on which Deng Xiaoping was criticised by radical nativists in 1975—76. One of the reasons for the cutback in several of the major projects the Chinese agreed with Japan, was the failure of China's oil production to expand at the rate anticipated in

1978. By an agreement signed with Japanese industrialists in February 1978, China was obliged to gradually increase its oil exports, so that by 1982 the total would reach 47 million tons. As it turned out, although oil output had grown by 11 per cent in 1978, it then began to stagnate and to level off at just over 100 million tons, so that China has had to cut back progressively on its projected oil exports. Rather than reaching a total output of 200 million tons by the mid-eighties, planners now expect production to fall steadily from 1982 until the end of the decade. Some experts even anticipate that China might have to become a net importer before the end of the decade. Meanwhile China, together with Western and Japanese companies, has begun to develop energetically the prospects for offshore oil. The potential seems very promising, but the oil is not expected to come on-stream on a commercial basis before the latter half of the eighties.

From the perspective of China's foreign policy another important question to be explored is the significance of China's trading relations with particular countries. There are two dimensions of importance here: the first concerns whether China has become economically tied too closely to one or more countries; and the second concerns whether China has become such a major trade partner of other countries that this could be translated into a source of effective diplomatic leverage. China has baleful experience of the high cost of its economic dependency on the Soviet Union when that country abruptly withdrew its assistance in 1960. According to Christopher Howe, 'the Soviet withdrawal, halfway through the agreed programme, virtually halted China's industrial progress for a decade in some sectors'.[32] As we shall see in the next chapter, China itself followed the same Soviet practice of trying to pressurise a recalcitrant ally when it ceased all economic assistance to Vietnam in 1978 with even more deleterious effects on that country, for China had been an important source of supplementary food supplies to Vietnam. Indeed China went even further by persuading other countries to desist from economic relations with Vietnam as part of its policy of isolating and pressurising the country into changing its policies in Indo-China.

With the exception of Hong Kong and Macao, which are in

any case tied to China, the Chinese authorities have gone to great lengths to ensure that never again would the Chinese economy be so dependent on one country as it was once on the Soviet Union. Arguably, China has formed such a relationship with Japan, its major trade partner, which accounts for something like 25 per cent of China's total trade. But that hardly compares with the 60 and 80 per cent of China's trade accounted by the Soviet bloc in the fifties. Moreover, special factors apply in the case of Japan, which does not espouse a foreign policy characteristic of great powers and is therefore highly unlikely to use its trade as a weapon to squeeze political concessions from China. On the contrary, it is China which is seeking to bend Japan to its larger strategic purposes in great power politics. In addition, it is China rather than Japan which has caused economic shock waves to the other side by cancelling or postponing previously agreed major projects in 1979—81. In any case China can turn to alternative sources of trade with other industrial countries. A similar point can be made about the United States, whether for agricultural produce or advanced technology. China is not exclusively dependent on either. To be sure there would be economic cost to be paid if for political reasons trade were severely cut back with any of China's major trade partners. But the critical point is that the cost would not reach anywhere near the proportions of that experienced as a result of the Soviet's sudden withdrawal in 1960. Perhaps more to the point is the influence of economic and political geography on the orientation of China's trade. The Asia—Pacific region has grown in importance. For example in 1978 Japan, the United States and the Southeast Asian countries accounted for 36 per cent of China's imports; by 1980 this had risen to 56 per cent. This trend is likely to be intensified unless the problem of Taiwan should become so acute as to cause the Chinese authorities to reduce the levels of their interactions with the United States. However, the economic orientation to the Asia—Pacific area should be seen less as the motivating factor for China's foreign policies in the region than as the consequence of that policy. Of course it is also a result of China's regional location in one of the high growth areas of the international economy.

As for the possibility of China's using its trade for diplomatic leverage, China hardly figures as a major trade partner for any of the great economic powers. It ranks as the sixth most important market and twelfth most important supplier for Japan. It ranks about thirtieth as a trading partner of the EEC and it is not a major trade partner of the United States either. However, China's importance for particular sectors of certain economies should not be discounted. China's importance as a grain importer has already been noted. Indeed the Chinese have at least on one occasion sought to use it as a political weapon. In October 1970 the Australian Wheat Board was unable to renew its annual contract for the sale of grain (which had been running at about $100 million a year) at a time in which the Australian government followed a harder line on recognising China than the Canadian government which was exploring a formula for diplomatic recognition.[33] However, since the rapid growth of China's international economic interactions, the Chinese authorities have constrained against using trade levers in such a blatant way. This is after all a double-edged sword which could rebound on China if it were to be perceived as an unreliable trade partner. Indeed China's leaders went to considerable lengths to try to persuade foreign traders that its cancellation of certain contracts in 1979—81 did not diminish China's interest in foreign economic relations or its creditability as a trader. China went so far as to pay compensation and to give various reassurances to the aggrieved parties about their prior claims in the event of these projects being resurrected at a later stage. On the other hand, China does seek to expand trade and aid to especially favoured countries and in recent years it has severed or cut back such relations with countries who have violated China's interests, such as Vietnam, Albania and the Netherlands (as the result of the latter's sale of two submarines to Taiwan in 1980). But such examples are rare. As China's trade continues to grow the resort to this as a weapon of diplomacy would be likely to raise more problems for China than could be gained by any short-term political advantages. Although China's credit rating is good and it still enjoys a reputation for honouring agreements, China is still not regarded as politically stable or as a reliable partner in the long term. While China's open-door policy is universally welcomed in the Western world, China still lacks the economic 'weight' or proven record of reliability to employ trade as an effective weapon in its diplomatic weaponry.

Another question that arises is whether China is likely to emerge as a major world trading power in the immediate future. Enough has been said about the domestic constraints to suggest that this is very unlikely. The political and economic impediments to rapid domestic reform are too great. At the same time China is unlikely to be able to continue the rapid rate of foreign trade expansion experienced over the last 4 years. It is perhaps realisation of this that has stopped the Chinese from utilising the $27 billion commercial and official lines of credit which have been available to them up to mid-1980. The cost of servicing such debts and the prospect of cheaper development loans from the International Monetary Fund, the World Bank, Japan and elsewhere have deterred the Chinese. Any loans would sooner or later have to be repaid out of exports. Generally, the Chinese since 1978 have preferred various forms of compensation trade, joint ventures, etc.

In fact the prospects for continued rapid expansion of China's trade seem limited especially because of the international economic recession and the prior claims which many other Third World countries have on the markets of the industrialised countries. This is especially true because the composition of China's exports has been gradually shifting proportionately in favour of manufactured goods. In 1975 they accounted for 37 per cent of total exports. But by 1981 manufactured goods (including products of the machinery, light and textile, chemical and metal industries) for the first time accounted for the bulk of China's exports by reaching 53.4 per cent of the total value.[34] Moreover it is the textile industry which is China's major industrial exporter. This is a pattern followed by other developing countries in which they enjoy a comparative advantage. But it also means that China is in direct competition with them and the prospects for the sustained expansion of this trade at present growth rates must necessarily be limited. China's long-term prospects in other spheres appear more promising, but these depend upon the success of the domestic economic reforms combined with a marked improvement in China's energy and transport capabilities.

Co-operative economic relations

The most significant departure from the previous patterns of foreign economic relations in the post-Mao era has taken place less in foreign trade itself than in the way China has opened up its doors to a variety of co-operative ventures with external capitalist companies. Thus after the fall of the 'Gang of Four' and the defeat of the foreign trade critics, it was still possible to argue for the necessity of foreign trade and the significance for the economy of imported turnkey plants while making the following assertion:

> We do not allow foreign capital to exploit China's resources nor do we run joint enterprises with foreign countries, still less beg them for loans. It is common knowledge that China now is free from both foreign and domestic debts.[35]

Even Deng Xiaoping in 1977 took the view that 'we now also accept instalment payment terms for machinery from abroad but only in the knowledge that we are capable of making regular payments. We must remain free from debts both at home and abroad, and go no further than that.'[36] However, the failure of oil production to expand, coupled with the consequences of the over-ambitious and ill-thought-out economic plan announced in February 1978, led to an unco-ordinated headlong rush by ministries and provincial authorities to negotiate their own foreign deals. In the realisation that the economy was over-centralised and grossly inefficient China's leaders had for the first time authorised these institutions to have more leeway in making their own investment plans and in concluding agreements with foreign countries and companies. As a result, a wild scramble ensued as provinces and industries, eager for prestigious foreign links, signed expensive deals with foreign businessmen who were caught up in a rush for the magnetic lure of a market of a billion customers. Huge projects were begun without feasibility studies and the economy began to lurch out of balance. The rate of domestic accumulation shot up to 36.5 per cent. As the *People's Daily* of 24 March 1979 noted, the scale of capital construction considerably exceeded the country's material and financial potentialities. The completion of all the projects already begun would necessitate the spending of all the funds allocated for construction in the next few years. Meanwhile China's shortage of foreign exchange was cruelly exposed. By 28 March 1979 the *Financial Times* estimated that China had already committed itself, in one way or another, to short- and long-term foreign purchases to the extent of $70 billion. China's leaders found themselves forced to accept credits and loans of various kinds in accordance with modern international banking and trading practices. Following the adoption of the policy of economic readjustment by the Third Plenum of the Communist Party's Central Committee in December 1978, China's leaders also moved to slow down their foreign trade commitments. Vice Premier Li Xiannian noted ruefully in February 1979 that 'it seems our ministers have a huge appetite [for foreign exchange]'.[37] That month China served notice of its intention to cancel six major projects including the great Baoshan steelmill of Shanghai, the agreement for which had been signed only 60 days earlier.[38] The following month China issued delaying notices for as many as 32 contracts with Japan with a total value of 560,000 million yen.[39] However, by September, China agreed to proceed with stage one of the Baoshan project and with many of the others, but at a slower pace and on different financial terms. In the following two years China cancelled the second stage of the Baoshan steelworks, several giant petrochemical complexes and chemical plants to the value of hundreds of millions of dollars. In certain instances China had to pay up to 10 per cent in compensation.

However, the requirements of modernisation necessitated the acquisition of foreign technology, management know-how, etc. Thus it was for pragmatic rather than ideological reasons that China's leaders turned to other means for achieving these ends. Two interrelated measures may be identified. First, the adoption of policies to encourage the old national-bourgeoisie with their close overseas Chinese connections (and hence the Overseas Chinese themselves) to play a greater economic role as entrepreneurs. The other was the encouragement of foreign investment, compensation trade, joint ventures, co-operative production, processing and assembling for foreign companies and so on. In June 1979 a law on joint venture was published. This was followed by a variety of other relevant laws including one on income tax. From January 1980 four special economic zones in Guangdong and Fujian Provinces were opened to attract foreign companies.

By the end of the first quarter of 1982 the Chinese central and local governments had endorsed about 1000 agreements of various kinds of co-operation arrangements with a combined Chinese and foreign investment of $2900 million.[40] Within the first year of operation the special economic zones had attracted more than 300 joint ventures, principally with firms from Hong Kong and Macao and concerned mainly with light industry.

What impact has this penetration of China by capitalist companies had on the Chinese economy and society? Has it facilitated China's capacity to absorb foreign technology? Is it currently or potentially of sufficient magnitude to draw China into the international economy? How far does it challenge existing social values and political controls?

These questions cannot be answered with precision. However, some broad-brush responses are possible. With regard to the impact of foreign trade, the general answer must be that the primary impulse for change in China continues to be internal rather than external. This does not mean that the open-door policy may not release countervailing tendencies within China. For example, the campaign against corruption, economic crimes and cultural decadence which has been evident in the Chinese press in the first quarter of 1982 has been linked with the growing contacts with foreigners. Ideologically, the two are linked in China's communist outlook because corrupt behaviour by officials has always been regarded as a manifestation of a bourgeois work-style. In fact, as we have seen, the incidence of 'backdoor practices', 'related households' and the 'study of relationships' is widespread in China and owes nothing to the new contacts with foreigners.

To be sure the links with foreigners involve access to foreign exchange and highly-prized foreign goods which enlarges the scope for corrupt practices. Guangdong and Fujian Provinces which are most open to foreign or rather overseas Chinese penetration, are notorious in China as centres of smuggling and other undesirable practices. One case which was highly publicised involved the Secretary of the Canton Municipal Telecommunications Bureau CPC Committee and Bureau Director, one Wang Weijing, who had profiteered through illegal foreign exchange dealings. Apparently his crimes had been exposed in early 1980 but because of what the *People's Daily* called 'bureaucratism, leniency and corruption' his case was not brought to trial until 2 years later.[41] On 20 January 1982 the *People's Daily* warned those who had contacts with foreigners to be on guard 'against the corrosive influence of bourgeois ideology' and 'the ideas of worshipping and having blind faith in foreign things'. Resorting to a high moral and patriotic tone the Party journal warned against certain kinds of contacts with foreigners which if heeded would necessarily limit their relations:

> Some personnel do not pay attention to guarding Party and state secrets in their foreign affairs work. Some even divulge secrets on purpose. Some have given away their aspirations for the sake of money. They have lost their moral integrity. . . . Some people have become weak kneed in the face of money. Some are blindly seeking a bourgeois way of life. They lack national self respect and a sense of pride.[42]

A Canton newspaper attacked certain kinds of foreign influence which, by its examples, was clearly aimed at Hong Kong and Macao Chinese. One concerned an advertisement by a restaurant run partly with foreign capital for handling wedding banquets and renting formal attire for weddings; another concerned a beauty parlour with high-quality foreign equipment at which 'female comrades' pay 15 *yuan* (or one-quarter of the average monthly wage) for a perm, and finally the opening of graveyards in Mainland China for sale to

Chinese in Macao and Hong Kong. All these were seen as inimical to socialism.[43]

Another example of the foreign impact which concerns the Peking leadership is urban Chinese predilection for foreign consumer goods. Of course high-level cadres and their families have always been able to purchase them at special stores. But in recent years other less exalted beings have begun to have access to such goods. The imports of finished manufactured goods other than machinery and equipment has grown at an average annual rate of about 70 per cent over 1976—80, almost twice the average 36.7 per cent growth rate of all imports. As a result Chinese watches are being overstocked and purchasers prefer foreign cars to the home-made variety which are of poor quality and uneconomic in their use of fuel. In February China took steps to restrict such imports in order to protect local industries. However, much of the competition is thought to come from the foreign trade establishment rather than foreign manufacturers. In any event China's planners recognise the value of these imports as a stimulus to domestic industries to produce more quality goods.[44]

These and other strictures against the bad effects of foreign influence such as those condemning 'decadent' Hong Kong pop songs or pornographic magazines go beyond objections to these developments as such. They suggest that there may be a concerted drive by more traditionally minded Communist Party officials against the open-door policy itself. Indeed a *People's Daily* article of 8 March 1982 directly addressed the issue by denying that smuggling was the inevitable consequence of the open-door policy. However, the article noted that there were in fact 'some people' who held that view. In many respects the undertones of the anti-corruption drive resemble those of the strictures of Party and Army stalwarts in 1980/81 against certain writers and poets who had dared to criticise aspects of the establishment as manifesting a 'liberal bourgeois' outlook. Here too there was the implication that it was the new policies of relative relaxation and of accepting foreign influence which were the real object of the strictures.

Another aspect of the special links between Guandong and Fujian Provinces and the outside world which has concerned the Peking authorities has been the need to establish tighter central controls. To this end the operations of the Special Economic Zones were placed under the direct administrative rule of the State Council from June 1982. This may be seen as an attempt to limit the sources of the growing governmental independence and changing identity of the two provinces. However, one can look in vain for significant examples of foreign economic penetration which have actually changed aspects of China's economic performance. The record of China's capacity to absorb foreign technology is at best mixed. It is true that in the fifties China successfully absorbed a massive infusion of technology from the Soviet Union. But special factors applied: firstly, China had practically no machine industry and heavy industry was sparse; secondly, China was also lacking in an administrative and managerial system so that the adoption of Soviet technology was accompanied by the establishment of such systems modelled closely on the Soviet example; and thirdly, China's First Five-Year Plan was also drawn from the Soviet model. By the seventies China already had an ongoing (albeit outdated) industrial foundation coupled with administrative and managerial systems which operated along altogether different lines from those of the West. Moreover, however much China's leaders wished to learn from the advanced West they neither wanted to, nor indeed could, model the country on the West. Thus the prospects for grafting advanced Western technology on the alien body of Chinese industry could not be promising.

A recent analysis by a Chinese economist of the results of the importation from the West (including Japan) of major plants incorporating complete sets of equipment suggests that these have been disappointing. Those introduced between 1973 and 1977 at a cost of $3500 million dollars have become operational. Almost none of the projects was completed on schedule and the majority are operating under capacity. For example, because of the different pace in the capital construction of its fittings, the ethylene project of the Peking Yanshan petrochemical company operated in 1979 at the rate of only 76 per cent. At another major plant difficulties in the supply of supplementary materials reduced the operational rate to 65 per cent. Six other major projects, including the Wugang steel rolling machine, the Inner Mongolia Yuan-baoshan power station and ammonia projects in Guizhou, Canton, Nanjing and Anjing had an energy utility rate below 50 per cent. Moreover, the returns on the investment on most of the projects were not good. Only one-quarter registered a comparative profit on the sum invested. The Wuhan steel complex, which initially could not operate because of a lack of electricity, in more recent times suffers from supply short-ages and the failure to keep up steel-smelting techniques. The result is that only seven out of twelve kinds of steel sheets and steel plates can be produced – and even then only in small quantities. The last six of the imported thirteen chemical fertiliser plants have faced the problems of insufficient supply of oil, gas, raw materials and the rise in the price of light oils. Moreover, even though the two plants in Hubei and Hunan were operating at full capacity, the rise in the price of light oils meant that they still suffered losses after paying taxes. Apart from these a good deal of machinery including the Spey jet engines, gas turbines, turbo compressors, indus-trial gas turbines and a few bearing plants, which cost about ¥2 billion, have still not begun production.

In 1978 contracts worth $6400 million were signed with foreign countries. Twenty-two were 'key projects' and were mainly metallurgical and petrochemical projects such as the Baoshan iron and steel plant, the Nanjing petrochemical complex and the Yizhang chemical fibres plant. Every year a further 12 million tons of oil and 20 million tons of coal were used up for these projects. Not only were the country's financial resources over-extended but its energy supplies were over-stretched. To make matters worse, it became necessary to import a great deal of raw materials simply to service many of the completed plants. Warehouses and other facilities had to be built 'to store hundreds of thousands of imported sets of equipment and materials' at the additional cost of some ¥10 billion. Finally, the cost of the equipment and hence its product is high. The average price per ton of the imported steel-rolling machines from West Germany for Baoshan is $16,000 while the domestic equivalent is ¥5000–6000.

The article lays the blame for much of this upon 'production departments [which] have put aside scientific studies, design and manufacture of equipment and have enthusiastically imported sets of equipment. As a result they are limited to importing one set of production equipment which has advanced technology'. This not only fails to help speed up the country's technological base, but is a positive harm. The article concludes with a strong plea for placing the emphasis on transforming the technology of existing enterprises by citing the positive experience of other departments. These have imported key equipment selectively, bought basic designs, co-operated with foreign companies or worked under the guidance of foreign experts.[45]

This analysis of 1981 strongly suggests that China's experience of importing major projects is not dissimilar to that of many other LDCs. It certainly deflates any suggestion that the heavy industrial sector of the Chinese economy has been significantly advanced by the large-scale importation of so-called turnkey plants since 1973. At the same time the article has also heralded the shift, later in 1981, towards emphasising the desirability of transforming existing enterprises or the investment in smaller-scale light industrial projects which can be completed quickly and yield rapid returns on capital. In June 1982 Chinese authorities put forward a list of some 160 enterprises to businessmen in Hong Kong to attract up to $900 million investment for renewing equipment. As we have seen a further priority is the development of energy resources and transport facilities. The agreements with Western oil companies for the development of China's offshore oil are in a somewhat different category, as these by definition are outside the Chinese milieu. The agreements are based on the principles that the foreign companies will be paid through production sharing and that the installations will revert to Chinese ownership after a certain number of years. Problems may arise with the provision of onshore facilities; but these are still for the future. Moreover, the areas with immediate potential are in the South China Sea where Hong Kong would play an important role and in the Gulf of Bo Hai which is near one of China's more industrialised areas with enough of a supportive on-shore infrastructure.

However, the reform of China's existing enterprises brings

more sharply into focus not only managerial inefficiencies of China's industrial system but also its enormous manpower problems. Part of the legacy of the Cultural Revolution is the low educational qualifications of a generation. China's industry faces deep problems because of the shortage of qualified engineers, technicians, workers and managerial personnel. For example, a survey conducted at 32 light industry enterprises in Kaifeng (Henan Province) showed that only seven managers had the necessary qualifications.[46] Another survey conducted in Peking in 1978 showed that out of several thousand employed in transport, communications and industry, only 4 per cent had higher and specialised secondary education, 17 per cent had been to senior middle school (about half had left before graduation) and more than 70 per cent had received only primary or junior middle school education.[47] Overmanning is rampant in Chinese industries. Labour productivity in the large (and most 'modern') of China's industries were judged in 1979 to be five times as low as in the industrialised countries.[48] Meanwhile it is estimated that between 12 and 20 million people are un-employed — or more technically, are awaiting to be assigned work by the state labour agency. In the absence of unemployment benefits, these young people do not qualify either for ration coupons for food, clothing and other necessities.[49] Although certain measures have been taken to alleviate the problem — for example, by encouraging the development of urban service co-operatives and the expansion of urban housing construction — other retrenchment measures which have cut back on heavy industry intensify the problem. Generally, however, this means that there are no easy or quick solutions to the overmanning of industry. Moreover the improvement of the technical and managerial skills in China's enterprises is also a question for the long term.

The more important changes in China's economic system do not, in fact, involve the external inputs very much. Thus the source of investment which used to be monopolised by the central authorities is increasingly shifting to bank credits and retained profits. The state's share of total fixed investment has declined from 50.6 per cent in 1978 to 27.1 per cent in 1981. The hope is that enterprises will use investment more efficiently as a result of having to pay interests on loans instead of having it provided cost-free by the state. They would have a powerful incentive to complete these capital construction projects as quickly as possible. This would also mean that investable funds could be recycled more quickly. Laudable as the scheme may be, it has so far encountered two major problems: firstly, the lack of sufficiently skilled personnel in enterprises or in banking; and secondly, the irrationality of prices which makes it impossible to arrive at a true criterion of economic efficiency.[50]

Student and other exchanges

The sending of students and others to be trained abroad has been important at various stages of Chinese modern history. The thousands of students sent to Japan after the 1894–95 war played a significant role not just as transmitters of modernity but in the intellectual–political life of the country. Those educated in the West or in Western schools in China in the three or four decades before the establishment of the PRC have played similar roles, and indeed the bulk of the older 'higher' intellectuals who have come to the fore since the end of the Cultural Revolution are the products of this experience. The 18,000 students, technicians and skilled workers trained in the Soviet Union, and the hundreds of thousands trained or guided by Russian experts in China during the fifties, have played key roles in the operation of the Chinese economy ever since. Thus one of the more important long-term effects of the new open-door policy may turn out to be less the direct impact of foreign companies in China than the sending of thousands of students to Western countries and other forms of exchanges of personnel.

The 1978 plan envisaged sending as many as 20,000 students abroad. With other aspects of the plan, this too was cut back. But by the end of 1981 there were some 7000 Chinese students enrolled at various American universities and colleges and about half that number distributed in other foreign countries. Over and beyond that the Academy of Social Sciences had sent 700 scholars abroad for study or exchange visits in the 3 years since its founding in 1979.[51] The Academy of Sciences had sent an even greater number. In addition, China has vastly extended the number of foreign students, teachers, scholars and consultants from abroad. It is far too early to assess the significance of these exchanges. But on the basis of previous Chinese experience the impact of such extensive and intensive exposure to foreign influence and intellectual currents will be of increasing importance — particularly if these exchanges should continue through the eighties.

Nevertheless, even in this regard, a degree of caution is in order. It is an open secret in China that nearly everyone who has been sent abroad to study is the son or daughter of high-level cadres. While this will ensure that they will be in positions to wield influence on their return to China, it also means that the benefits of the exercise are limited to a narrow social sector with privileges to defend. Significantly, the demands for political change voiced at Peking's 'Democracy Wall' from December 1978 until the crackdown in March/April 1979[52] did not come from those who up to that point had had direct contact with foreigners or the outside world. Through access to *Reference News* (the daily journal for internal distribution which reprints extensive extracts from the world press and journals, and is thought to be read by 20—30 million) and foreign broadcasts, Chinese can be quite well informed about the outside world. But without experience of living abroad or having fully open relationships with foreigners in China, younger Chinese can only interpret this news from within Chinese perspectives. Since the political authorities have shown themselves time and again to be able to limit and control the kinds of contacts which Chinese can establish with foreigners inside China, it would be decidedly premature to place too much confidence on the modernising influences which may flow directly from visiting foreigners. The success of the authorities in the Spring of 1979 in putting an end to the open interchange between Westerners and Chinese, that journalists had found so refreshing, suggests that the time-honoured distinctions between Chinese and outsiders cannot be easily broken down. The occasional indiscretions of foreigners and the temptations which their presence has offered to Chinese to gain access to highly prized consumer goods, or even as potential marriage partners, has already given opportunities to more fundamentalist Chinese and certain political groups to play on traditional antipathies or ideological orthodoxies to attack aspects of the modernisation programme as bourgeois Westernisation.

There can be no question but that external influences are growing in China and that the returned students will play important roles in the future. But these influences, as in the past, will be mediated through the patterns of China's political culture. The nineteenth-century dilemma of *ti* and *yong* ('Chinese learning for essence and Western learning for practical application') has by no means been resolved.

Defence and the open door

One of the primary (if not indeed the principal) reasons for China's leaders' commitment to modernise the country is the perceived need to upgrade its military equipment and train its armed forces to be able to fight modern wars. This is seen as absolutely necessary if China is to retain its independence in the long run and not become subject once again to bullying and humiliation by foreign powers. However, the modernisation of the PLA poses immense problems. Even if it had a sufficient number of adequately trained personnel and effective command, control and communication systems (which it certainly does not have), the costs of importing advanced weapons sufficient to develop a credible deterrent force against either of the two superpowers would be stupendous.[53] It would certainly wreck the prospects for achieving sustained economic growth. The problem, therefore, centres upon selective priorities. Within a broad framework of a long-established agreement that the modernisation of the equipment of the PLA would have to wait until an adequate industrial base had been built as the first priority, the PLA has been divided between those who emphasised military professionalism and those who advocated important political roles for the armed forces as befits a people's army. Overlapping this axis of conflict has been one between those who have advocated the immediate acquisition of particular advanced weapons and those who have objected to this by stressing the prior claims of economic development.[54] Meanwhile important resources have been allocated to China's nuclear and space programmes which have never come under the direct administrative control of the armed forces. The nuclear deterrent has been seen as complementary to the general strategy of defending China by people's war. The latter, however, is very flexible and can incorporate many different kinds of force profiles.

The fall of the 'Gang of Four', in which certain key regional military commanders played a critical role, marked the official ending of the Cultural Revolution and led to the formal withdrawal of military men to the barracks from which they had been reluctantly summoned in 1967/68 to maintain order as the only functioning arm of government.[55] This withdrawal was accompanied by a new emphasis on professionalism. Following four national military conferences in February 1977 Hua Guofeng outlined in March a plan for a smaller, more streamlined PLA, with more advanced weapons, tougher discipline and a more centralised line of command.[56] Military commentaries began to refer to the concept of 'people's war under modern conditions'. It was argued that:

> the suddenness of an outbreak of modern war, the complexity of co-ordinating ground, naval and air operations, the extreme flexibility of combat units and the highly centralised, unified, planned and flexible command structure — all these factors make it necessary for our army to have modern equipment.

These decisions led to the despatch of scores of military shopping expeditions to the West. These in the end turned out to be mainly shop-window exercises. Very few contracts were actually signed. By the end of 1980, as budgeted investments funds were sharply cut back, visits by these delegations dwindled away almost to nothing. At least 85 such visits were made in the 2½ years after January 1977. However, the demands of the civil sectors of the economy were such that after the decision of the Third Plenum at the end of 1978 to readjust the economy, Deng Xiaoping told United States Senator John Glenn that 'defence modernisation has a lower priority than the other three modernisations'. The implication was that China was not going to embark on an international shopping spree for modern weapons. This has been borne out notably by the Chinese decision in 1979—80 not to purchase the British Harrier Vertical Take-off and Landing jet aircraft despite having come so close to doing so that it had been the focus of diplomatic controversy involving sharp opposition from the Russians.

Nevertheless modernisation of the PLA has gone ahead in many important ways in which the 'open door' has played a significant part. Firstly, closer study of advanced military experience in other countries and in modern conflicts such as the 1973 Arab–Israeli war, combined with the effects of the shop-window expeditions and the establishment of a separate institute of strategic studies in Peking, have helped to familiarise China's military planners with the requirements of modern warfare. The experience of the 1979 war with Vietnam highlighted many logistical, command and co-ordination deficiencies of the PLA.[57] Secondly, China has acquired from the United States important advanced radar, computer and other civil—military advanced technology equipment related to surveillance, air defences and aerospace. China now operates two sophisticated American-supplied installations which monitor Soviet military activities in Central Asia. China has also purchased helicopters and anti-tank infantry-operated missiles from France and West Germany as well as up to 1000 heavy-duty trucks and other equipment designed to improve China's logistics. Thirdly, China's naval capabilities, which have been greatly upgraded, have drawn on selective foreign purchases made earlier in the seventies.

China's 4,750,000-strong armed forces not only require re-equipping with modern weapons, but they require training and reorganising for modern warfare. With respect to the latter there is much that can be done within the country. Indeed significant progress has been achieved in enhancing the professional qualities of the armed forces. Officers now have to attend courses at military academies before qualifying for promotion. Last year a large-scale military exercise was held in north China in which for the first time, skill was demonstrated in combined operations.

Because of the competition for scarce resources in a context of growing professionalism China is beginning to demonstrate a degree of inter-service rivalries common to all other major armed forces. For example, there have been arguments about the respective merits of maritime and inland defence, which (for the time being at least) appear to have been won by the navy.[58] China seems to be on the verge of going beyond coastal defence. In May 1980 the Chinese for the first time sent a naval task force several thousand miles into the Pacific Ocean as part of support operations for its first 8000—10,000 mile range intercontinental ballistic missile (ICBM). Much has been made of the longer-term significance of the naval venture in the Chinese press. In March 1982 it was announced that a Chinese submarine had returned from a test in which it spent 'tens of days and nights' submerged — thus suggesting that it was nuclear-powered. It has also been made public that China has been training pilots for operations on aircraft carriers, thus indicating very clearly China's future intentions.[59] It can be argued that the expansion of the navy would have taken place eventually, regardless of the open-door policy. However, the new orientation to the outside world has clearly enhanced the need for better naval defences. China's current long-term economic strategy places much emphasis on the coastal regions and on international trade. The development of offshore facilities at a time in which China has unresolved disputes with neighbours over the division of the continental shelf, and indeed over the sovereignty of various islands, all point to the need for a more modern and ocean-going naval capability. The growing Soviet naval presence in the area also calls for a Chinese response. Thus, although the Chinese navy is not based on the acquisition of modern ships from the West, the open-door policy has been an important factor in the high priority it has enjoyed in recent years.

As for the other services, and indeed China's nuclear arm, there can be little doubt that but for the shortage of finance and the prior claims of other sectors of economy, a considerable number of purchases would have been made. The nuclear and aerospace arms are largely independent of the PLA, but a number of important breakthroughs have been achieved related to the long-distance ICBM. Meanwhile there is much that can be done in improving China's ability to fight the electronic war that has become typical of the modern battlefield. The production of Chinese domestically generated electronic systems (associated with its nuclear and aerospace programmes) combined with the imports of advanced electronics and computers from the West should enable China's more modern sections of the PLA to upgrade their knowledge and capabilities in these essential features of modern warfare. However, the sheer size of the PLA, and of China's problems, suggest that progress will not be rapid. Over and beyond that there are important elements in the armed forces who still adhere to more pristine views of people's war and who are resistant to the new changes. Of China's 169 divisions only 11 are armoured and a further 40 are artillery. More than 100 divisions are still old-fashioned, foot-slogging infantry. After the Cultural Revolution the prestige of the PLA has plummeted and the agricultural reforms have given such incentives to able-bodied young men to work with their households that for the first time the PLA faces problems of recruitment.

This is not to imply that the PLA is seething with inner conflict or simmering in potential revolt against the new policies and the new political order. It is, however, to suggest that there are various conflicts of interest within the PLA and that the political and structural constraints to rapid reform elsewhere in China can also be seen within the PLA. The tension in the PLA between the modernising professional tendency and that which still adheres to the guerrilla people's war traditions has a long history, as does the conflict of priorities between the military and civil budgetary appropriations. It is too early to identify the patterns by which these issues in their contemporary guise interact with the policy debates in the civil sector, but the implications for China's foreign policy seem more evident. Since the general modernisation of the PLA must await the modernisation of the economy which in turn is to be measured in decades, it follows that China's domestic requirement for a long period of international peace can only be established if at all, by diplomacy. That strongly suggests that the international strategic implications of China's economic reforms and the open-door policy should be to reduce tensions with the Soviet Union.

However the social and economic dimensions of China's foreign relations do not in the final analysis determine the strategic and international dimensions of foreign policy. Just as the initial détente with the United States was not occasioned by economic considerations, the question of improving relations with the Soviet Union will be determined primarily by strategic/diplomatic judgements. China's domestic requirements are obviously an important factor in these calculations, but ultimately they are unlikely to be decisive. On the other hand, as has happened before in China's history, the socioeconomic consequences of the kind of open-door policies being currently pursued can lead to a sociopolitical backlash from more fundamentalist elements which in turn could lead China back to a neo-isolationist position. That would doubtless have important implications for China's international/strategic relationships, but whether it would fundamentally alter China's place in the balance of world power is doubtful.

5

Strategic and International Politics Since Mao

Perhaps the most striking aspect of this dimension of China's foreign policy is its continuity with the Maoist era. Despite signs of greater flexibility in the conduct of policy and a major change in ideological perspectives, the general pattern of Chinese approaches to the strategic dimensions of international politics has not markedly changed in the 10 years since the early seventies. Notwithstanding the deepening links with the international economy, China's leaders have continued to perceive international politics within the highly conflictual framework of Mao's 'geopolitical thought' (see Chapter 3). Mao's theories of revisionism and his ideological criticisms of the Soviet Union may have been jettisoned, but the Soviet Union has continued to be regarded as the most dangerous and expansionist of the superpowers. The discarding of Mao's ideological objections to the Soviet Union has been caused by domestic changes in China and the rejection of the theoretical considerations which underpinned the Cultural Revolution. It has not been caused by a re-evaluation of the international role of the Soviet Union. Indeed the current analyses of the strengths and weaknesses of the Soviet Union as an expansionist imperialist power are precisely those which Mao himself advanced in his famous 'paper tiger' thesis on the nature of imperialism. According to this thesis, while militarily powerful in the short run, an imperialist power is weak in the long term because its expansionism leads to over-commitment which in turn accentuates the political, social and economic contradictions of its domestic society. Such a power necessarily will encounter increasing local resistance to its foreign adventures and it will also become more isolated internationally. Both tendencies combine to exacerbate its domestic social tensions. In this view there comes a point at which the imperialist power either retracts and settles for a defensive posture or it is broken by an unpopular war. It is this mode of analysis which has led successive Chinese leaders since the beginning of the seventies to argue that the American failure in Vietnam was its turning point, and that thereafter it has been thrust generally on the defensive. The Soviet Union, it has been argued, took advantage of the American involvement in Vietnam to improve its relative military power so that it was able to replace the United States as the major global expansionist power. However, implicit in the Chinese analysis is that in time the Soviet Union too will find the costs of sustaining its expansionist role to be too great.

It follows from the Maoist thesis that the expansionist imperialist superpower can only be checked by universal opposition to its policies and by resolute resistance in the countries it is seeking to dominate. Any moves to conciliate it or to acquiesce in its latest expansionist enterprise are by definition self-defeating. Thus, like Mao before them, China's leaders in the late seventies and early eighties have been highly critical of certain Western approaches to détente, regarding them as little short of appeasement. Similarly, they have argued that local conflicts in the Third World only provide opportunities for intervention by the Soviet Union, and that therefore these should be settled as quickly as possible and without using 'the good offices' of the Russians.

Another example of following Maoist precepts concerns the approach of the post-Mao leaders towards Vietnam. Obviously, no-one can know how Mao or Zhou Enlai personally would have handled relations with Vietnam, but there can be little doubt that the Chinese approach since 1978 closely accords with Mao's strategic thought. The objective of Chinese policy is to keep up military pressure on Vietnam, support the insurgent resistance to it in Kampuchea, and isolate Vietnam internationally with a view to compelling Vietnamese society to reach a breaking point at which Vietnam would have to revise its attempt to control the whole of Indo-China. Some have argued that China's policy has the result of driving Vietnam into closer relations with the Soviet Union. They suggest that the object of policy should be to make Vietnam less dependent on the Soviet Union as a prelude to encouraging Vietnam to modify its policy in Indo-China. Indeed it is often pointed out that the Vietnamese have already expressed misgivings about their exclusive dependence on Russia.[1] The recognition of differences between Vietnam and the Soviet Union towards the end of 1981 has not led the Chinese leaders to change track on the grounds advocated by some in the West that possibilities exist for weaning the Vietnamese from the Russians. The Peking argument is that to offer the Vietnamese alternative sources of aid at this stage would only promote much needed relief for the government and thereby actually strengthen the current policies of occupation to which the Chinese leaders object. On the contrary, almost in Maoist fashion, Chinese policy suggests that the maintenance of the pressure on Vietnam damages the Soviet Union too because the burden of aiding Vietnam is an extra drain on those resources used by the Soviet Union to maintain its expansionist role. The Chinese suggest that the relief of the Soviet burden would actually serve the joint current interests of Vietnam and the Soviet Union without necessarily bringing about a change in Vietnamese policies in Indo-China. The Chinese approach may be contrasted with traditional Western diplomatic norms which emphasise both conflict and harmony, and which seek to find points of compromise with an adversary in order to draw it into observing international diplomatic norms favoured by the traditional great powers.

The general pattern of continuity with the early seventies extends beyond the question of modes of analysis to that of specific policies. Thus much of China's foreign policy has continued to be devoted to the building of an anti-Soviet international coalition. Although the importance of the partnership with the United States has grown, the essential guidelines were established during the reception by Mao and Zhou of Nixon and Kissinger in the early seventies. Indeed even the tensions and ambiguities in the Sino-American relationship in the early eighties reflect those of the previous decade. These concern the Taiwan issue, Chinese suspicions of aspects of American relations with the Russians, and

Chinese criticism of aspects of United States policies towards Third World countries. China's leaders have continued to be concerned lest China should be used as a pawn in the Washington—Moscow dialogues and they have not abandoned Mao's long-standing fear of a Soviet—American condominium — especially on nuclear matters. Similarly, the patterns of China's relations with Western Europe have not greatly changed. Chinese approaches to Third World countries, and to movements of national liberation, have declined somewhat in intensity, but even that reflects a trend that had begun earlier in the seventies. Moreover, the Chinese posture towards the Third World as a whole in the early eighties is still recognisably that which was manifested 10 years earlier. China's relations within the Asia—Pacific region have been characterised by several important new developments involving closer relations with Japan and the countries of ASEAN (Association of South East Asian Nations), but especially the emergence of the conflict with Vietnam. Nevertheless the genesis of Chinese policies in the area may be traced to the last few years of the Mao era.

Within this general pattern of continuity of Chinese approaches to international politics, however, there have been important new developments, particularly in what might be regarded as China's diplomatic style.[2] China's more open door practice of economic development has been accompanied by greater foreign access to Chinese society and by a greater willingness of the Chinese authorities to 'learn' from the outside world. This has meant that Chinese domestic affairs have begun to be better understood outside China and that Chinese diplomacy reflects a sharper appreciation of the perspectives and interests of others. In short, China's diplomacy has acquired a greater flexibility. As will be shown later in this chapter, the new flexibility is particularly evident in Chinese attempts to woo the countries of ASEAN within a framework of a rather rigid and unyielding Chinese policy towards the conflicts of Indo-China. Chinese diplomacy may be said to reflect the fruits of the experience of a more active participation in the international diplomatic community and of the acquisition of a better-informed and sophisticated understanding of the politics and policies of other countries. However, another important contributory factor to this development is the rejection of much of Mao's ideological line of his last 20 years. The domestic keynote slogan since the end of 1978 has been 'learn truth from facts', and this has been reflected in the style of Chinese approach to the external world. The Chinese official news agency no longer publishes reports from other countries couched exclusively in the terms and concepts of Chinese politics. Instead they tend to be more factual presentations of the issues and institutional structures of the relevant countries. Similarly, but perhaps more importantly, China's diplomacy has dropped much of its hectoring didactic tone in favour of a style which takes more into account the sensitivities and constraints affecting the behaviour of other governments. Thus for example, Chinese diplomats have stopped lecturing their West European counterparts on their supposed obligation to unite Europe better; they no longer 'instruct' NATO (North Atlantic Treaty Organisation) members as to how they should react to the latest manoeuvres by the Soviet Union. Instead they have sought to improve their own understanding of the workings of the European Community and the reasons for NATO's difficulties in advancing a common front on certain salient questions.

Developments in Chinese approaches to international politics

Like the foreign policies of all major countries those of China are a product of a multiplicity of factors involving a complex mix of interactions between what might be called the domestic and external environments. Given the extent of the changes which have taken place in both sets of 'environments' since the beginning of China's new direction in international politics in the late sixties and early seventies, perhaps the most pertinent question about Chinese foreign policy in what has been called here the strategic domain is why such a high degree of constancy has been maintained through to at least the early eighties.

The constancy is all the more remarkable if consideration is taken of the magnitude of the changes which have taken place. In the words of Thomas W. Robinson: 'the 1970s . . . saw changes in the general international system that were more revolutionary than in any of the decades of the twentieth century, save perhaps those associated with the two world wars. . . '[3] In particular he drew attention to five major trends: the rise of Soviet military power and the relative decline of the United States; the replacement of Cold War bipolarity by a more relaxed and diffused East—West relationship which included greater trade and elements of co-operation; the growth of interdependence in the West, including Japan, and the increasing importance of economic questions, especially concerning energy and oil; the emergence of the so-called north—south problem; and the militarisation of Sino-Soviet relations. Earlier in the same article Robinson drew attention to the significance of some of the changes in the international relations of Asia during the decade: 'The emergence of six "modern" rapidly growing, capitalist developed states or city-states along the eastern periphery of the continent' — South Korea, Taiwan, Hong Kong, Singapore, Japan and ('possibly') Malaysia (as we have seen, the first named on the list have been referred to in China as 'the four little tigers'); the final American defeat in Vietnam in 1975 and its partial withdrawal from Asia; the new activism by China and Japan; and finally the new activism by the Soviet Union which has brought it militarily and economically into maritime Asia and which in turn has transposed the lines of conflict in Asia.

More could be added to Robinson's list, but he has surely captured the most important of the changes in the international environment especially as they affect China. If to these are added the extensive domestic changes which China underwent during the decade, the general constancy of China's position on the strategic—international plane must seem all the more remarkable. It suggests that major interests of the Chinese state as perceived by successive Chinese leaders are served by this posture. It also suggests that what Mao and Zhou identified as the most important international trend (i.e. the new relative defensiveness and offensiveness of America and Russia respectively) when they first developed this posture, has been seen to be persistent and overriding by China's leaders.

The one overriding strategic issue for China's leaders

throughout this period, and stretching into the 1980s, has been the rise and extension of Soviet military power coupled with the relative decline of the United States. Not even the death of Mao and the removal of his ideological objections to the Soviet Union fundamentally changed the Chinese position. To be sure the demise of the great protagonist towards the Soviet Union has led to some new nuances in Sino-Soviet relations. Yet the essence of Mao's view as reported by Henry Kissinger from his conversations of 1973 are remarkably similar to those of the official Chinese position 9 years later. Kissinger reported Mao as urging the United States to play a more effective role in constructing an anti-Soviet coalition. American military deployments in Asia were criticised as being 'too scattered'. Mao and Zhou were said to have stressed the importance of close American co-operation with Western Europe, Japan, Pakistan, Iran and Turkey. America should build up its defences and focus on the fundamental (Soviet) challenge rather than squabble with allies over short-term differences. Soviet expansionism, Mao asserted, was 'pitiful' for Soviet courage did not match its ambitions. Moscow looked strong, Mao argued, but as early as 1973 he asserted that it was actually over-extended. It had to be wary of Japan and China; it had to keep an eye on South Asia and the Middle East; and it faced another front in Europe, where it had to maintain forces larger than those facing China. Kissinger quoted Mao as concluding that the Soviet Union would be unable to attack China 'unless you let them in first and you first give them the Middle East and Europe so they are able to deploy troops eastward'.[4]

Despite the profound changes in international politics since then, including the expansion of Soviet military power both directly and indirectly in Africa, the Middle East, Southwest and Southeast Asia, the central thrust of Mao's analysis is still echoed by China's leaders and official commentators: namely, that the Soviet Union is the main threat to world peace, but it is beset with difficulties, while it poses a threat to China, an attack on China is not imminent. In Zhou Enlai's words of August 1973, China was too 'tough a piece of meat' and the Soviet Union was only 'making a feint to the East while attacking in the West'.[5] Following the military conflicts in

Indo-China and the Soviet invasion of Afghanistan, coupled with Soviet naval and airforce deployments in Southeast Asia and the Indian Ocean, the Chinese have publicly acknowledged that these developments pose threats to China, but they nevertheless still assert that the primary threat is to other regional states and to Japan and the United States.[6] Moreover Mao's implied point that the defeat of Soviet expansionism would depend to a large extent on the United States and the success of establishing an anti-Soviet international coalition, rather than primarily on China, has remained a persistent theme of China's approach to these global issues. It is suggested that China has a role to play, but it is essentially a modest one. Neither Mao nor his successors have claimed a pivotal role for China in the global strategic balance. Similarly, although Mao's successors no longer adhere to his view that a new world war is inevitable, neither he nor they had in mind a war between China and the Soviet Union, but rather between the two superpowers.[7] Interestingly, the point at which the global situation might be changed was also implicit in Mao's comments. That point would be reached when Soviet expansionism should finally catch up with its domestic weaknesses so that its over-extendedness would impose impossible burdens upon its own societal capabilities. These are certainly the terms within which the Chinese began to debate the issue in 1980–81.[8]

At the end of the sixties Chinese analyses of international politics were marked by confusion and uncertainty which in part reflected the domestic factional struggle, but which also flowed from ambiguities and inconsistencies in the Mao/Zhou approach to international issues. This was a period of transition for China in which the American threat was being replaced by a different kind of menace from the Soviet Union.[9] This was also paralleled by an ending of the revolutionary isolationism of the early stages of the Cultural Revolution as China reached out for improved diplomatic relations, first with Third World states, and second with the small and medium capitalist states. Interestingly some of the first states involved were Yugoslavia (hitherto reviled as the progenitor of revisionism and a Trojan horse for the introduction of capitalist and American influences into the socialist camp) and the Soviet neighbours Turkey and Iran. The beginnings of the attempt to construct an anti-Soviet coalition were already becoming clear. But at this stage both superpowers were still being condemned as arch-imperialists in roughly equal measure. It was not until the early 1970s, after the opening to the United States, that Chinese analyses began to acquire coherence. The demise of Lin Biao signalled the end of the dispute as to whether collusion or contention was the major characteristic of relations between the two superpowers. The victory of Mao and Zhou meant that henceforth contention was to be regarded as the predominant characteristic of their relations. It followed that China should seek to exploit their conflict and compromise with the United States to block the Soviet Union. Nevertheless the 1972 New Year editorial of China's leading newspapers still proclaimed that 'the characteristic feature of the world situation can be summed up in one word "chaos", "upheaval" or "global upheaval" '. In fact it was not until 1974 that this chaos was said to have resolved itself into a division of the world into three groups, or as it was put, into three worlds. That is, the superpowers, the small and medium capitalist powers (coupled with the East European countries under Soviet dominance) and the Third World.[10]

There were, however, tantalising signs of other modes of analysis being considered by China's leaders before the emergence of the new orthodoxy. Interestingly, some of these were to re-emerge at the end of the decade and in the early 1980s. One such view was that the world could also be regarded in terms of a five-power balance. In a semi-private interview the late Guo Moruo (then Chairman of the Standing Committee of the National People's Congress and head of the Academy of Sciences and a man who had often been close to Mao) in an analysis of the current state of world politics depicted its essential features in terms of a 'five-pointed star' with the points made up of the US, the USSR, the EEC, Japan and China.[11] When asked to endorse this view Zhou Enlai replied guardedly without explicitly disagreeing, 'we admit that we can develop in some decades into a strong prosperous country. But we have declared that we will never be a superpower, neither today nor in the future.'[12] The implication was that it was wrong to equate China with the superpowers. Two years later in 1973 the then Assistant Foreign Minister Zhang Wenjin refuted the 'five-pointed star' by noting the unequal distribution of power between the countries that made up the five points.[13]

The three worlds theory which eventually emerged in April 1974[14] was not fully endorsed by the Gang of Four,[15] and although it was largely in accord with Mao's approach to international affairs no statement of his support was released publicly before his death. A year later a lengthy theoretical defence of the theory claimed that Mao had outlined the key elements of the theory to Zambia's President Kaunda on 22 February 1974 during his visit to China. The theory had doubtful Marxist credentials as it focused almost entirely upon state behaviour in international affairs, to the exclusion of class analysis or socialistic criteria.[16] It also played down one of Mao's more cherished revolutionary — if typically elliptical — precepts of the early seventies that 'countries want independence, nations want liberation and the people want revolution; this has become an irresistible trend of history'. Indeed after Mao's death little further was heard from Chinese sources about this allegedly 'irresistible trend'.

There were certain ambiguities in the theory, at least in so far as it was meant to offer operational guidelines for China's foreign policy. Perhaps the most important of these concerns the two superpowers which as the 'first world' constitute the heart of the three worlds theory. In theory there is little to distinguish between them as the contemporary 'biggest international exploiters and oppressors' and as 'the source of a new world war' except that the Soviet Union was said to be 'especially vicious', mendacious, perfidious, 'self-seeking and unscrupulous' (all these are abusive epithets rather than analytical categories). Yet as we have seen, Mao, Zhou, Deng Xiaoping himself and other Chinese leaders in practice drew much sharper distinctions between the two superpowers and treated the United States as a strategic partner in combating Soviet hegemonism. In fact the theory shed remarkably little light on the actual operational concepts employed by China's leaders in managing their complex relations with the superpowers; nor does it help to explain China's successive leaders' persistent search for an international anti-Soviet (not anti-superpower) coalition.

The high strategic significance allotted the Third World in theory as the major centre for effective resistance to super-power dominance has not been reflected in Chinese diplomacy, which has focused its attention far more on relations with the West and Japan as well as the countries in China's Asian region.

The theory of the three worlds has had a rather chequered career since its first enunciation in April 1974. At that time there was a certain Chinese disenchantment with the United States after the heady enthusiasm of the previous 2 years. China's leaders were critical of aspects of the new Soviet–American détente associated with the Strategic Arms Limitation Talks (SALT) and exemplified by the first SALT agreement. They were also concerned lest some Western leaders were seeking to stabilise the European sector in order to encourage the Soviet Union to move eastward. Another high point of the advocacy of the theory was in 1977 when Chinese dissatisfaction with the Carter Administration was marked.[17] But from 1978 when the alignment with the United States was cemented in the context of the conflict with Vietnam and in the euphoria of normalisation, it did seem as if the three worlds theory had been quietly abandoned. However, it has since been resurrected in 1981–82, largely as a consequence of the incipient rift with the Reagan Administration over projected arms sales to Taiwan. This account strongly suggests that the three worlds theory with its equal treatment of the Soviet Union and the United States is something of an embarrassment when relations are judged to be warm and productive with the United States. Nevertheless the theory does attest to ambiguities in Chinese official attitudes towards the United States. On the one hand it is perceived as a strategic partner of long-term significance, but on the other it is also regarded as an imperialist power with whom China has deep differences so that their partnership could not but be limited and temporary.

Even as the three worlds theory was reappearing in Chinese publications, senior Chinese writers in the Academy of the Social Sciences were advancing new perspectives on world politics and economics that owed little to that theory. Thus the deputy director of the Institute of West European Studies argued in an article that the world should best be seen in multi-polar terms. The United States, the Soviet Union, Western Europe, Japan and China were perceived as independent centres with their particularities of strengths and weaknesses. The fact that the article was broadcast implied that it was of more than academic interest and that this essentially power-political mode of analysis found favour with at least some political circles in Peking.[18] An even more senior figure, Huang Xiang, Vice-President of the Academy and a former high official of the Ministry of Foreign Affairs and associate of Zhou Enlai, analysed the economic recession in Western countries in terms of the capitalist countries as a whole rather than by distinguishing sharply between the first and second worlds. The article was even more prominently publicised through publication in China's premier foreign-language journal. He argued that:

unless it is stimulated by external factors, the Western economy will remain at a low level. Its period of relative stability has gone for ever. In the coming decade, instability and frequent crises will prevail in the capitalist world.[19]

Nevertheless there was no shortage of Chinese official pronouncements to the effect that China would for ever belong to the Third World and that the three worlds theory was still relevant. Although the theory may have been a convenient way for classifying different forces in world politics, it is clear that if it were a guide to Chinese decision-makers it was only at a high level of generality. As far as the immediate practicalities of China's foreign policy-making, other considerations came to the fore. It is also instructive that the theory received more emphasis in proportion to the deterioration of Sino–American relations. From a Chinese perspective the American overtures to Taiwan were manifestations of underlying imperialist tendencies.

The non-inevitability of war

Perhaps the greatest departure from Mao's legacy was the disavowal or partial disavowal of his theory of the inevitability of war. While Mao conceded that a new world war could be postponed, he nevertheless held in Leninist fashion that war was an inherent characteristic of imperialism and that sooner or later such a war would break out between the Soviet Union and the United States. Only if revolutions were to take place in the two countries could it be avoided. This was one of the issues on which Mao broke with Khrushchev. Mao strongly disputed Khrushchev's argument that the advent of nuclear weapons and the emergence of nuclear deterrence required a modification of Lenin's stands on the inevitability of war, the impossibility of peaceful transition from capitalism to socialism, and the irreconcilability of the conflict between the forces of socialism and imperialism. In Mao's view that was the starting point for the emergence of revisionism in Russia. To assert that mutual Soviet–American nuclear deterrence could prevent a global war meant that the two powers should seek patterns of co-operation and arrogate unto themselves a special position over and above all other countries. It also meant that just revolutionary wars would receive less help lest they should escalate into regional wars involving the two great powers which in turn could lead to the breakdown of deterrence. On the other hand, Khrushchev implied that mutual nuclear deterrence would inhibit the greatest imperialist power from intervening in civil wars or aiding the reactionary side, thereby paving the way for the peaceful transition from a capitalist to a socialist society without having to follow the revolutionary path of the Bolshevik Revolution. All this was held by Mao as signifying the abandonment of Leninist revolutionary principles and the slide towards revisionism and reformism.

There is no evidence to suggest that despite the opening to the United States Mao ever changed his mind on the inevitability of war. He did, however, imply that it could be postponed for a long time into the future if imperialist expansion were firmly resisted by an international united front. He never abandoned the view he had first advanced in 1946 that a world war would not break out between the two superpowers until one or other had mastered the intermediate zone of the many countries between them. Thus the way to hold back Soviet expansionism in the seventies, according to Mao, was the establishment of a broad coalition of resistance; and the more effective this was, the better the chances of postponing the global war. His last statement on the subject was on 20 May 1970: 'The danger of a new world war still exists, and the people of all countries must get prepared. But revolution is the main trend in the world today'. This view was echoed in Deng Xiaoping's address to the United Nations of April 1974 which first spelt out the theory of the three worlds: 'The contradiction between the two superpowers is irreconcilable. . . . Either they will fight each other, or the people will rise in revolution.' Zhou Enlai also repeated this theme in his speech to the Fourth National People's Congress in January 1975. Both superpowers were regarded as equal threats to world peace and 'their fierce contention [was] bound to lead to war some day'.

Beginning in October 1980 Chinese leaders revised this view. Hu Yaobang declared:

It is our view that if all peace loving countries and people unite and take firm steps to curb the hegemonists' aggression and expansion, it is possible to postpone *or even to prevent* the outbreak of a great war [emphasis added].[20]

The Foreign Minister, Huang Hua, repeated the point in December:

We should make a sober estimate of the Soviet Union's military capability and adventurism. Likewise we should see its weaknesses and difficulties. The Soviet Union's southward thrust can be frustrated and war can be postponed or prevented.[21]

Deng Xiaoping returned to this theme in a somewhat different way in his talks with the then United Nations General Secretary General, Kurt Waldheim, in June 1981:

The present international situation is even more turbulent and unstable than before, with an increasing number of danger spots . . . all forces opposing hegemonism and cherishing peace [should] unite so as to deal with the difficult situation and defer the outbreak of a major war. If such a war can be prevented so much the better.[22]

The suggestion that a global war was not necessarily inevitable was based on different considerations and on theoretical premises altogether different from those which led Khrushchev to advocate that view some 15 years earlier. China's leaders argued that the possible prevention of a world war depended less on understandings between the great powers than on the united opposition to 'hegemonists' by 'peace loving countries and peoples'. The view of the nature of international conflict and how it could be circumscribed still owed much to Mao's consistently expressed thesis that peace cannot be won by making concessions to an aggressive great power, or by great power diplomacy alone. It could be won only by determined resistance to the aggressor by as many social groups and countries as possible.

The emergence of the new view on war can be traced to three developments in Chinese assessments of the international situation. The first was the identification of the Soviet Union alone, rather than the two superpowers together as the major source of a new world war. This view gained momentum especially after the final American debacle in Indo-China in April 1975.[23] The second was China's success in effecting an anti-Soviet coalition with Japan and the United States in late 1978, which was a contributory factor in restraining the Soviet Union from opening a second front on China's northern borders during the Chinese attack on Vietnam in February— March 1979. Linked with this was the growing diplomatic isolation of the Soviet Union arising out of the Vietnamese military occupation of Kampuchea and the Soviet invasion of Afghanistan. Both were opposed by huge majorities in the United Nations, and the latter in particular evoked sharp hostility by the Islamic world. The third development was Chinese appreciation of the growing burden on the Soviet Union arising out of its international activities and the high cost of its military build-up. Chinese commentaries from early 1980 began to highlight the costs to the Russians of sustaining the Vietnamese and the Cubans, the problems arising out of the Afghani resistance to the Soviet occupation and Soviet difficulties in Eastern Europe as epitomised by the Polish crisis.[24]

Indeed the recognition of Soviet difficulties had been a factor in Chinese readiness to begin inter-governmental talks with the Soviet Union in Moscow in September 1979 with the stated aims of improving relations. But the Soviet invasion of Afghanistan caused the Chinese to postpone the next round of talks due to begin in Peking in early 1980. A year later it became evident in April 1981 that a debate of sorts was taking place in Peking as to whether or not the Soviet Union had begun to decline. A 7 April *Xinhua* commentary acknowledged the increase of Soviet power but questioned whether it was superior to that of the United States. Other articles dwelt on the problems the Soviet Union was encountering in its 'southward drive'. On 31 July Hu Yaobang asserted that although the Soviet Union was threatening in appearance, 'in reality it [was] very feeble'. At the same time other articles pointed more sharply to Soviet strength and assertiveness.[25] The debate may be seen as reflecting a certain duality or ambiguity in Chinese analyses of the Soviet position, especially after the invasion of Afghanistan. On the one hand, further incidences of Soviet expansionism were perceived as adding to the Russian burden and increasing the difficulties it would encounter in carrying on the policy of intervention and expansion. This would suggest that the Soviet leaders might become more constrained in the exercise of their foreign policy. On the other hand, examples of Soviet expansionism could also be seen as proof of the unlimited insatiable ambitions of Soviet hegemonism. If the first interpretation were to predominate it would follow that room could exist for the improvement of Sino-Soviet relations; if the latter, very little room for such manoeuvre could exist. Both sets of attitudes were evident in Chinese commentaries which examined the likelihood of a Soviet intervention in Poland during the second half of 1980. For example, on 4 September a *Xinhua* commentary argued that in the light of Soviet 'embarrassment' because of Afghanistan, the Russians 'could not afford another stormy international reaction', and it concluded 'judging from Moscow's past behaviour, it could have made another adventurous move at this critical moment, yet it had to be very cautious before making such a move'. By 6 December, however, *Xinhua* warned that 'the shadow of outside intervention [in Poland] looms large'. The uncertainty about the Soviet response to Poland persisted throughout the following year. In the event, unlike the Western governments, China did not condemn the imposition of martial law on 13 December as equivalent to Soviet intervention. Nor was the apparent Soviet restraint interpreted as a sign of weakness. On the contrary, after a few official commentaries in the autumn of 1981 which drew attention both to Soviet strength and to the difficulties which confronted the Soviet Union, a highly publicised article entitled 'Is the Soviet Union Declining' of 25 December 1981 concluded decisively that it was not. Despite its difficulties Soviet economic and military strength was said not to have been weakened and in many respects it was said to be better placed than the United States; moreover the current Soviet overseas burden was calculated as far below that shouldered by the United States in Vietnam. The article finished on a rather guarded and cautious note:

To overestimate or underestimate the present Soviet strength and difficulties will lead to the wrong judgement on the Soviet political and military tendencies and the world situation. To underestimate the serious difficulties being faced by the Soviet Union and to overestimate the Soviet hegemonic power and to reach a compromise will be unfavourable to world peace. The Soviet Union has not been on the decline because of present difficulties, nor has it renounced its global strategic offensive. Even if it is confronted with greater difficulties, Moscow can act with prudence or make a reckless move. Military adventures launched by the warmongers in history often took place in a period of economic crisis and not of economic prosperity.

Therefore, it is harmful to the maintenance of world peace to think that the late coming superpower is on the decline and thus lose vigilance against it.[26]

The implications for China from this line of analysis were clearly to continue to emphasise defence preparedness and to be very wary of resuming negotiations with the Soviet Union.

One problem with Chinese public analyses of Soviet problems at this stage was that in arguing that Soviet expansionism could only be stemmed by resolute opposition by the rest of the world they could hardly suggest at the same time that the Soviet Union had lost its forward momentum and that it was possible to negotiate a relaxation of tensions with it. The Chinese dilemma was that while they dearly sought a peaceful environment in which to concentrate on domestic economic development, they could not negotiate an agreement with the Soviet Union which left all its threatening military deployments in place. They, or those leaders who sought to withstand the demands of the military (or certain sections of it) for a greater claim on China's economic resources, had a special interest in detecting signs of Soviet decline or of difficulties which would constrain Soviet adventurism. A corollary to this was that these leaders would have to rely very much on the continued opposition to the Soviet Union by the international coalition China had built up. Therefore they resolutely rejected any suggestions that the Soviet 'peace offensive' of the early eighties was anything other than a piece of 'trickery' to take advantage of the European peace movement to drive a wedge between the United States and its Western European allies. Chinese official statements tended to be highly ambiguous in the sense that they combined warnings about Soviet aggressiveness with emphases on its growing difficulties.

This ambiguity was evident in the address to the U.N. General Assembly by Vice Foreign Minister, Zhang Wenjin on 23 September 1981:

International realities do not bear out the view that the Soviet Union launches a 'peace offensive' because it is on the defensive and that its own difficulties are causing it to retreat.

Facts in the past year have shown that the Soviet Union has not given up its bid for world hegemony. . . . However, because of repeated setbacks and its own vulnerabilities, the Soviet Union, while adhering to a policy of aggression and expansion, has increasingly resorted to political tricks . . . another so-called 'peace offensive' . . . 'political solutions' and proposals for disarmament and so on, which are designed . . . to disguise its hegemonism and to deceive or lull the people of the world.[27]

Recognition of Euro-Communism

On first consideration the reversal of the stand by China's leaders in April 1980 on the question of the so-called Euro-Communist Parties of Western Europe might be thought to be of little strategic significance. After all their impact on China's national security concerns is minimal in the extreme. Deeper consideration, however, suggests several important consequences which attest to a subtler appreciation of world politics and to a greater degree of diplomatic flexibility by China's leaders. The new development also involves an important shift in the perceptions by Chinese leaders of their country's place in world affairs. Finally, the cultivation of relations with these Communist Parties is an important dimension in Sino-Soviet relations as it provides another pressure point with which to constrain the Soviet Union.

The initial severance of relations with the West European Communist Parties in the late 1950s and early 1960s had been a function of the Sino-Soviet dispute. Interestingly, Chinese criticisms of the Soviet Party in 1956—57 had been an important contributory factor to the emergence of polycentrism among the Western European Parties. But these were soon to be condemned by China as revisionist Parties who had abandoned the revolutionary road in favour of the reformist Parliamentary way to power — i.e., the 'peaceful transition' which had been one of Khrushchev's revisions of Leninist doctrine. By the 1970s the Western European Communist Parties had also come to be seen by China's leaders as fifth columnists who would serve Russian interests.

Thus even after Mao's death and the dropping of his ideological theories of revisionism the hostility to the Euro-Communists remained. On 23 October 1977 Deng Xiaoping said that China 'would not like to see the Communist Parties of

France, Italy and Spain come to power or even to participate in government'. They would, he claimed, carry out a 'policy of appeasement' towards the Soviet Union.[28] As late as March 1979 a *Xinhua* commentary which was also published in the *Beijing Review* cast doubt on the assertion of independence from Moscow by the Communist Party of Italy (CPI) and favoured its exclusion from government. The commentary noted:

> Italy's Western allies cannot but pay more attention to the situation in Italy at this time when the Soviet Union is stepping up its arms expansion and war preparations and looking menacingly at Western Europe. Recently the PCI has come out publicly in favour of the Soviet-supported Vietnamese aggression in Indo-China. Italian public opinion has taken note of this.[29]

Whether or not Italian public opinion 'took note' of that, China's leaders certainly noted the CPI's condemnation of the Soviet invasion of Afghanistan. Within a context in which Chinese economists were drawing upon the experience of reforms in Hungary and Yugoslavia, and in which debates were being held as to whether the Soviet Union was a socialist country, the *People's Daily* in early April 1980 announced that the nine Chinese commentaries on the international Communist movement, that had been at the core of Sino-Soviet polemics in the early sixties, were incorrect on the questions of economics and revisionism. This fuelled speculation on the prospects for Sino-Soviet relations until Deng Xiaoping made a brief but blunt statement in May that the Soviet Union was not a socialist country but a social imperialist one, on account of its expansionism and interventions in other countries. The true import of the change (which had not taken place even to honour President Tito on his visit in 1977) became clear when a CPI delegation led by its General Secretary, Enrico Berlinguer, visited China from 14 to 23 April 1980 and restored Party relations with the Chinese. China's leaders stressed the international importance of the CPI in Europe and in the international Communist movement. The major point of agreement between the two sides was respect for each other's independence and the rejection of the right of any one Party (i.e., the Soviets) to assume patriarchal airs and seek to impose its view on others. The point was made even more forcefully when relations with the Communist Party of Spain were restored in November of that year, Hua Guofeng declared that 'all Communist Parties are independent and equal. They should integrate the universal truth of Marxism with their own revolutionary practice and formulate their own political line, principles and policies.' The Spanish Party leader went even further and he was published in the Chinese press claiming that 'the thoughts of our great masters' must be developed lest the Communists should 'lag behind or change from revolutionaries to conservatives'. Moreover, he asserted that 'there are no prescriptions valid for all' countries. He went on to argue that 'a socio-economic formation like socialism could have different superstructures and political systems as in the case of capitalism'.[30]

An even more surprising development was the establishment of Party relations with the Socialist Party of France in February 1981 as, unlike the Euro-Communist Parties, it did not even claim to be a Marxist Party. The *Beijing Review* stated that the CPC was interested in establishing friendly relations with other European Socialist parties. 'As the hegemonists expand and make troubles everywhere, it is not possible to rely on a few countries and political parties to effectively check the hegemonists' aggressive and expansionist acts and defend world peace.' And in a new version of Marx's famous cry, in the name of the CPC the journal declared: 'All countries and political parties that uphold justice, oppose aggression and work for social progress and world peace should unite and resolutely struggle against the hegemonists' acts of aggression and expansion.'[31] Interviewed a year later in January 1982, Deng Xiaoping noted that the Chinese had not adequately studied the developments of the Communist and workers' movement. He found the international situation to be changing and complicated. Nevertheless he did not think that problems could be resolved 'according to a pattern or even to two or three patterns. Our basic position is that Marxists in every country must resolve their own problems on the basis of their independent analyses and assessments and on the basis of the actual situation in each country.[32] During his meeting with the Chairman of the Communist Party of the Netherlands on 7 June 1982, Hu Yaobang put forward four principles which the CPC has since advanced as the only acceptable basis for inter-Party relations. These are, independence, full equality, mutual respect and non-interference in each other's internal affairs. These 'principles' not only imply criticism of the Soviet approach, but they also imply a repudiation of the CPC stand of the early sixties.

In part this new inter-Party diplomacy was designed to develop a new constituency with which to increase the diplomatic pressure on the Soviet Union. The cultivation of the Communist and workers' movements in Western Europe has always been an important if not decisive element of Soviet diplomacy. But the new development was also conceived as a significant attempt to reach out to groups with which the Chinese Communists have only had fleeting relations in the past. It demonstrated a closer appreciation by China's leaders of the complexities of European politics. Perhaps by their new emphasis in explaining their foreign policy as being designed to safeguard world peace, China's leaders sought to reach an understanding of and with the European peace movements which hitherto they had tended to condemn as appeasers of the Soviet Union. However, in so doing China's leaders have amended their diplomatic style and indeed their general diplomacy considerably. The general goals of Chinese foreign policy may not have radically changed, but the new flexibility and the less self-righteous diplomacy has extended the appeal of China's stand against 'hegemonism' and, if it should be continued, it promises to be an important if not decisive contribution to China's strategy of trying to isolate the Soviet Union internationally.

Relations with the countries of Europe

The main patterns of China's relations with the countries of Western Europe were well established in the early seventies and they have not significantly changed since. Although both sides recognise the importance of the other in world affairs, neither can exercise much influence over the other. The geographical distance between the two areas, and the essentially regional deployments and regional effectiveness of their armed forces, has meant that neither impinges directly on the other's national security interests. Although they may be said to share a common adversary in Moscow, their respective attitudes and policies towards it differ in many respects. Although there are variations as between the Western European countries, they all seek accommodation with the Soviet Union on the basis of a shifting mix of co-operation and adversity as expressed by the concept of détente under conditions of deterrence. Although China's leaders may choose to portray the Western European countries as common members of the anti-Soviet hegemonist united front, few of these governments would describe their relations with the Soviet Union in these terms. There is a relationship between the Soviet western and eastern fronts, but it is by no means an obvious and clear one. The Soviet deployments in Europe and the Far East are independent of each other. In other words neither force is drawn from the other. The deployment of up to one-quarter of the Soviet armed forces in the Far East did not lead to any reduction in the West. This means that short of a rapid escalation of hostilities or the significant reduction of tensions in one of the sectors, neither the European nor the Chinese side can affect the position of the other.

As we have seen, Western Europe has been an important source for China for access to advanced technology, but the significance of this trade can be exaggerated. Despite the growth of trade in 1980 China still ranked only as 31st in the list of countries to which the European Community (EEC) sent exports in terms of value and it ranked 29th as a source of imports. The EEC ranked 4th among those trading with China and although EEC–China total trade had more than doubled between 1975 and 1980, the EEC's proportion of China's trade had dropped from about 18 per cent to 11 per cent. Moreover, as China's trade with countries of the Asia–Pacific region continues to grow at a rapid rate, the EEC proportion of China's trade is likely to decline still further.[33] Doubtless the EEC will remain an important alternative source for advanced technology for China, if only to ensure that China does not become unduly dependent upon one or two sources. That lesson of 'self-reliance' is unlikely to be lightly abandoned.

Within these constraints the attention given to Western Europe by China's leaders may seem disproportionate. However, the Chinese have consistently depicted Western Europe since 1973 as the focal point of Soviet strategic interests and as the main centre of Soviet—American competition. Even the alleged 'southward drive' of the Soviet Union in Asia and the Middle East has been described by China's leaders as an elaborate outflanking movement ultimately aimed at Europe. Thus the cultivation of close diplomatic relations with the Western European countries is seen as essential in view of their strategic importance for the Soviet Union and hence for China. It is worth recalling that in 1964 China's leaders turned briefly to Western Europe as a possible partner in restraining American adventurism. It is not strange, therefore, that China's leaders should attach significance to Europe in the seventies and eighties when they are seeking diplomatic leverage against both superpowers and the creation of an anti-Soviet coalition.

As with other countries Chinese interactions with the Western European countries have increased substantially if measured in terms of the number of visits of delegations and exchanges of all sorts.[34] Perhaps the most important of these was the European tour of the then CPC Chairman and Premier, Hua Guofeng, who visited France, the Federal Republic of Germany, Britain and Italy from 15 October to 6 November 1979. Various agreements were signed and the visits were notable for the way in which the Chinese leader was able to make his points about the need for a common stand without embarrassing his hosts with regard to their relations with the Soviet Union.[35]

The one area in which the Western Europeans and the Chinese could translate their expressed mutual interests in the others' strength and prosperity was in Chinese purchases of advanced weaponry. But despite various missions by military personnel and by ministers empowered to sign contracts, no major agreements about arms transfers were made. In fact the largest arms deal that took place was the British sale of a Rolls Royce jet engine plant, the contract for which was signed in 1975. At the cost of $200 million the plant was duly completed in 1980, but as the Chinese did not have a suitable airframe for the advanced Spey engine the plant is not turning out a supply. Indeed, one rumour has it that its high-precision manufacturing equipment has been converted for the making of bicycles. More typical was China's interest in purchasing the British Harrier Vertical Take Off and Landing jet aircraft. Interest was first displayed in 1977. The Soviet Union sought to prevent the sale, but first the Labour and then the Conservative Governments agreed to sanction the sale when the Chinese side finally withdrew in 1980 on the grounds of cost and the consequences of the domestic economic policies of readjustment. Unconfirmed reports claimed that some French anti-tank HOT missiles had been sold to China in early 1978.[36] However, despite the large number of military delegations which visited Western Europe in 1977–80 and the amount of diplomatic attention they attracted – not least from the Soviet Union – no major sale has been confirmed.

In July and August of 1982 there emerged reports of a Chinese interest in the French advanced military aircraft Mirage 2000. One reason was that Chinese attempts to trial produce their own advanced fighter aircraft had been unsuccessful. As of September 1982 no agreement had been reported. Judging by previous experience the Chinese side is likely to seek an arrangement that would involve the purchase of a limited number of the aircraft combined with the establishment of an enterprise that could manufacture them under license in China. Also judging by past experience the relevant negotiations are likely to be prolonged and complex.

Chinese diplomacy with regard to the Eastern European countries showed most development and change in the post-Mao era. As in other respects the genesis for the change can be traced to the earlier period. For example, the initial overtures to Yugoslavia were made as early as 1968 in the wake of the Soviet invasion of Czechoslovakia, and relations with Romania were never broken. However, the more active diplomacy and the domestic economic and ideological changes combined to accelerate China's interest in these countries. The Chinese were particularly interested in the economic reforms of Yugoslavia and Hungary. The Hungarian experience of market socialism was seen to be of especial relevance to the reforms contemplated by Chinese economists. Romania, however, was of interest not because of its domestic economic system, which was a tight command economy of precisely the kind from which the Chinese sought to move away themselves, but because of its foreign policy which stressed independence from Soviet controls. Doubtless privately the Chinese understood as much as others that Romania's independent foreign policy within the framework of the Warsaw Treaty Organisation was possible because of its peculiar geopolitical position and because its domestic political and economic system did not challenge Soviet orthodoxy. Moreover, just as with regard to the other East European members of the Warsaw Treaty Organisation, the reason why Romania is a Communist country and why that cannot be challenged is because of the Soviet domination of Central and Eastern Europe since the end of the Second World War. It cannot be known whether China's leaders have understood that despite its relatively independent foreign policy the survival of the Romanian political system is ultimately dependent on continued Soviet dominance of the region.

Chinese foreign policy towards the Eastern European countries, after Mao, reflected a unique combination of both strategic and domestic interests. Once these countries were no longer perceived as hotbeds of revisionism, the similarities of the political-economic systems with those of China became obvious. All had developed more or less out of the Soviet model which they had followed willingly or unwillingly in the early fifties. The one essential difference was that China and also Yugoslavia had made their revolutions independently from within, whereas the others had it brought to them by the power of the Soviet Red Army. These post-war arrangements had been sanctioned more or less by the agreements of the great powers during the latter stages of the Second World War despite Western alarm at the 1948 pro-Communist coup in Czechoslovakia. These developments indirectly affected China's strategic interests, for Soviet controls over Eastern Europe were both a source of Soviet strength and of weakness. Since the death of Stalin the Russians have intervened military in Eastern Germany (1953), Hungary (1956) and Czechoslovakia (1968) and they hovered on the brink of Poland several times (1956, 1970 and 1980–81). Chinese policy towards these events has varied according to the dictates of their relations with the two superpowers. Thus in the fifties they supported the Russians, and indeed they have boasted that they were instrumental in dissuading the Russians from marching into Poland and in pushing them into Hungary in 1956. But since then the Chinese have opposed Russian interventionism. The invasion of Czechoslovakia and the Brezhnev doctrine of limited sovereignty was perceived as providing the ominous justification for a Soviet intervention in China.

There is no other region in the world where the Chinese theory of three worlds would seem less applicable than it does to Eastern Europe. As explained by Deng Xiaoping in 1974, and as elaborated by the *People's Daily* in 1977, Romania and Yugoslavia belong to the Third World and the other Eastern European countries belong to the second. China itself has been consistently described as a socialist member of the Third World. It will be recalled that the first world was identified as the imperialistic superpowers; the Third World consisted of those countries which had suffered from colonial oppression and which sought economic development to escape from their backwardness and the second world consisted of the developed countries in between them. From the outset it was by no means clear why, except for the temporary convenience of Chinese foreign policy, Romania and Yugoslavia should belong to the Third World and the other Eastern European countries to the second world of the small and medium capitalist countries. When pressed for an explanation Chinese officials tend to suggest that the Eastern and Western European countries are both developed economically and that the Eastern Europeans are dominated by one superpower and the Western Europeans by the other superpower. The inadequacy of the explanation is highlighted by China's own foreign policy which constantly exhorts the Western Europeans and Japan to unite more closely with the United States while dwelling on the malevolent consequences of Soviet-imposed unity on Eastern Europe. In fact, as Chinese officials and academics will privately concede, Romania and Yugoslavia have far more in common with the other Eastern European countries than either has with any country in Asia, Africa or Latin America. Moreover the systemic problems in Eastern Europe have little in common with those of Western Europe, let alone countries like Australia, New Zealand, Canada and Japan — to which the theory of the three worlds has consigned them.

Despite appearances to the contrary, these problems are well understood by Chinese officials and academicians. Chinese publications for open distribution may not reflect necessarily Chinese thinking on the affairs of Eastern Europe and Chinese policy towards these countries. Consider, for example, the Chinese response to the events in Poland since the emergence of the independent Solidarity trade union followed by the introduction of martial law in Poland on 13 December 1981. Chinese official *Xinhua* commentaries have dwelt exclusively on the danger of a possible naked military intervention by the Soviet Union. The sparse Chinese pronouncements on Poland since the introduction of martial law only reiterate the standard Chinese line that the Poles must be allowed to settle their own affairs by themselves. China's leaders have refused to join the Western governments in condemnation of the suppression of Solidarity as a measure engineered by the Russians. China's reticence can be explained more readily by reference to Chinese sources meant for internal circulation in China only, and to which I have had but fleeting access. Unlike the official news agency reports these were replete with information about developments in Poland and they reflected a certain distaste for Solidarity lest a similar independent trade union might emerge in China. The organisation of the Chinese economy and the structures of Chinese enterprises may differ in certain important respects from those of Soviet Eastern Europe, but there are sufficient similarities for the Chinese leaders to fear the emergence of a similar independent trade union movement to that of Solidarity in Poland.

There is then a double-edged sword quality about Chinese policy towards the countries of Eastern Europe. In one sense China's leaders encourage nationalistic assertions of independence from the Russians, but in another they are concerned lest the particular forms which these may take might also have repercussions in China. The post-Mao period is not the only time in which this ambivalence has been apparent. The events in Poland and Hungary in 1956 had a profound effect in China. Mao's analysis of their causes and effects played no small part in the unfolding of the Hundred Flowers policy towards intellectuals in the Spring of 1957, the consequent anti-rightist movement and indeed on the theorising that led to the Cultural Revolution in 1966. Similarly, the Party's stalwarts' reaction to Mao in 1956—57 was also heavily influenced by their understanding of the significance of the events in Russia and the Eastern European states in 1956.[37]

Nevertheless Soviet difficulties in Eastern Europe were seen by China's leaders as an important restraining influence on Soviet expansionism elsewhere in the world. The then Chairman Hua Guofeng visited Romania and Yugoslavia in August 1978 on the tenth anniversary of the Soviet invasion of Czechoslovakia. He also went on to visit Iran and the exercise may be seen as part of a Chinese attempt at counter-encirclement of the Soviet Union after the beginning of the close Soviet—Vietnamese relationship as established by Vietnam's having joined the CMEA on 29 June 1978. The visits to Romania and Yugoslavia also served a wider purpose. As became apparent from the themes of the speeches of Hua in both countries, his concern was to deny any Soviet right to exclusive spheres of influence in which it could impose its own will. Notwithstanding the growing tensions in Sino-Soviet and Sino-Vietnamese relations China could still reach out to countries near the Soviet Union and establish common understandings. The point was not lost on the Soviet Union, and the China factor may be said to have increased its pressure on Eastern Europe.[38] China's more sophisticated diplomacy has been displayed in lending such support as it can to improving relations between the countries of Eastern and Western Europe while distinguishing these sharply from those designed to improve Soviet—Western economic relations. The former were seen as possibly loosening Soviet dominance over Eastern Europe, whereas the latter were portrayed as feeding the Soviet war machine.

The enduring aspect of China's relations with Europe, both

Eastern and Western, has been shown to be one in which Chinese aspirations and policies fall very short of Chinese capabilities to significantly determine outcomes on issues that are perceived to be of considerable importance for China's global strategy. Moreover the disparity between interest and influence is likely to persist for a long time to come.

China and the superpowers

China's relations with the superpowers continued to be the main, but not the only, determinant of its foreign policy. The relationship has continued to shape not only the general formulation of policy, but it has also, for example, affected very strongly China's relations with its neighbours. China's policies in the Asian region can only be understood within the context of Chinese perceptions of the roles of the two superpowers. Local and regional issues have always been seen by China's Communist leaders in conjunction with the need to resist the superpower judged to be most active and expansionist. Conflicts with neighbouring countries have been perceived as threatening to China's national security only if the local adversary has been backed by either the United States or the Soviet Union. This was true, for example, of the conflicts with India in the sixties and early seventies, and is especially true of the conflict with Vietnam beginning in the later seventies.

Chinese preoccupation with the balance of forces between the United States and the Soviet Union suggests that its leaders have long operated diplomatically in fact, if not in name, along tripolar lines. Put rather crudely, China's strategy may be seen as having moved from a reliance on the Soviet Union in the 1950s against the American menace to a reliance on American countervailing power against the Soviet threat in the seventies and eighties. The period of China's most acute vulnerability, as seen from Peking, was the sixties when the superpowers were perceived to be in collusion against Chinese aspirations to great power status. There is a sense in which the more the adversorial relationship between the United States and the Soviet Union is marked by conflict rather than by co-operation, the greater is their readiness to concede China's claims to independent great power significance. China's period of self-isolation in the sixties, which reached its zenith in the early years of the Cultural Revolution, was predicated on Chinese assumptions of collusion between the superpowers and of an attempt by them to impose their condominium on China.[39] The *rapprochement* with the United States was based on claims by Mao and Zhou that the relative decline of the United States, matched by a growing expansionist tendency of the Soviet Union, had created a new situation in which relations between the two would be characterised by conflict rather than collusion. Throughout the seventies and into the eighties, China's leaders have consistently deprecated any Soviet–American moves towards détente. One of the clearest examples of Chinese continued fears of a superpower condominium can be seen from Chinese praise of the initiative by the late President Sadat of Egypt in declaring his willingness to go to Jerusalem in late 1977 in search of peace. In so doing he had successfully defeated a combined move on the Middle East by the superpowers as expressed in a joint declaration by Foreign Minister Gromyko and Secretary of State Vance only a few days earlier.[40] China's leaders were also concerned by the prospect of tacit agreements between the Americans and Russians to acknowledge each other's rights to special zones of influence. They condemned in public the 1974 Helsinki Agreements, Kissinger's détente diplomacy and the so-called Sonnenfeldt Doctrine (which suggested that the United States should recognise Soviet dominance in Eastern Europe and assist it to establish an 'organic' relationship there in order to strengthen stability in Europe) as analogous to the appeasement of Nazi Germany in the 1930s. Indeed they also suggested that in 1977 a new Munich-type agreement might be in the offing, by which the West sought stability on the European front in order to divert the Russians eastward. Privately, however, the Chinese leaders still feared a superpower condominium. Following the agreement to normalise Sino-American relations of December 1978, a high-level document meant for internal circulation only claimed that as a result, 'we have . . . managed to win over the United States and [we] have successfully prevented the backstairs deal between the two superpowers to divide the world between them'.[41]

China's strategic significance to the superpowers arises out of their respective global strategies. During the fifties and the sixties — the decades of American global ascendancy — American global strategic dispositions were based on the need to be able to conduct 'two and a half wars'. That is, a possible war in the West involving the Soviet Union and another in the east involving China, leaving the capacity to fight a 'half war' against lesser challenges in other parts of the world. In the seventies the Russians faced a similar situation with up to a quarter of their forces stationed in the Far East. China's strategic significance, however, masks a very great asymmetry in power between itself and the superpowers. If they possess the capacities to project their military force to all parts of the world, China's capacity to influence events by its military power is limited strictly to its own region. Moreover, even in this context China still lacks the capabilities to project its forces much beyond its borders. Despite considerable efforts to upgrade its naval forces during the seventies, China still lacks an ocean-going military fleet comparable to that, say, of India, let alone one which could match American or Soviet naval power in the seas of East and Southeast Asia. Thus in a very real sense China depends upon the American Seventh Fleet to counterbalance the growing pressure of Russian naval power in the region. China's principal sources of strength continue to derive from such traditional geopolitical factors as its vast size, massive population, strategic location in Asia and political unity under an effective government (that is, effective in the traditional foreign policy terms of being able to organise the population in accordance with its strategic and foreign policy goals).

Although the two superpowers have tacitly conceded China 'candidate superpower' status (to use Jonathan Pollack's distinctive phrase),[42] China's role in the great strategic triangle necessarily differs from theirs. As giant nuclear and conventional military powers, and as leaders of major alliances with world-wide spreads of varied interests and commitments, both Russia and America are constrained to manage their adversorial relationship in order to keep it below the threshold of nuclear conflict. The United States in particular is obliged to take into account the interests and perceptions of its allies, some of whom in Western Europe have their own reasons for seeking to reduce tensions in Europe and eschew Chinese policies of confrontation with 'hegemonism'. China, by contrast, has what might be called global policies without global commitments; it has policy without power. Therefore the inherent complexities of international politics which militate against the implementation of logically consistent and simply conceived policies become apparent in Chinese policies only within in its own region. Thus the complexities of China's relations with the superpowers can be seen less in the grand strategic formulations of tripolarity than in Chinese manoeuvrings to sustain 'a long-term strategic' relationship with the United States while simultaneously carrying on with it the long-standing disputes over Korea and Taiwan. China is an ally of the Democratic People's Republic of Korea and it is formally pledged to support its position on Korean re-unification which includes calling upon the United States to withdraw its forces from the south. But at the same time Chinese officials privately concede that the American presence there serves other interests which are important to China. It is a component part of the American continued strategic commitment to Japan and to the seas near China, and it is seen as a restraining influence against the renewed outbreak of warfare on the Korean peninsula. These are all seen as important to China.[43]

The Taiwan problem raises more complex and deep-seated issues for China. But the same American right-wing impulses that have propelled the Reagan Administration towards a less compromising line with the Soviet Union are those that cause it to be less yielding to the Chinese position on Taiwan. Clearly it is one thing for the Chinese to call upon other countries to temper their local conflicts to meet the needs of an anti-hegemonist united front, and it is quite another for the Chinese to do likewise. Moreover, specific Chinese policies towards the Soviet Union do not always reflect the hard line of Chinese international declaratory policy. For example, at China's initiative governmental talks were held in 1979 to improve relations. Although little was achieved at the talks and they were indefinitely postponed after the Soviet invasion of Afghanistan, the Chinese initial proposals were advanced without the usual insistence on prior conditions of Soviet troop withdrawals from Mongolia and from the disputed areas along the border — preconditions which had always been rejected by the Russian side.

The death of Mao was a far less significant factor in shaping the development of China's relations with the superpowers than the alteration of China's international environment which began to take shape in 1975. This was the year in which the Soviet capacity to extend its military power to far-flung areas of the world began to be made dramatically evident by the despatch of thousands of Cuban troops to change the course of events in several African countries from Angola through to Ethiopia and the Horn of Africa. Nearer to home, the final American debacle in Indo-China raised the prospect of a rapid increase of Soviet influence in Southeast Asia. It was at this point that China's leaders, who had hitherto blamed both superpowers for the world's 'intranquillity', began to warn that the Soviet Union was 'far more dangerous' as a source of war. Two weeks after the fall of Saigon a *People's Daily* editorial noted with alarm, 'The Soviet social imperialists . . . are leaving no stone unturned in their efforts to replace the U.S. imperialists at a time when the latter are becoming increasingly vulnerable and strategically passive.' In June and July Deng Xiaoping publicly cautioned visiting leaders from Southeast Asia 'to beware of the tiger coming from the back door while pushing out the wolf from the front door' and he explicitly warned the Thai Premier of Soviet designs on South Vietnam and its bases.[44]

These developments gave greater salience to Chinese fears of a grand Soviet geopolitical strategy of encirclement that they had claimed to detect the previous year. They claimed that the Soviet Union sought to control Southeast Asian sea lanes and straits in order to link up its Vladivostok-based Pacific Fleet with that in the Indian Ocean and then with the Soviet forces in the Mediterranean as part of a deep-seated design to outflank Europe. The Chinese also asserted that the Soviet encroachments in Africa (through their Cuban 'mercenaries') were part of a component scheme to control the sea lanes carrying oil from the Middle East, and that the African adventure was also linked to Soviet alleged expansionist designs in the Indian Ocean and Southeast Asian areas.[45]

Meanwhile both China and the United States were engulfed in their own domestic traumas. It was not until 1977 that the newly constituted Chinese leadership and the Carter Administration were able to begin talks at a high level. The United States Secretary of State, Cyrus Vance, visited Peking in August 1977 just after the conclusion of the Eleventh Congress of the CPC at which Deng was formally reinstated. But little progress was made on the Taiwan issue. Moreover, when assured by Vance that America was still strategically superior to Russia, Deng bluntly replied: 'We Chinese people do not believe it.'[46] The American government at this stage was very much divided between those who sought to improve relations with the Soviet Union through the diplomacy of détente and those who favoured a harder, more confrontational, approach. Vance represented the more conciliatory approach and after his visit Chinese commentaries began to warn against the dangers of appeasement and of a new Munich by which the West would make concessions in Europe to deflect the conflict to the East. Ironically, Deng represented an approach within China which argued that economic development should take precedence over the rapid acquisition of military technology and he therefore stood for a less alarmist interpretation of likely Soviet military moves. Earlier in 1977 commentaries associated with the armed forces in China had called for the rapid acquisition of modern armaments on the grounds that China was engaged in a 'race against time' because of the imminence of Soviet pressure to 'subjugate' the country. Deng and his civilian colleagues successfully repulsed their claims on China's precious resources and they maintained that what China needed was to buy time rather than race against it.[47] This could be achieved only by the establishment of a more solidly based anti-Soviet international united front which included the United States. Thus within China there was a tendency in the official press to downplay the Soviet threat and to magnify it in Chinese publications and commentaries beamed to the outside world. Rüdiger Machetzki has computed the ratio between anti-Soviet articles published exclusively in the English-language edition of *Xinhua* and those which were also reproduced in the *People's Daily* for the years 1977–79 (to September). In 1977 only 76 out of a total of 1205 anti-Soviet articles were printed in the *People's Daily*. In 1978 and January–September 1979 the proportions were 56 out of 1207 and 32 out of 668 respectively. The 'domestic' share of these articles represented no more than 4–6 per cent.[48]

As the tensions and conflicts in Indo-China escalated the Chinese began to call more openly for a united front with the United States. Meanwhile the Carter Administration began to ease step by step the barriers on transferring military technology to China. The initial steps in 1978 removed American objections to the deliveries of so-called defensive weapons and the corresponding know-how by Western European countries. Following the visit by the Presidential National Security Adviser Zbigniew Brzezinski in May, who emphasised the long-term strategic character of their association, Sino-American relations appeared to improve. But events in Indo-China were developing at a rapid rate leaving China for a period in the summer of 1978 feeling isolated and insecure in the face of Soviet encirclement. Between 29 June — when Vietnam was admitted to the Soviet-dominated economic system, CMEA — and the signing of the Sino-Japanese Peace and Friendship Treaty on 12 August, China's leaders had cause to feel particularly exposed. It was at this stage that they first began to refer to a 'plot' by which the 'Soviet superpower with its own hegemonic aims provides cover and support for the Vietnamese authorities to serve as a junior partner for the Soviet Union'. Not surprisingly, this was also protrayed as part of 'Moscow's global strategic plan . . . to outflank and encircle Europe and isolate the United States', but this was qualified by the fact that for the first time reference was made to a Soviet design to 'encircle China'.[49] The Chinese were clearly appealing to the Americans to recognise that their interests were parallel if not identical: The encirclement of China, it was implied, was damaging to the long-term strategic interests of the United States. For good measure China's premier foreign-language journal ran an article on appeasement and its 'adverse effects' which pointedly criticised those who allegedly sought 'by trying to divert the Soviet peril eastward . . . to pacify the aggressor and have it "all quiet on the Western front" '.[50] Meanwhile the Chinese Defence Minister took the opportunity to write an article in the Party's main theoretical journal calling for the 'high-speed' acquisition of 'new type conventional equipment and sufficient ammunition as well as better atom bombs, guided missiles and other sophisticated weapons'. Although he repeated the then accepted view in Peking that while a world war was inevitable 'we do not mean that it is imminent'. He nevertheless returned to the earlier military argument that China was engaged in a 'race against time'. He also emphasised the dangers of war as far as China was concerned in ways that civilian Party leaders like Deng and Li Xiannian did not: 'What Soviet social imperialism has done is doubtless spearheaded against the United States and aimed at Japan, but this also shows that it has stepped up its preparations for launching a war of aggression against China.'[51]

Deng Xiaoping, whose commitment to the priorities of an economic development which would allow even fewer resources for military preparedness was even stronger than the previous year, took a different view from the Defence Minister. If the latter emphasised the threat to China while acknowledging the more global dimensions of the Soviet challenge, Deng reversed the emphasis as a means of eliciting the diplomatic support of others against the alleged Soviet menace. At a press conference in Bangkok on 8 November Deng acknowledged that this 'military' treaty (i.e., the Soviet-Vietnamese Treaty of Friendship and Co-operation signed 5 days earlier) was directed at China, but he argued that it had other targets: It 'constitutes an important component part of the Soviet Union's global strategy in the Asian—Pacific region'. He went on to refer directly to the question of China's encirclement and added: 'I have told foreign friends on many occasions that China fears no encirclement. To a greater extent, the treaty means the threatening of peace and security in the Asian—Pacific region and even the world.'[52]

China's international position was significantly changed by the agreement to establish normal diplomatic relations with the United States, as signed on 16 December. Deng had taken a lead in the negotiations and despite Chinese objections to America's publicly stated intention of selling arms to Taiwan, China nevertheless signed the agreement which involved certain mutual concessions. A confidential report by Political Bureau member and the then Secretary General of the powerful Military Affairs Commission of the Party, Geng Biao, was delivered on 16 January 1979. Although it was specifically directed towards the situation in Indo-China the report was also revealing about Chinese attitudes to wider issues of international politics. The agreement to normalise relations with the United States was regarded as having 'completely changed the balance of power in the world'. The report suggested a greater China-centred view of world politics than was apparent from Chinese open commentaries. China's diplomatic successes, the trade and technology agreements with Western countries and their readiness to assist in the military modernisation of China were described as 'severe blows' to the Russians. He also argued that as the Soviet Union was 'most afraid' of the emergence of a vigorous modernising China it would endeavour 'to stand in the way and interpose obstacles'. That was described as the 'immediate target' of Vietnam and the Soviet Union.

The United States was described in a highly ambiguous way by Geng Biao. He depicted it as the 'secondary enemy' which had been drawn into the united front against the Soviet Union. As has already been noted, Geng claimed that China had blocked 'the backstairs deal between the two superpowers to divide the world between them'. The establishment of diplomatic relations with the United States was seen as further proof 'that American imperialism is in essence a paper tiger and not a sheet of iron', which because of its present difficulties 'it is easy to win over to our side'. Yet the essential ambiguity of Chinese attitudes was amply brought out by his next sentence: 'However, we should know that the United States, though lacking a magnificent goal of political strategy, is rich and advanced in science and technology, modern weapons and economic resources.' In stark contrast with another secret speech given by him 2½ years earlier, when Geng Biao talked of discarding America once it had performed its allotted role of holding off the Russians until China had built itself up,[53] Geng now conjured up a picture of the 'joining of the two forces together'; that is, an alliance in all but name between China and the United States.[54]

In an interview with *Time* magazine which had named him 'man of the year', Deng Xiaoping actually called for an 'alliance' with the United States.[55] The precise terms of the new Sino-American relationship were to exercise the minds of both sets of leaders for the next year and a half, but the Taiwan issue promises to fester as an open sore between the two sides well into the eighties. The ambiguity of part derision and part awesome respect for the power, opulence and modernity of the United States was reflected in the Chinese television and newspaper coverage of Deng Xiaoping's visit there in late January and early February 1979. On the one hand, Deng's press conferences, in which he lectured his American audiences on the 'realities' of dealing with the Soviet Union, were beamed back live to China by satellite, courtesy of American technology, and on the other hand, Deng, was shown visiting the homes of American skilled workers rich beyond the dreams of anyone in China. During his visit Deng called for 'realistic and practical steps' including the United States, China, Japan, Western Europe and other countries 'to deal with Soviet hegemonism'. He also warned of the need to teach Vietnam a 'lesson' — a point he repeated in Tokyo on his stopover en route back home.

The Chinese attack on Vietnam had a significant impact on the triangle of Chinese—American—Soviet relations. The Russians, already alarmed by the implications of the burgeoning association between China, Japan and the United States based on anti-Soviet 'hegemonism' at first accused the Americans of connivance at the Chinese attack. But a week later, on 26 February, Foreign Minister Gromyko in effect called upon the United States to place a higher priority on its relations with the Soviet Union. He warned that the Chinese objective was 'to set the Soviet Union and the United States at loggerheads' and that 'the development of Soviet—American relations is being throttled under their influence and the attitude to this serious question changes in Washington as quickly as the weather in the North Atlantic'. On 5 March, when the Chinese announced the beginning of their withdrawal of forces from Vietnamese territory, a *Pravda* commentary detected signs of American understanding of the long-term objective of their new 'ally' and it congratulated the Soviet leadership for having seen through 'the treacherous scheme of the Peking leaders in time' and for not having fallen for 'their provocations, the purpose of which is to get us into collision with the United States'.[56] In other words, the Soviet leaders explained that they did not open up a second front along China's border lest that should lead to a Soviet—American confrontation, and they also warned the Americans of the dangers to both superpowers of too close an alliance between China and America.

By the same token, Soviet forbearance on the Chinese border also paved the way for China's leaders to explore the possibilities of improving relations with the Soviet Union later that year. So far the Chinese have not explained the underlying rationale for initiating the governmental talks held in September 1979. The first round of talks were held in Moscow, but no agreement was reached except to hold another round in Peking early the following year. They could not even agree on the agenda as the Chinese wanted a broadly based one (including also Indo-China) and the Russians wanted it strictly limited to bilateral state relations. The next round of talks was indefinitely postponed by the Chinese because of the Soviet invasion of Afghanistan. When pressed for an explanation a senior member of one of the institutes of the Chinese Academy of the Social Sciences told me in April 1980 that 'we Chinese will not negotiate on our knees'. This suggests that China's leaders had calculated that their new alignment with the United States, having deterred the Russians during the Sino-Vietnamese war, had also sufficiently strengthened China's negotiating position with the Soviet Union to relieve the Russian general strategic pressure on China. But the Soviet invasion of Afghanistan demonstrated that the Soviet Union was still 'hegemonist' and that the time was far from ripe for negotiations.

The main Soviet diplomatic objective concerning China, beyond settling outstanding bilateral questions on the basis of the *status quo* on the borders, appears to be to wean it away from the alignment with the United States. Thus President Brezhnev's negotiating offer of 24 March 1982 was couched precisely in terms to take advantage of Chinese disenchantment with the United States over Taiwan. The curt official Chinese response 'noted the remarks' of the Soviet leaders on Sino-Soviet relations (which had been cast in conciliatory terms), but it rejected his 'attacks on China' — a reference to his criticism of China's association with 'imperialism' — and concluded with the observation that 'what we attach importance to are actual deeds of the Soviet Union'.[57]

An article by a 'special commentator' of China's Journal of International Studies on Sino-American relations and the Taiwan question claimed that a deterioration of Sino-American relations would not necessarily lead to an improvement in Sino-Soviet relations. He referred back to the sixties when China broke with the Russians without reducing its opposition to American imperialism. The Chinese explanation for the Sino-American *rapprochement* has always been that they responded to American initiatives, and indeed the Nixon Administration had taken various concrete measures (such as reducing its patrols of the Taiwan Straits) in 1969 and 1970 before Dr Kissinger visited Peking in July 1971.[58] If this pattern is any guide the Chinese would refrain from a *rapprochement* with the Soviet Union until there were specific signs that Soviet conciliatory words were similarly translated into actual 'deed'.

The United States officially deplored the Chinese attack on Vietnam, while at the same time recognising the importance of continuing to develop the momentum of Sino-American relations. Although there was considerable and continuing debate in Washington about the new stage of the strategic triangle, there was a sense, as Joseph Camilleri has pointed out, in which

the China card endowed American diplomacy with much greater flexibility, enabling the United States to speak with two voices and to combine in its dealings with the Soviet Union elements of hostility and conciliation, the relative weights of which could be varied depending on domestic or external circumstances.[59]

Thus while Brzezinski focused on the significance of the new relationship with China for American security interests in the Asia—Pacific region, Secretary of State Vance was instrumental in negotiating the SALT II Agreement with the Soviet Union in the spring of 1979.

Just as the Soviet invasion of Afghanistan was instrumental in blocking the tentative improvement of Sino-Soviet relations, it also increased American hostility towards the Soviet Union and brought about a closer degree of Sino-American partnership. United States Secretary of Defense, Harold Brown, visited Peking in early January 1980 and in consequence of the Soviet invasion he promoted wider security links with China and agreed to increase substantially American military aid to Pakistan. He and the Chinese leaders resolved to carry out 'complementary actions' of 'a down-to-earth and practical' character. In May Deputy Premier Geng Biao visited the United States and agreement was reached on the procedures by which the so-called 'non-lethal' military equipment could be sold to China. American firms would be allowed to set up factories in China to produce helicopters or computers and the sale of communication equipment, radar, transport and other 'dual-use' military equipment was agreed.[60]

By this stage both sides had reached broad agreement on the character of their relationship. The Chinese had never been pleased with the way in which some in Washington had regarded them as a factor to be used by the United States in modulating Soviet behaviour. Geng Biao and Harold Brown spoke of a common strategic perspective and of 'a long-term strategic policy'. Geng used the term 'friendship', carefully avoiding the word 'alliance', for in his words the Americans and the Chinese 'do not share the same day and night'. The American Assistant Secretary of State for East Asia and the Pacific, Richard Holbrooke, issued a major statement on his government's policy towards China in which he said that although ties were being 'consolidated and institutionalised' and 'our perspectives and our policies may be parallel from time to time, they will rarely be identical'. China and America were 'friends, rather than allies'. He also declared in a passage that particularly pleased the Chinese that the strategic triangle was 'no longer an adequate conceptual framework' as Sino-

American ties were 'not a simple function of our relations with the Soviet Union'.[61] The Chinese had always objected to the Carter Administration's previous policy of what an 11 June *Xinhua* commentary described as 'equidistant relations'.

The 'consolidation and institutionalisation' of Sino-American ties soon found expression by an agreement in July to hold regular consultations at defence-deputy ministerial levels and by the endorsement by the Carter Administration of over 400 licences for exporting auxiliary military hardware and modern military electronic equipment.[62] Meanwhile an unofficial secret agreement had come into effect by which the United States sent China communications equipment and technical experts in exchange for intelligence on Soviet military actions collected by means of American radar and electronic bases installed near the Soviet border.

The advent of the Reagan Administration, however, brought to the fore underlying tensions in Sino-American relations. The American commitment to the 'people of Taiwan' stemmed from the web of close ties established over the previous 30 years which included trade, investment and arms sales whose value exceeded that of Sino-American commercial relations even at the end of the seventies.[63] However, in addition to these more 'practical' aspects of American—Taiwan relations, the Taiwan issue had long been an important one in the politics of the American right. To be sure, the old 'China Lobby' of the fifties no longer existed as a major political force. Nevertheless American political conservatism as represented by Ronald Reagan's election to the Presidency was determined to resurrect American military power relative to the Soviet Union and it was as resolutely anti-Communist as ever. In one sense this strengthened the strategic bond with China on anti-Soviet grounds. Thus the new Secretary of State, Alexander Haig, informed the Chinese leaders of his government's readiness to sell them offensive weapons. In another sense, Sino-American relations became strained because of the new Administration's determination to stand by the people of Taiwan against a forcible Communist takeover. The immediate issue centred on the question of American arms sales to Taiwan. The same impulses that drove the

Reagan Administration to take a hard line against the Soviet Union also sustained its position on Taiwan. Moreover, as demonstrated by the passage of the Taiwan Relations Act by the American Congress earlier in 1979 (to which Peking also objected as an infringement of Chinese sovereignty and as a violation of International Law)[64] there was in America a consensus on the question of 'not abandoning the people of Taiwan' that extended beyond the American right to other parts of the political spectrum. Peking's claims to Taiwan, however, also involve fundamental beliefs and political values which transcend immediate strategic issues. The cause of the unification of the country is one of the most deeply felt in China that goes back to before the turn of the century and which has been intensified by the uncompleted civil war between the Communists in control of the mainland and the Nationalists (with American backing) in control of Taiwan. The ultimate aim of the Chinese reforms to modernise the country is to ensure its security and independence. Any leader who compromised Peking's claims to sovereignty over Taiwan would not only be vulnerable to the charge of national betrayal, but he would endanger the very programme of modernisation and the new Sino-American ties that such a compromise may have been designed to promote.

The Taiwan issue has complicated and slowed down the development of Sino-American relations for the more than 10 years since the Nixon—Zhou Communiqué of February 1972. Both sides have been impelled to examine the strategic significance of their relationship at every stage of the unfolding of the Taiwan saga. But the issue has not blocked the ever-tightening of Sino-American ties and at every juncture both sides have demonstrated sufficient flexibility to assure the continuation of their strategic co-operation without fully conceding to the other side on Taiwan. Since China's capacity to exercise sufficient pressure on Taiwan's rulers to accede to re-unification is likely to remain very limited for the immediate future (certainly for the rest of the eighties), the Taiwan question is likely to persist as an irritant in Sino-American relations. But if the pattern of policy over the first decade of Sino-American relations is repeated through the second, neither the American nor the Chinese leaders are likely to so threaten the other's basic position on Taiwan as to risk the Sino-American strategic alignment. That alignment serves too many of their parallel interests not only in confronting the Soviet Union, but also in the Asia—Pacific region as a whole.

Thus following repeated Chinese protests and protracted negotiations, President Reagan wrote personally to China's three most prominent leaders in May 1982. But the most significant breakthrough occurred with the issuing of a joint communiqué on 17 August on the question of American arms sales to Taiwan. In this carefully worded document the United States pledged not to increase arms sales to Taiwan beyond levels of recent years and that such sales would be gradually reduced 'leading, over a period of time, to a final resolution'. The United States government also came very close to accepting Peking's view that Taiwan's future could only be reunification with the mainland. However, Sino-American differences on Taiwan were by no means completely resolved. The American government still linked the question of arms sales to the Taiwan Relations Act by which it was mandated to sell arms for defence of the island if the American government assessed it necessary. For its part the PRC government rejects any linkage with that Act and it professes concern lest the agreement embodied in the communiqué should not be implemented smoothly. Nevertheless, despite the continuation of certain Sino-American differences it was clear that rather than precipitate a serious deterioration in relations, both sides still found ways of reaching still another transitional understanding.

Just as Sino-American common global and regional strategic interests have facilitated compromises over a bilateral issue such as Taiwan, so divergent Sino-Soviet global and regional strategic interests have blocked progress in ameliorating their bilateral relations. Nevertheless since the threat of a Sino-Soviet war receded after the Kosygin—Zhou agreement of September 1969, the two sides have maintained an uneasy *modus vivendi* along their 4500-mile borders. Both sides at various times have proposed ways of settling some of the outstanding issues between them, and a basis does exist for defusing some of the tension along the border and increasing trade. Indeed agreements have been possible on aspects of river navigation and fishing. One barrier to improved relations so far has been Chinese insistence upon some tangible indication of a reduction of Soviet deployments along the border. Moreover, the abandonment in China of Mao's ideological objections to the Soviet Union and the disappearance of many of the issues of the sixties has doubtless eased the pathway for a more conciliatory approach. The substantive issues of the Sino-Soviet conflict had long since shifted to those of high strategy and foreign policy. There are those in the Soviet Union who would favour a military conflict with China while the military balance is still weighted overwhelmingly in the Soviet favour. Even President Brezhnev, who has consistently spoken in favour of a negotiated settlement of outstanding bilateral questions under these conditions, once warned that Russia could obliterate China with nuclear weapons before any of its Western associates could do anything and thus present them with a *fait accompli*.[65] A less apocalyptic scenario was that the Soviet Union could take advantage of Chinese problems in running their minority borderlands to establish buffer states in Xinjiang, Inner Mongolia, Tibet and Manchuria which would be linked to adjoining Soviet Asian republics.[66] Precisely because of the adverse balance of power China's leaders have so far resisted Soviet blandishments. The adverse balance may be changed in the Chinese view by the prospect of increased Soviet difficulties in sustaining the high cost of its 'hegemonistic' policies, possibly combined with an improvement in China's strategic situation arising out of the strategic alignment with the United States. There remains therefore the ironical prospect that the Sino-American *rapprochement* which arose out of the Sino-Soviet conflict may become a contributory factor to the reduction of Sino-Soviet tensions.

Relations with Japan

Aside from the two superpowers possibly no country has been more important to China than Japan. In addition to the historical and cultural ties, Japan's trade potential and strategic importance for China have ensured that Sino-Japanese relations have figured large in China's foreign relations. Thus despite, or perhaps because of, Japan's alliance with the United States and its close association with Taiwan, China's leaders throughout the fifties and the sixties endeavoured to develop trade and — through trade — political ties with Japan. China's object was to weaken the link with the United States and to disengage Japan from Taiwan. China's leaders were able at certain times to play on the sentiments felt towards China by certain circles in Japan.[67]

Moreover the memories of Japan's past imperialist power directed in large part towards China from 1895 to 1945 have inclined China's leaders to believe in the military potential of the country. Indeed the decade of the seventies opened with Chinese professions of alarm at what they claimed was the revival of Japanese militarism. Japan was depicted as a resource-poor country dependent on external sources of supply which it would now seek to protect militarily because of the weakening of the American presence in the Asia—Pacific area. At the same time China's leaders also looked to the technologically advanced Japanese economy as a source for the import of industrial plant and machinery. They also feared possible Japanese participation in the economic development of the Russian Far East which would pose obvious strategic dangers to China. The worst kind of scenario, which at that stage was by no means totally implausible, would have left China dangerously exposed to a rampant Soviet Union linked economically to a re-militarised Japan in a rapidly changing international environment that was by no means necessarily favourable to China.

The character of Sino-Japanese relations was immediately changed (as was China's general international position) by the Sino-American *rapprochement* that was scaled by the Nixon—Zhou Communiqué of February 1972. Normalisation of relations with Japan soon followed. But from China's perspective the die had been cast a year earlier in July 1971 as a result of the path-breaking first Kissinger visit to Peking. After August 1971 Japanese political groups visiting Peking no longer found their hosts repeating the usual call for the removal of American bases from Asia. China had come to see the continued American presence as an important counterweight to the

emerging Soviet thrust into the area. Thus after the establishment of Sino-Japanese diplomatic relations Zhou Enlai not
only publicly assured the Japanese of Chinese support for the
continued Japanese—American alliance, but he also criticised
Kissinger for not paying it sufficient attention. Zhou argued
that that alliance was even more important than the new
Sino-American relationship.[68]

The normalisation of Sino-Japanese relations also brought
to the fore important differences between the two countries.
Unlike China Japan was a highly advanced industrialised
country whose political system and economic relationships
placed it firmly in the Western world despite its long historical
and traditional cultural ties with the Confucian world of
China's past. Moreover the position with which Japan emerged
after the war and the American occupation, as enshrined in
its postwar Constitution, was one which eschewed the path
of militarisation. Japan's postwar economic 'miracle' was
predicated on the security provided by the United States and
on its economic relations with America, as well as on its
economic pre-eminence in the Asia—Pacific region as an
importer of raw material resources. Japanese interests and
popular sentiment called for, as far as possible, a conflict-free
approach to foreign policy. This was to be expressed after the
normalisation of relations with China as the search for an
'omni-directional' foreign policy. Just as the Chinese endeavoured to draw Japan into a nexus of relations aimed at restraining the Soviet Union, so the Japanese in turn sought to avoid
having to take sides in what was perceived as the Sino-Soviet
dispute.

One of the long standing issues in Sino-Japanese relations
had been the question of Taiwan and the Japanese treaty
with the Chinese government on the island. By the terms of
the establishment of diplomatic relations with Peking the
Japanese government expressed its 'full understanding and
respect' for the 'reaffirmation' by the PRC that Taiwan was
an 'inalienable part' of its territory and it pledged itself to
'comply' with Article 8 of the Potsdam Proclamation by
which the great powers formally agreed on the political rever-
sion of Taiwan to China. This still left legal ambiguities about
the status of Taiwan as far as Japan was concerned. It also

facilitated the remarkable arrangement by which Japan and Taiwan were able to develop non-official relations ostensibly to handle trade and people-to-people ties. In fact Japanese trade with both China and Taiwan grew substantially after 1972. By 1978 two-way trade with China had quadrupled in value, to reach $5130 million (nearly 27 per cent of China's total trade). Over the same period Japan's trade with Taiwan had also grown, to reach $5270 million. At no point did Peking suggest that the Japan—Taiwan trade should be reduced. The normalisation agreement declared that the state of war had now been terminated, but it looked forward to the signing of a peace treaty in due course.

After this further agreements on fisheries, communications, aviation and trade were made between the two sides, but negotiations for the peace treaty became bogged down over China's insistence that it should contain a clause pledging both sides to oppose hegemony. Although such a commitment had been included in the normalisation agreement of 1972, it did not have then the strong anti-Soviet connotations which both the Chinese and the Russians gave it thereafter. It was not until the deterioration of Soviet—Japanese relations by early 1978 that the Japanese were ready to move closer towards the Chinese position. The contracts which Japanese companies had hoped to sign for the development of energy and other resources did not materialise because of difficulties on the Russian side. But more importantly, the Soviet government appeared to harden rather than soften its line on the question of the four islands to the north of Japan which the Russians occupied as part of the Kuriles chain ceded to them at the end of the war, and which were claimed by Japan. Japan had hoped to be able to sign a peace treaty with the Soviet Union as well as with China as part of its 'omni-directional' foreign policy. The Russians instead, in January 1978, offered a treaty of 'good neighbourliness and co-operation' which would have meant tacitly conceding the Soviet claim to the islands. Negotiations were then suspended and in February, a week after a major Sino-Japanese private trade agreement had been concluded, the Russians published their proposed treaty, presumably to put pressure on the Japanese government. The attempt backfired as it aroused the indignant opposition of nearly all political circles in Japan. This development, coming on top of a number of occasions on which the Russians had displayed an undiplomatic disregard for Japanese susceptibilities, paved the way for Japan to move towards a treaty with China only. At the same time complex factional manoeuvres within the ruling Liberal-Democratic Party in Japan also contributed to the final push towards the treaty. Washington too favoured the treaty and, as we have seen, the Chinese also had their reasons for a speedy resolution of the issue.[69]

The Treaty of Peace and Friendship was finally signed on 12 August. It involved mutual concessions by both sides. Although the Chinese duly obtained the 'anti-hegemony' clause, its anti-Soviet implications were weakened in three important respects: first, the Chinese draft had referred specifically only to hegemony in the Asia—Pacific region while the Japanese draft had referred to hegemony in the world at large; the final text included both ideas. Second, at Japanese insistence that clause was qualified by another which stated that the treaty would not affect either's position with regard to third countries. Third, the Chinese had sought to give the treaty the quality of an alliance by setting a fixed time limit, whereas the Japanese sought directly to avoid giving any such impression and their draft excluded any such temporal restriction. Once again the text included both ideas. Rather oddly, Article 1 of the treaty commits both sides to 'relations of perpetual peace and friendship' while Article 5 set the treaty a life span of 10 years to be automatically renewed unless either side gave a year's notice of termination.

Although the Chinese did in fact seek to interpret the treaty as an anti-Soviet alliance, they did not dispute the Japanese claim that it was not. As Wolf Mendl has pointed out, the treaty is within an East Asian tradition in which

the emphasis is not on defining a strict contractual and legal relationship, so characteristic of western concepts of international relations, but [it] makes clear that the effectiveness of the Treaty will depend very largely on the sincerity and trust which both parties bring to its implementation.[70]

Nevertheless the treaty, coupled with the normalisation of Sino-American relations at the end of the year, brought into being a nexus of relations involving China—America—Japan that, with all its ambiguities and differences of approach by the parties concerned, had the effect of powerfully bolstering China's position with regard to the Soviet Union and to Vietnam in Southeast Asia.

The new relationship with Japan also conjured up the possibility of the emergence of a complementary economic partnership between China and Japan of wide-ranging significance both regionally and globally. Chinese leaders began to dwell on this theme after Japanese euphoria about the enormous prospects for trade and investment in China receded in the wake of the February 1979 postponement and then cancellation of several giant contracts worth several hundred million dollars. Thus Vice Premier Gu Mu, on a visit to Japan in September 1979, sketched out a Chinese view of the possibilities:

An economically developed and technologically advanced Japan and a gradually prospering and modernised China co-operating with other friendly countries in the Asia Pacific region would in a very large measure ensure stability in the East. . . . The overwhelming majority of the nearly 1,100 million Chinese and Japanese people who desire to live on the best of terms and co-operate closely in the fields of economics, trade, technology and culture constitutes a mighty force, a tide which no one can dam.

Deng Xiaoping on 12 December 1979 repeated the point more pithily: 'If Japan and China co-operate, they can support half the Heaven.'[71]

While Sino-Japanese economic relations did greatly expand, their relative significance to both countries can be judged from the fact that the value of their two-way trade in 1980 ($9401 million) came to over 24 per cent of China's total trade and only 3½ per cent of Japan's. The limitations of the Chinese economy discussed in the previous chapter will severely restrict the development of a Sino-Japanese economic bloc for a very long time to come. Moreover, the continued expansion of Sino-Japanese economic relations is likely to continue to reflect the uneven Chinese dependence on Japan without any corresponding rise in Japan's dependence on China. Apart from the uncertainties regarding the long-term stability of China's current political arrangements and its economy, the stagnation of China's oil production and the difficulties China has encountered in significantly boosting its coal exports to Japan have seriously affected China's capacity in the short term at least to pay for the import of Japanese plant and technology. Prospects do exist for the development of offshore oil, but its scope for export remains yet to be seen, particularly in a context in which China is experiencing severe shortages of energy in the domestic sector. Thus China has appealed for loans from Japan, as elsewhere. This has caused alarm in some of the ASEAN countries, in part because China is emerging as an international competitor to their own light industrial exports. Conscious of this, Japan agreed in September 1979 to offer China only $1500 million development loans instead of the $5000 million which the Chinese had originally requested. Nevertheless within these various constraints Japan is likely to continue to be China's major trading partner and source of advanced technology for a long time to come.

The bilateral issues in dispute between China and Japan such as the Sengaku (or Tiaoyudai) islands, the allocation of the continental shelf between them and the questions of Taiwan and South Korea (the settlement of which may very well have to precede a final resolution of the former) have been contained and not been allowed to obstruct the development of their economic and political relations. But they remain as potential sources of conflict for the future.

The new expanded relationship with Japan has served China well, not only in bilateral terms, but also in regional and global ones. The genesis for the new relationship clearly goes back to the Mao era and in the sense that it is a continuation of trends begun then, it may be regarded as fairly stable. But despite Russian accusations of this being an alliance, the new relationship is clearly something less than that. As yet no military ties exist between the two countries and Japan is

not directly involved in the Sino-American evolving strategic—
military relationship. Japan's foreign relations continue to be
based on the link with the United States and to be low-key
reactive rather than initiatory. Its chilly relations with the
Soviet Union are caused primarily by the dispute over the
four northern islands and the growing Soviet military presence
in the Asia—Pacific region rather than because of any shared
perspective with China. The place of Japan in China's foreign
relations, however, is far more significant. The two countries'
respective relationships with the United States may be said to
be the cornerstone of China's policies in the Asia—Pacific
region. It undoubtedly plays a very major role in the execution
of China's policies in Indo-China and elsewhere. Any increase
in the Soviet military presence in the area will be seen as
unwelcome by all three, and it thus reduces somewhat the
Soviet threat from the sea if not from the land. In short, the
new ties with Japan are an integral part of the Chinese strategy
of buying time.

Encirclement and counter-encirclement in Southeast Asia

China's policy towards this region, where its influence as a
military power has been greatest, has been characterised less
by the urge to *acquire* control of adjacent countries, for
example, by the imposition of client buffer states, than by
the concern to *deny* control of the area by its major superpower adversary. In the 1950s and 1960s China sought to
deny America use of this zone as part of its ring of containment, and in particular China aimed to prevent the establishment of American bases in countries with which it shared
borders. It was the American military thrust into northern
Korea towards the Manchurian border with total disregard of
Chinese warnings to desist that prompted China's military
intervention in 1950. During the Vietnam war in the 1960s
the Americans were more circumspect; nevertheless during
the war in the period from October 1965 to March 1968,
China claims to have sent up to 320,000 men into northern
Vietnam (for air defence, engineering, railway and logistics
work) with the aim of indicating to the Americans China's
determination to prevent their conquest of the north.[72] In

the 1970s and 1980s the object of Chinese concern has shifted to the fear of Soviet dominance of its periphery. That was one of the factors which led to the Chinese punitive attack on Vietnam in early 1979.

Yet at no point have the Chinese sought to transform either North Korea or North Vietnam into client régimes. Relations with these two smaller but proud Communist neighbours have never been as harmonious as official statements tended to imply. Major problems, however, arose with the shift of China's strategic adversorial relations away from the United States and towards the Soviet Union. The principal adversary for both the smaller countries remained the United States. However, it is a measure of the real political independence enjoyed by these smaller neighbours, for whom much Chinese treasure and blood has been spent, that they have asserted foreign policy lines very different from those of China. It remains to be seen whether the pattern of conflict that has emerged between China and Vietnam, which extends beyond the question of the Soviet Union to conflicting strategic imperatives about Indo-China as a whole, does not lead China to arrogate to itself, in effect if not openly, the right to determine the pattern of relations among the countries to its south. Meanwhile, however, China's policy is determined largely by its perceptions of the roles of the superpowers.

It is that perception which has shaped to a considerable extent Chinese approaches to the countries of the region at one remove from its borders. As late as August 1969 Chinese publications openly derided the governments of the five member states of ASEAN (Malaysia, Indonesia, the Philippines, Singapore and Thailand) as 'Asian lackeys' of America who had received a 'shot in the arm' through a 'so-called "regional economic co-operation" organisation'.[73] But by 1971 China began to support the claims of Malaysia and Indonesia to administer the Straits of Malacca against the internationalisation demands of the major maritime powers — except that the Chinese focused their attention mainly on the objections raised by the Soviet Union. In the course of the following year the Chinese government encouraged various initiatives in trade and sporting links towards the ASEAN countries, especially Malaysia, Thailand and the Philippines.

By 1973 Chinese officials formally expressed approval for the Malaysian proposal subsequently endorsed by ASEAN for the establishment of Southeast Asia as a Zone of Peace, Freedom and Neutrality.

Chinese relations with the states of this region, however, have been complicated by a variety of factors. China has a long and complex pattern of historical associations with a number of the countries that affect modern perceptions in many important ways. Most of the principalities and kingdoms in the area before the advent of the Europeans used to pay periodic tribute to the Chinese court, and some of them from time to time sought Chinese imperial legitimation for their claims against rivals for the local throne.[74] Some, like Burma, Nepal or Korea, had belonged to what has been called the inner ring of tribute-bearers, and as late as the 1930s some Chinese nationalists (including Mao Zedong) claimed these as belonging territorially to the modern Chinese state.[75] Vietnam was perhaps unique in having been an integral part of the traditional Chinese administrative system until it broke away in about AD 900 during the disintegration of the Tang Empire. Although it was subsequently subject to occasional invasion by imperial Chinese forces, it was also periodically a security threat to China and its court sometimes aspired to be the southern imperial court (that in China being merely the 'northern court') and in that capacity claimed tribute from its neighbours.[76] These pre-modern patterns of relations have become sources of tension and suspicion in the twentieth century. They do not relate easily to the norms and concepts of the contemporary international system; and the rise of nationalism with competing claims to nationhood and sovereignty have led to divergent readings of the contemporary significance of the pre-modern era. The passing of colonialism which was finally confirmed by the defeat of America and its client régimes in Indochina in 1975 brought to the surface these latent conflicts as the countries of the region sought to establish a new regional order.

What the Chinese call rather slightingly 'problems left over from history', such as conflicting claims to islands and to territory, abound in the area. Chinese claims to the island groups in the South China Sea are particularly extensive and their forceful assertion of sovereignty over the Paracel Islands in 1974 was regarded as potentially ominous throughout the region, but of course especially by the Vietnamese. To a certain extent it is the very vagueness of Chinese traditional claims to superiority which excites apprehension in modern times by many in Southeast Asia. Simple Chinese disclaimers of their past are welcomed, but they are not entirely persuasive. The Chinese, like leaders of other countries, have used selectively traditional ties to advance modern claims when this has suited them. Besides this, a nation can still be shaped by its past even though its leaders may claim to have broken utterly with that past in the inauguration of a new era. There are those in the Indonesian government, who fear that once China should acquire the capacity to project its military power into maritime Southeast Asia the Chinese may revert by instinct and tradition as much as by great power aspirations to playing a dominant role. There is, therefore, a tendency in Indonesia to regard Vietnam as a buffer against the possible expansion of Chinese power.

This apprehension is further intensified by the presence of Overseas Chinese in the region who play a vital economic and commercial role out of proportion to their numbers. The character of their importance varies from country to country, but in none is their presence totally free of strife and tension. The advent of a united and internationally significant China has stirred doubts in the region about their fundamental loyalty. This has been exacerbated by continued Chinese sponsorship of local Communist Parties (predominantly made up of ethnic Chinese) committed to insurgency against the established régimes. The PRC has gone further than previous Chinese governments (including that on Taiwan) to assuage local fears. It has developed laws of citizenship and nationality which are no longer based on *jus sanguinis* and which expressly rule out dual nationality, so that Overseas Chinese are required to take out local nationality and citizenship or to retain their Chinese nationality — in which case they are enjoined not to take part in local politics and to observe all the laws of their country of residence. Nevertheless ambiguities exist even in the approach of the PRC. Overseas Chinese of all hues are encouraged to maintain ties with China and to send remittances to relatives still in China. Special educational facilities are offered in China for the children of Overseas Chinese. Beyond that ties of sentiment continue to be present as the Overseas Chinese take pride in China's newfound great power status, and China's leaders at times have been known to wax eloquently about the common ties of the 'great Chinese family' extending from the people in China to the 'compatriots' in Taiwan, Hong Kong and Macao, and beyond them to all the Overseas Chinese (Hua Qiao) wherever they may be.[77]

In recent years China has taken a low-key interest in the communal problems of the area. But this has not always been so. Although the PRC chose to downplay the significance of the anti-Chinese rioting in Malaysia in 1969 there can be little doubt that the PRC maintains a close watch on the communal problems of the region. The problem is particularly acute in Malaysia where the Chinese constitute up to 38 per cent of the population and various quota systems have been introduced to ensure Malay dominance of the institutions of state. Indeed the reasons as to why Malaysia was the first of the ASEAN countries to establish diplomatic relations with the PRC (1974) had as much to do with its particular domestic communal structure as with international politics. At the same time Malaysia, for these reasons, shares with Indonesia an apprehension over a possible increase in China's influence in the region. This shapes the way in which both countries tend to be more accommodating to Vietnamese interests. Thailand, however, has been able in the past to pursue a relatively successful policy of assimilation with the Overseas Chinese, so that the issue is far less pressing in Sino-Thai relations. Both Thailand and China, unlike Malaysia and Indonesia, share (from their different positions) more pressing strategic objections to Vietnamese dominance of the Indo-chinese peninsula.

A further problem affecting China's relations with the governments of ASEAN is China's continued support for the Communist Parties carrying out insurgency struggles in the region. China's leaders have refused to dissociate themselves from these parties which are dedicated to the violent over-throw of the governments with which the same leaders are seeking to cultivate good relations. Chinese claims that Party and State relations are totally different have not been accepted by a single government in the region. Although China's material support for these parties has been reduced to negligible proportions its propagandist endorsement of them contributes significantly to their legitimacy and perhaps to the Chinese Party's sense of its own political legitimacy as a Marxist—Leninist Party genuinely committed to revolutionary internationalism. At the same time, however, the Chinese position is hardly calculated to win over the confidence of the local governments. Deng Xiaoping's argument that it is better that China should sponsor these parties than Russia or Vietnam may make sense to the ASEAN governments as the lesser of two evils, but if they had hoped that their own association with China would have led to the withering away of the insurgencies, they have been disappointed. Moreover, they are aware of the Burmese experience in which the Chinese seem to have used their support for the White Flag Party across their border as a means for exercising pressure on the established government.

As elsewhere in China's foreign relations, the main trends in Chinese foreign policy in the region were established in the first half of the seventies before the death of Mao. The establishment of diplomatic relations with the ASEAN countries followed a slower pace than with the rest of the Third World. Malaysia broke the ice in 1974 and the Philippines and Thailand followed suit in 1975. Singapore's Prime Minister visited China in 1976, where he found understanding for the island's special position as city-state with a population of 97 per cent ethnic Chinese. It was agreed that recognition would be delayed until Indonesia had resumed relations with China. Although China and Indonesia have many sources of contact and trade, the Indonesian government has so far resisted Chinese requests for the resumption of relations.

But if the ramifications of China's new foreign policy and the Sino-American *rapprochement* opened the way for the improvement of China's relations with the countries of ASEAN, they also drove a wedge between Peking and Hanoi. In 1968 the Vietnamese refused to join the Chinese in condemning the Russian invasion of Czechoslovakia; still less did they agree with the assertion that the Soviet Union had become an imperialist power and that the socialist camp had ceased to exist. For Vietnam, America was the primary enemy and the Sino-American *rapprochement* came as a bitter blow. It signified how far the strategic imperatives of China and Vietnam had begun to diverge.

The victories of the revolutionaries in Indochina and the final debacle of America in April 1975 transformed the situation and brought to the fore the hitherto incipient clash of Sino-Vietnamese interests. New patterns of conflict and encirclement emerged involving a complex web of global, regional and local relationships. The old cold-war rivalries were finally replaced by a realignment of power which brought the Sino-Soviet conflict into the region. This complemented rather than replaced the Soviet-American global adversorial relationship. If China was to come under pressure by the opening of a front in the south in addition to that in the north, the Soviet Union and Vietnam faced a new alignment between China, America and Japan. At the regional level Vietnam replaced a combined opposition between China and Kampuchea with a strategic *de-facto* alliance between its traditional Thai and Chinese protagonists. Vietnam also faced diplomatic isolation orchestrated by China to the north and the ASEAN countries to the south. At the same time local adversorial relationships combined paradoxically both to exacerbate the larger lines of conflict and to introduce degrees of flexibility into them; for while none of the ASEAN countries was prepared to condone Vietnam's forcible imposition of a client régime in Phnom Penh, none sought the re-establishment of the Pol Pot government (to which each was technically committed in diplomatic terms) as the ruler of Kampuchea. Moreover, Malaysia and Indonesia in particular have not sought the humiliation of Vietnam as has been sought by China.

These patterns, however, did not fully emerge until after the Vietnamese conquest of Kampuchea and the Chinese punitive attack on Vietnam. Before 1978 the character of the incipient Sino-Vietnamese conflict was largely hidden from public view. Indeed so rapid was the escalation of that conflict in 1978 that it is possible that neither was in control of events. As late as November—December 1977 it was still possible that the deterioration of Sino-Vietnamese relations might be held within certain limits. It was then that the last high-level visit by Vietnamese leaders to Peking failed to reach any agreement on any of the outstanding issues. There is evidence to suggest that it was only in December 1977 that the Chinese concluded that because of the Kampuchean issue Sino-Vietnamese relations were set on a collision course.[78]

China's support for Pol Pot's Kampuchea from the outset was closely linked with the Sino-Soviet conflict. While Russia developed relations with the Lon Nol government which had displaced Sihanouk in an American-assisted coup in 1970, China became the chief sponsor of the Sihanouk-led united front government in exile. In 1973 the Vietnamese forces in Kampuchea (still called Cambodia at that point) withdrew presumably to regroup for the final onslaught on south Vietnam, leaving the country to pitiless American bombing and abandoning the revolutionary resistance to the fiercely anti-Vietnamese forces of the Khmer Rouge led by Pol Pot. Thus China became the only external supporter of the Pol Pot forces which seized victory in 1975. China had already indicated that it was opposed to Vietnamese domination of Indo-China. Indeed the Chinese leaders were none too keen to see the re-unification of Vietnam and at one point they publicly endorsed the idea that the north and the newly liberated south Vietnam might be admitted to the United Nations as separate entities. Although China's leaders had already indicated their concern at the close links being consolidated between Vietnam and the Soviet Union, they were unwilling to pay the high price in aid to buy influence in Hanoi. Zhou Enlai specifically told Vietnam's leaders in 1975 that now that peace had been established China would not honour its 1973 pledge of assistance because China needed the putative aid for its own modernisation drive. The Vietnamese then went on to Moscow where they received an offer of $2600 million aid for the 1976–80 Five-Year Plan.[79]

Nevertheless China's leaders still appeared to think that, bad as Sino-Vietnamese relations had become, they were not yet cast upon the kind of collision course which emerged 2 or 3 years later. In September 1975 they were already anxious at the prospect of Soviet bases in Vietnam, yet reportedly that was not seen as likely to be 'a lasting arrangement'. At that time Mao took the long-term view that 'the Vietnamese had not been fighting the French and then the Americans for thirty years only to be run by the Russians'.[80] Given the opposing strategic perspectives and conflicting needs of China and Vietnam, as well as the points of conflict between them on the border and possession of the Paracel and Spratly Islands, the management of their tense relations would have required great sensitivity and balance in order to ensure that their antagonism could be kept below certain thresholds. However, their tense relations were exacerbated by the pressures of their respective domestic crises coupled with the impact of international events beyond their control, notably the developments in Pol Pot's Kampuchea. The Chinese succession crisis of 1976 and Vietnamese difficulties in absorbing the south (coupled with a Party Congress which by demoting pro-Chinese elements moved the Party closer to the Soviet Union) precluded the search for a manageable *modus vivendi*.

In retrospect it seems clear that from mid-1977 Sino-Vietnamese relations were set inexorably on a collision course in which the global, regional and local dimensions of their conflict interacted in ways that neither was able to control. Certainly neither side appeared to display the kind of sensitivity to the security concerns of the other that could have prevented the continued escalation of their conflict even at this late stage. One important reason for this may have been the acute sense of betrayal which both sets of leaders felt towards the other. The Chinese claimed to have extended to Vietnam no less than $20,000 million of aid since the fifties at considerable cost to itself including half a million tons of oil, 1 million tons of rice and some $300 million in other aid annually since 1970.[81] The Vietnamese were regarded as greedy, ungrateful and treacherous. The Vietnamese for their part felt that the heavy costs and sacrifices of their countrymen's long war with the United States which had protected China from war, and which had benefited China greatly, was now being used by the Chinese to subordinate their country to Chinese great power interests. Ironically the emotions involved on both sides were not dissimilar from those engendered during the Sino-Soviet rupture. Soviet—Chinese feelings at that time parallel contemporary Chinese—Vietnamese attitudes. If the Russians then (the Chinese now) felt betrayed and their generosity abused, the Chinese then (the Vietnamese now) felt their independence threatened and their war efforts used against them.

The Sino-Vietnamese road to conflict is best seen as a series of rapid actions and counter-actions which neither sought to halt. In August 1977 Vietnam cemented its dominance of Laos with a 'Treaty of Friendship and Solidarity'. The following month Pol Pot visited China against the backcloth of a major Khmer offensive which penetrated deep into Vietnamese territory and during which unspeakable atrocities were committed. China for its part had not only supplied the Khmers with war materials but it had also sent in advisers and instructors who played an important part in the Kampuchean war effort. Pol Pot took the opportunity of his Peking visit to deliver a vitriolically anti-Vietnamese account of his Party's history. Meanwhile, Vietnam had begun to clear its northern border areas of Chinese and suspect hill people in preparatory moves to militarise the border region. Border incidents were increasing in number and intensity. Sino-Vietnamese talks in late 1977 broke up in disagreement. Vietnam by this stage had secured new arms deals with the Soviet Union. On 31 December Kampuchea broke off relations with Hanoi, precipitating the latter to decide upon the necessity 'to assert rather than negotiate the special relationship to which it had long aspired for the whole of Indochina'.[82] At the National People's Congress in February 1978 China's Premier Hua Guofeng dropped any semblance of neutrality by accusing Vietnam of seeking regional hegemony. In April the Chinese protested for the first time at the expulsion of vast numbers of ethnic Chinese from Vietnam. By the time that China closed the border in June 160,000 refugees had fled to China. On 29 June Vietnam joined the Soviet-dominated Council for Mutual Economic Assistance (CMEA or Comecon). On 3 July China terminated its remaining aid and withdrew all its experts, supposedly to pay for the settlement of the influx of refugees. In August China signed the Treaty of Peace and Friendship with Japan. In November Vietnam and the Soviet concluded a treaty of friendship which pledged 'consultation' with a view to practical assistance in the event of an attack or the threat of an attack upon the other. Although there was no automatic pledge of Soviet assistance, a Vietnamese diplomat expressed confidence in the insurance provided by the pact against any possible 'adventurist' acts by China.[83] On 16 December China and the United States agreed to normalise relations as from 1 January 1979. On 25 December Vietnam invaded Kampuchea, and by 7 January it had installed a puppet régime in Phnom Penh. On 17 February (the day before Hanoi and Phnom Penh signed a treaty of friendship) China launched its punitive attack on Vietnam, ostensibly because of continued border 'provocations', and after the capture of the fifth provincial capital in the border region (Lang Son) on 5 March it commenced the withdrawal of its forces, which was completed 11 days later on 16 March.

China's attack on Vietnam has been extensively reviewed and variously interpreted by scholars in the West.[84] The account here has stressed the uncontrolled slide to war since mid-1977 against the emergence of conflicting strategic interests since the turn of the decade. However, an important insight into Chinese perspectives on the eve of the attack on Vietnam has recently become available in the West in the shape of a secret report by Political Bureau member and the then secretary-general of the important Military Affairs Commission of the Party, Geng Biao, dated 16 January 1979.[85]

The report, entitled 'On the Situation of the Indo-Chinese Peninsula', depicted Vietnam's leaders (including Ho Chi Minh) as having long desired dominance over Indochina, but as having been held back by the war with the United States. The Kampucheans were described as faction-ridden and their troops ill-disciplined, but they were now stated to be in a good position to carry out prolonged resistance to the Vietnamese invaders. The Vietnamese were described as having long been associated with the Soviet Union so that their treaty merely increased Vietnamese arrogance. But Soviet aid was derided as 'something that cannot be eaten, worn or used'. The United States was held partially responsible for the new situation by having sponsored the Lon Nol coup against Sihanouk. Nevertheless Vietnam was described as having got itself into a 'mire' of its own making. Geng Biao looked forward to important co-operative endeavours with the United States, including access to intelligence on Soviet and Vietnamese naval movements in the area and various unspecified moves to limit the growth of Soviet influence. Deng Xiaoping was reported as likely to explore these matters with the Carter Administration during his visit to America later that month.

Perhaps the more interesting and significant aspects of the report concerned possible actions which were contemplated by the Chinese at the time. Apparently, the head of the Chinese navy and Political Bureau member, Su Chenhua, suggested despatching a Chinese fleet to Kampuchean waters and Xu Shiyu, commander of the southern region and also a member of the Political Bureau, proposed an attack with his troops from Guangxi Province. But 'after careful consideration' both suggestions were rejected for several reasons which give a fascinating insight into Chinese political and strategic calculation of costs and benefits:

(1)   It was against Chinese principles to station troops on foreign territory and it would cause China to be seen as just another kind of hegemonic power — 'such a big mistake, once committed, is hard to be remedied';

(2)   It would damage the common international front of condemnation of Vietnam, for China would also be in the dock;

(3)   China lacked the strength to fight a war in Indochina unless it first abandoned the modernisation programme; and

(4)   The Soviet Union wanted such a Chinese intervention so that China would become bogged down in conflict and isolated from its Western friends from whom it sought assistance for modernisation. Moreover Russia would have a pretext to attack in the north.

Aid, however, could and would be given to the Kampucheans. The report disclosed that up to 1500 Chinese advisers had been unable to leave and that they had volunteered to take Kampuchean nationality and stay on to fight the Vietnamese. Aid could be sent from the sea or by using the Thai Communist Party by land across Laos. Geng also looked forward to using the remanent Kuomintang forces (in the Golden Triangle) for this purpose. Either tacitly or openly Thailand would enable the Chinese to send supplies to Pol Pot's forces and he frankly described the alliance of convenience about to emerge between China and Thailand as based on a shared perspective of the new security threat posed by the Vietnamese to the Thai border and the northeastern part of Thailand.

As for the future, Geng Biao stressed the significance of building up the international front against global and regional hegemonism and of the necessity of alerting others to the danger that Kampuchea is but the 'first step of the Soviet Union to enhance its expansion in Southeast Asia'. But he also dwelt on the possibility of an armed response by the Chinese. Referring to the border incidents with Vietnam he claimed that China's restraint was 'absolutely not a manifestation of weakness . . . we say that we do not fight now. But that doesn't mean that we won't in the future.' That would be done if 'we have no other choice'. This somewhat cautious approach was superseded by the subsequent explanation that no attack had been launched so far, firstly because of the need to cultivate world public opinion in China's favour; secondly, because 'in essence' the struggle is between 'social imperialism and socialist China' and it is only on the surface that it is a Sino-Vietnamese conflict; thirdly, there is still the hope, albeit a 'small' one that Vietnam may change its mind. Meanwhile Geng Biao emphasised the significance of the Sino-American agreement which had 'changed the balance of world power'.

It will be seen that the report depicted Vietnam as having been long determined to control Kampuchea and as having been deeply wedded to the Soviet Union. That may explain why China's leaders did not pursue policies designed to wean Vietnam away from its Soviet link. Chinese policy, in fact, could not have been better calculated to push Vietnam ever closer to the Soviet Union even if that had been the Chinese purpose. The reasons advanced in the report for not sending in troops to Kampuchea which, interestingly, had been proposed by military leaders, suggest a fascinating interplay between international political considerations and a shrewd grasp of China's military weaknesses. However, only two of the reasons would have applied to the question of the punitive attack on Vietnam: fear of the Soviet Union and fear lest it damage the modernisation programme. Unlike much of the rest of the report neither of these figured at all in Chinese public pronouncements. But the report underscores the importance attached to the new relationship with the United States and to the significance of Deng Xiaoping's impending visit there. Much seemed to depend on the kind of understandings and arrangements that he might make in America. It is also interesting that no reference was made in the report to the expulsion of the ethnic Chinese, yet at several points Geng referred to the ingratitude of the Vietnamese. Finally it is worth noting the use China hoped to make of the Thai Communist Party and the cavalier way in which Chinese advisers simply assumed Kampuchean nationality. Neither point could be welcomed in Southeast Asia.

There can be little doubt that Deng Xiaoping was the key decision-maker in launching the punitive attack on Vietnam. While there is no evidence to suggest that his frequent public declarations on the need to 'teach Vietnam a lesson' were endorsed in Washington or Tokyo, they were not repudiated either. In view of the imminence of Soviet—American negotiations on SALT II Deng was careful to state in Washington that he was not opposed to superpower negotiations as such, but he expressed concern lest too much reliance should be placed upon them. In retrospect this appears to have been a well-calculated ploy to indicate that any Chinese action against Vietnam would not be designed to damage Soviet—American relations, but any Soviet counter moves against China could indeed lead to that. Moreover by claiming that the Chinese punitive action was based entirely upon bilateral issues rather than involving Kampuchea or Sino-Soviet questions (although it was quite clear from Geng's report and subsequent Chinese diplomacy that both were involved) Deng had made it easier for other governments to avoid involvement.

In the event Deng appeared to have judged the international reaction correctly. The Soviet Union, to the disappointment of the Vietnamese,[86] did not open a second front in the north, and the Western countries carried on their assistance to China's modernisation efforts despite apprehension and even formal disapproval of China's military attack. China's problems arose from the less than distinguished performance of its armed forces.[87] China's diplomatic skills were not matched by its armies. Nevertheless it was clear that having committed itself to the field of battle, the Chinese would not allow themselves to be defeated, and sufficient soldiers were held back in reserve to be used if necessary in order to ensure a victory of sorts.

Despite unease in Malaysia and Indonesia where there was underlying suspicion that it was China rather than Vietnam that was the long-term enemy, China has so far held the ASEAN countries to the line of isolating Vietnam until its forces should be withdrawn from Kampuchea. The Soviet invasion of Afghanistan in December 1979 and the exodus of the 'boat people' from Vietnam undoubtedly facilitated China's diplomatic task. At the same time the Chinese have successfully cultivated a special relationship with Thailand which has coincided with American interests in the region. While maintaining a hard-line policy of 'bleeding Vietnam' by pressure and isolation, the Chinese have demonstrated skilful flexibility on the question of Kampuchea itself. Thus, ASEAN initially sponsored the notion of a trilateral united front of the Kampuchean resistance forces and, when this showed signs of faltering, the Chinese took up the issue themselves by lending all their weight and prestige to sponsoring such a development in Peking and eventually such a front was established under ASEAN auspices in July 1982. At the same time, despite many predictions to the contrary, the Chinese have been able to ensure the continued occupation of the Kampuchean seat at the United Nations by the universally execrated Pol Pot régime. This has been achieved, it should be noted, without the Chinese having to assume the position of front runner. The relevant General Assembly resolutions have always been sponsored by ASEAN countries.

Nevertheless the Chinese position is weaker than the foregoing account may have suggested. It is a position that depends more on the performance of others than upon its own actions. China has no alternative but to rely upon the continued capacity of the Pol Pot forces to resist the Vietnamese in Kampuchea and on the persistent isolation of

Hanoi by the international community. Peking is also having to pay a price for the bestial if not genocidal policies of the Pol Pot régime in the past, for it seems that however much the Vietnamese may be disliked in Kampuchea, the return of the Pol Pot régime is feared even more. Moreover China still lacks the military and diplomatic weight to ensure the compliance of others to its diplomatic strategy against Vietnam. Should the Vietnamese display signs of 'breaking' or changing course, it is very possible that the ASEAN countries might find means of effecting a 'political solution' that would fall short of Chinese demands. It is doubtful whether even Thailand would welcome a broken-backed Vietnam with the corollary of enhanced Chinese influence in Indochina. So far Chinese inflexibility on Vietnam and the alleged Soviet menace has been matched by even greater intransigence on the part of Vietnam. The forward military presence of Vietnam on Thai borders is an unacceptable intrusion (from Thai perspectives) into its national security concerns and it also threatens the territorial integrity of Thailand's northeast provinces (only acquired in the 1830s). But a political solution which involved significant Vietnamese military withdrawals from the border region may well be acceptable to the Thais. Meanwhile there has been no such sign from Vietnam and despite indications of Soviet—Vietnamese differences Chinese diplomacy has been successful in perpetuating the isolation of Vietnam.

China and the Third World

One of the ironies of Mao's legacy in the strategic dimensions of foreign policy is that the articulation of the 'theory of the three worlds' which accords pride of place to the Third World as 'propelling the wheel of history forward', has coincided with a period in which China has come to rely less and less upon the Third World as the main force for its putative anti-Soviet international united front. China's principal efforts in this regard, as in its foreign economic relations, have been directed towards the Western world. Although China's leaders continue to claim a common identity with the Third World the main focus of their attention is directed towards the

United States and its allies in Europe and in the Asia—Pacific region. Even the Chinese argument that the Soviet Union is concentrating its expansionism upon Third World countries is qualified by the suggestion that its purpose is to outflank Western Europe as part of its superpower contention with the United States for 'world-wide hegemony'. Thus the main target for Chinese diplomacy is the Western world. The Chinese regularly beseech the United States in particular to respond more positively to the nationalist and developmental aspirations in the Third World, especially in the Middle East, southern Africa and Central America.

Chinese policy towards Third World countries is predicated on the assumption that local conflicts create opportunities for Soviet intervention. Therefore Chinese diplomacy consists largely of exhortations to participants in such conflicts to settle their differences. The limitations of Chinese power have reduced many of these pleas to ineffectiveness — even in areas of geopolitical significance to China such as the Gulf where the Iran—Iraq war is perceived in Peking as potentially very serious. But in southern Asia, where Chinese power and influence is far from negligible, Chinese diplomacy has been instrumental in reducing the intensity of local sources of conflict. In the wake of the Soviet invasion of Afghanistan in particular, the Chinese government has demonstrated a new flexibility in seeking to solve the long-standing border dispute. It has also encouraged policies of accommodation between India and Pakistan and it has sought to reduce the tensions involving Sino-Indian relations with regard to the smaller Himalayan states.

Thus the mainsprings of Chinese foreign policy continue to be determined by Peking's perceptions of the global roles of the two superpowers and the character of the threats which they have posed to China. Chinese policy towards the rest of the world continues to be dependent upon that. However, the domestic changes within China and the repudiation of the ideology of the Cultural Revolution has witnessed a profound change in China's diplomatic style. China has joined the main institutions of the international system and it is seeking to play a more vigorous role in the international economic system. These developments have helped to make clear (what some have long argued) that essentially China is only a regional power, albeit of global significance. In other words, the range of China's effective power and influence is confined to countries within close range of its borders. Yet because of China's significance to the central balances between the superpowers it remains paradoxically a country of much greater global significance than, say, India with which it might otherwise be compared. Whatever the extent of the changes in the post-Mao era in China and in certain aspects of its foreign relations, there can be little doubt that the geopolitical thinking underlying the strategic dimensions of foreign policy are still very much within the framework established by Mao. Whether or not this will be continued by the successors to Deng Xiaoping and the other leaders of his generation remains to be seen. Deng Xiaoping, it should be remembered, belongs in a very real sense to the generation of leaders who were among the architects and leaders of the Chinese revolution from the late 1920s and early 1930s. Perhaps the 'real' succession will take place only after the demise of Deng and his generation.

Conclusions: Problems and Prospects

By treating separately the societal and strategic dimensions of China's foreign policy it has been possible to examine more closely the continuities and discontinuities since the passing of Mao. This study has shown that the continuities are most marked in the strategic realm. This is true both of the general policies and the outlook on international politics which underlie them. It is in the societal aspects of foreign relations that the change is most evident. Although it is possible to exaggerate the extent of the change which has taken place, it is nevertheless clear that the policy of the 'open door' has exposed China to a degree of Western influence that was unimaginable in the early seventies.

Reform and the open door

As was discussed in Chapter 4, the modernisation programme also involves an attempt to establish a new political and economic order. The opening to the West is seen as necessary for the economy, but it is also seen as a threat to the political order. The transformation of a political system always raises acute problems as it necessarily affects the distribution of power and influence in society. In China the problems are especially deep-seated. The legacy of the Cultural Revolution includes a widespread disillusionment with politics and collectivist values, especially among the young. It has left up to 100 million people with inadequate educational training and technical skills and it has left bitter divisions between social and political groups. Corruption is widespread and most people pursue private rather than collectivist goals. Indeed the current economic policies accentuate the promotion of private interests both in industry and in agriculture. At the same time China's leaders are engaged in trying to restore the organisational norms and general morale of the Communist Party. The years 1981 and 1982 have witnessed a widespread campaign against corruption and economic crimes. These crimes are perceived as caused by 'bourgeois liberal' influences. As a result there is a tendency to link that with the growing foreign influence. Whether or not this will bring about a counter-tendency to narrow the opening of the door to the outside world remains to be seen, but already there have been greater pressures on ordinary Chinese to restrict their dealings with foreigners. At the same time China's leaders repeatedly assert that the 'open door' is an integral part of the modernisation programme and that foreign economic relations will continue to expand.

In this programme of reforms China's leaders are confronted with very real political dilemmas. On the one hand they want to establish a legal order, clear lines of organisational responsibility and a system by which economic decision-making at the enterprise level in industry and at the grass roots levels in agriculture can be separated from 'administrative' decision-making by the hitherto all-powerful local Party Committee and its secretary. On the other hand they wish to enhance Party leadership and 'socialist morality'. The experience of the Soviet Union in trying to institute similar reforms is instructive. This kind of decentralisation leads to the erosion of Party authority and to acute problems of managing centralised planning. We have already seen that in order to reduce the rate of capital accumulation in China in 1980 and 1981, the central leadership had to curtail some of the limited powers it had previously given to Provinces and major enterprises. The attempt to grant more decision-making powers to enterprise managers, for example, while simultaneously seeking to enhance the authority of a demoralised Party seems fraught with problems and unlikely to succeed.

If the Soviet experience is instructive in these domestic reforms, then China's own nineteenth century experience is important with regard to the 'open door'. The 'ti-yong' dilemma (see pp. 11–14) in which China sought then to absorb science and technology from the West for the purpose of 'self-strengthening', and in order to maintain its separate social values, failed. That does not mean that it will necessarily fail again in the very different circumstances of today; but it is as well to recognise the immense problems inherent in the exercise. There can be little doubt about the strength of patriotic or nationalistic sentiments in contemporary China. Although the same cannot be said for the attachment to socialist values, there are powerful institutional interests to be found in the Party and the armed forces opposed to aspects of the new reforms and of the 'open door' policy. It is striking how frequently the press and radio in China repeat the point that corruption and economic crimes are not the inevitable consequence of the 'open door'. It suggests that there are many people of political weight who link the two.

There is, therefore, a danger that a backlash against the 'open door' could occur. If that did happen it could very well spill over into the strategic dimension of foreign policy. It could, for example, seriously affect China's alignment with the West. Indeed the strains that have emerged in Sino-American relations which are primarily focused on the Taiwan may already reflect such a tendency. That is to say that Deng Xiaoping may have found his freedom for manoeuvre on the issue severely curtailed because of domestic opposition to some of his reforms and because of problems that have arisen in societal relations with the West.

Problems of succession

At this point it is as well to recognize that the succession issue is far from resolved within China. It is true that the immediate question of 'after Mao what?' has been settled. It is also true that once Deng Xiaoping had established his ascendancy the new Party leadership was able to deliver an official verdict on Mao and the great man's role in history. But an examination of these 'new' Party leaders as established in the Standing Committee of the Political Bureau immediately shows that apart from Hua Guofeng and the two men promoted under the aegis of Deng, Zhao Ziyang and Hu Yaobang, the rest are not new at all. Ye Jianying, Chen Yun, Li Xiannian and Deng Xiaoping are all men who have been prominent leaders of the CPC since the late 1920s and early 1930s. In a very real sense they belong to the generation of leaders like Mao and Zhou Enlai. Indeed they draw much of their authority from being old revolutionary veterans closely associated with Mao and Zhou who have extensive networks of followings amongst other leaders of substance in the Party, the armed forces and the state bureaucracy. There are still others of their generation and standing in the Political Bureau and the Central Committee. These are all people now in their late 70s and early 80s. The question that arises is what will happen once they pass away. Will Zhao Ziyang and Hu Yaobang command similar respect and authority? It seems unlikely. Hua Guofeng, who was by no means lacking in proven administrative ability and who had experience as a successful Provincial leader, a good record in handling agriculture and as a minister of Public Security, found in the end that possession of the formal trappings of power as both Premier of the State Council and Chairman of the Party could not protect him from the informal and real authority wielded by Deng Xiaoping.

It is one thing for veteran authoritative leaders like Deng Xiaoping and Chen Yun to challenge established procedures and to undermine the positions of power-holders of substance; it will be quite a different exercise for new generational leaders like Zhao Ziyang and Hu Yaobang. Much will depend upon the circumstances and manner in which this generational succession will take place. There is not, in the Political Bureau of the Communist Party of today, the kind of raw conflict between factions that existed when Mao died. But the attempt to establish a new political and economic order has encountered resistance and difficulties. These could well be magnified with a leadership that commanded less authority than Deng Xiaoping, Chen Yun *et al*. Because of the advanced age of these veteran leaders the generational succession cannot be long delayed and it is possible that the expectation of that is already having an effect on Chinese politics. People at all levels of the bureaucracy may be less ready to commit themselves fully to current policies if they lack confidence that the direction from the top may change or lose effectiveness in the not-too-distant future.

Consideration of the generational succession issue probably affects the societal dimensions of foreign relations in the first instance because they have an immediate impact on the interactions between domestic Chinese society and the outside world. But, of course, they also affect the strategic dimensions. A leadership which cannot command full authority at home is unlikely to be able to act with full confidence in foreign policy. A 'strong man' in such a position may seek to consolidate his position at home by engaging in a foreign adventure such as a war. But a 'collective leadership' such as seems more likely to emerge in China tends to follow existing patterns of more 'conservative' policies — 'conservative', that is, within its own institutional and political cultural traditions. In so far as Mao's legacy may be considered to be the 'conservative' norm, it would suggest that notwithstanding the bilateral strains of Sino-American relations, the broad pattern of the strategic dimensions of China's foreign policy would come under less challenge in a succession crisis than the societal dimensions associated with the 'open door'.

The end of isolationism?

In what senses can the increasing interactions which China has developed with the outside world since the passing of Mao be described as having ended its period of relative isolation? Any answer to the question will depend upon one's understanding of the concept of 'relative isolation'. In the second half of the twentieth century no country can be fully isolated from the rest of the world. All countries are influenced either directly or indirectly by the broad sweep of events affecting the world as a whole. No country is immune from the influence of superpower rivalry upon its region, or indeed from the global implications of the character of the central strategic balance between the United States and the Soviet Union. Similarly all countries are affected to a greater or lesser degree by the changes which have taken place in the operation of the international economy. The advances in science and technology recognise no national boundaries and any country that deliberately limits the access of its scientists and technologists to that growing international fund of knowledge will end up by causing its people immense harm.

In what ways then could China under Mao be described as isolationist? Clearly on the strategic plane of foreign policy China was not only greatly affected by the relationship between the Soviet Union and the United States, but it was an active participant in the shaping of the balances of power between them. Mao and his colleagues had their own distinctive approaches to international politics and to strategic questions, but these involved very careful calculation of the changing currents of international affairs. Indeed in some respects their approach to world politics alerted them to the significance of important changes in the international system earlier than most. For example, they were quick to seize upon the significance of the rise of the Third World (of which their revolution was a part) as a challenge to the existing order. They were also among the first to recognise the change in the balance between the two superpowers at the end of the 1960s.

Nevertheless there were aspects about China's strategic stance and the theories of its leaders that suggested it was separate (if not isolated) from the developments in military technology and strategic theorising which shaped the main developments elsewhere particularly with regard to Soviet—American strategic relations. This was, of course, particularly evident after the rupture of Sino-Soviet relations. The building of China's defence posture on the twin pillars of people's war and a relatively small nuclear capability meant that the country took a lone path in two important respects. First, the capacity to fight a people's war depends upon a politicised 'people's army' backed by a politically mobilised self-reliant peasantry. Although a people's war strategy does call for the existence of a relatively professionalised corps of main forces able to fight positional warfare, it does not envisage using such a corps until relatively late in the war. This strategy was not only different from those of all the other major countries, but in so far as it stressed the importance of political mobilisation it also meant that it would be desirable to limit heterodox foreign influences to a minimum. Second, by challenging the nuclear monopoly of the two superpowers China was in effect deliberately withdrawing itself from the processes of nuclear arms limitation talks and agreements in which the two were engaged, and on which the rest of the international community vested much hope. Mao and his colleagues were disputing the right of the superpowers to act by virtue of their overwhelming power as the custodians of nuclear weapons on behalf of all mankind.

At the same time it should be recognised that for much of this period China was deliberately excluded from many of the international organisations and conferences by the United States and its allies. Perhaps the most remarkable fact about the first two decades of its existence, when the PRC was excluded from the United Nations and other major institutions of the international community, was how few of the norms and customs of the inter-state system were challenged or violated by its government. Only during the first 2 years of the Cultural Revolution (1966—68) could China be said to have flouted these norms. But immediately the Chinese leaders signalled their intention to return to 'normalcy' and actively sought diplomatic relations with other countries, a large number of countries responded without delay. That implied that China was recognised to be an influential member of the world community and that its mystifying behaviour of the previous 2 years was not regarded as particularly damaging to its international credibility.

There is, however, another aspect of its international political role in which China may be said to have been perhaps relatively isolated. Again this applies especially to the sixties period, although elements of it may be detectable before then. Apart from the time of the close alliance with the Soviet Union, China has been free from the cross-cutting pressures of interdependence or allied relations which have become characteristic of the situations of the other major powers. As a result China has appeared to have exercised a greater freedom of international manoeuvre than most. It has shifted its alignment from East to West and, over the years, it has blown hot and cold over relations with Third World countries. This capacity to act as something of a 'loner' may be said to be derived in part from the legacy of imperial Sino-centricity and in part from Maoist geopolitical theory, but it has been made possible by a largely self-sufficient economic system. The PRC has been able to provide for most of its own food, energy and raw materials, and until recent times only a small proportion of its GNP was devoted to foreign trade.

There can be little doubt that it was in its societal relations that the PRC's relative isolation was most marked. To be sure this is not true of the early years of the Sino-Soviet alliance. Mao himself once divided the history of the PRC into two periods, remarking that it was only from 1957 that China began to follow its own path. Although Mao was not xenophobic and he always argued for the need to learn from abroad, the logic of his position from the early sixties became increasingly isolationalist in societal terms. From 1962 he never wavered in his view that the Soviet Union had gone revisionist and that China had become the principal centre of socialism in the world. His theory of continuing the revolution under conditions of socialism (on which the Cultural Revolution was based) stressed the importance of continued class struggle. That theory held that one of the sources for the generation of class enemies within China was the influence of class enemies abroad. At the same time Mao approved of the importation of advanced technology from Western countries. He also had foreign friends – notably Edgar Snow. Nevertheless both the political system over which he presided and the socialist values which he espoused meant that foreign influences were inevitably closely circumscribed.

In what respects has this 'relative isolation' changed in the 5–6 years since Mao's death? In the strategic realm China is still something of a loner, but to a lesser degree than before. China's defence posture has been modified by greater emphasis on professionalism. Under the rubric of the need to prepare for a people's war 'under modern conditions' China's leaders have encouraged the adoption of more modern means of communication and better training in combined operations. There is a greater readiness to study the combat experiences of other armed forces. However, there is simply insufficient funding available to meet the enormous costs of purchasing advanced weapons from abroad. Therefore China's armed forces will remain significantly inferior in all aspects of its military equipment to that deployed by their Soviet adversaries for the foreseeable future. As a result China's defensive posture will continue along the lines of people's warfare but with increasing elements of professionalism and modernity.

As for China's role in the strategic dimensions of international politics, China continues to exhibit a high degree of manoeuvrability. Despite the closer links with the United States and Japan, and despite the complex pattern of Sino-Soviet encirclement and counter-encirclement, China is not tied institutionally to any alliance pattern. Its leaders continue to retain the capacity to change the country's alignments in the manner of their predecessors. As has been argued in Chapter 5, the post-Mao leaders have continued to operate along the previous approaches to geopolitics, but a greater degree of flexibility and sophistication has been added to China's diplomatic style.

It is in the realm of societal relations that the greatest changes have been made. Under the slogan of the 'open door' China's foreign economic relations have been transformed. The value of foreign trade has leapt to account for 16 per cent of GNP, and although China's low domestic price structure undoubtedly exaggerates the figure it still constitutes a significant increase on the 3—6 per cent of Mao's era. Special Economic Zones have been opened, more than 300 joint ventures have begun operation, and a wide variety of compensation trade deals have become effective. China's banking system has been adapted to meet the requirements of the international market. Foreign models have been studied for their application to the running of the Chinese economy and the management of its enterprises. Over 7000 students are studying abroad. An extensive range of scientific and cultural exchanges are maintained with many countries. Tourism has been greatly expanded.

Nevertheless it is premature to conclude that China's relative isolation is over. Although certain regions and certain sectors of light industry have become closely linked with the international market it is patently clear that China has not become as dependent on trade as the major Western countries or the newly industrialised countries on its periphery. For example, although the United States ranks as China's second most important trading partner, its leaders' threats to down-grade Sino-American relations over the Taiwan issue are credible in a way that could not possibly be true for these other countries. However, it is possible that if current trends continue China could become so reliant on the international market that the domestic economic costs of changing or downgrading partners would be too great; but that point has yet to be reached.

China's Communist political system itself is a great barrier to the full ending of isolation. There have already been signs of the limited tolerance extended to personal relations be-tween Chinese citizens and foreigners. So-called 'liberal bourgeois' influences on Chinese political and cultural life have been criticised and certain writers and dissidents have paid heavy penalties for exceeding official tolerance. Dif-ferent points of view on these questions can be identified in the Chinese political elite and the political climate varies over time, but it is clear that no major threat to Party dominance will be allowed in the long run. Since the economic reforms have by no means run smoothly, and they all involve a greater pluralisation of decision-making in China, they have evoked opposition from certain sections within the Party. Much of the corruption in China has been blamed in certain quarters on the growing foreign influence. The new foreign economic relations have also altered the balances of economic power between certain regions and the centre — especially in the case of Guandong Province. There is evidence, too, that difficulties have been experienced in absorbing foreign technology. Thus it seems that the new relationship with the outside world is closely associated with the reform pro-grammes of Deng Xiaoping, and its continuance is very much dependent on those reforms. But even Deng himself is fully committed to ensuring Communist Party dominance of the political system. That in itself will set certain limits to the range of interactions with the Western world.

It can be argued that once again China is back to the 'ti-yong' dilemma, but in a new guise. China's modernisation programmes require access to advanced foreign technology and they need a greater involvement with the international market. However, the object of the exercise is to promote and develop a socialist China, which minimally means a China controlled by its Communist Party. The dilemma in domestic terms is how to introduce Western 'practicality' without undermining the Party 'essence' of socialist China. In foreign policy terms the dilemma is how to establish deeper and more extensive links with the international economy without finding that the country's freedom of international manoeuvre has become limited by the ties of interdependency experienced by nearly all the other major countries.

Notes and References

Preface

1. 'Resolution on Certain Questions in the History of Our Party Since the Founding of the People's Republic of China', *Beijing Review*, no. 27 (6 July 1981).
2. *Ibid.*, p. 24.
3. For an account of this see Michael B. Yahuda, *China's Role in World Affairs* (London, Croom Helm, 1978), chapter 6.
4. 'Great Internationalist Fighter' in *Beijing Review*, no. 12 (24 March 1978) pp. 19—26. See also the July 1981 issue of the journal *Guoji Yanjiu (International Studies)*, Beijing, on Zhou's diplomatic style, translated in *SWB/FE/6774*.

Chapter 1: Introduction

1. See the arguments by Hedley Bull, *The Anarchical Society: A Study of Order in World Politics* (London, Macmillan, 1977) pp. 16—20.
2. For a useful discussion of the elements involved in the related concept of national interest see Joseph Frankel, *The National Interest* (London, Macmillan, 1970).
3. See *Da Gong Bao* (Hong Kong, English edition) 1 April 1982 for extract of Peng Dehuai's autobiography in which Mao is depicted as arguing alone at a meeting in favour of intervention. See also Chou Ching-wen, *Ten Years of Storm: The True Story of the Communist Regime in China* (Connecticut, U.S., Green Wood Press, 1960) p. 117; where he states that Mao 'paced up and down for three days and nights before he came to the decision'.
4. For an argument to that effect, see Michael B. Yahuda, *China's Role in World Affairs* (London, Croom Helm, 1978) pp. 275—81.
5. See the argument in J. R. Levenson, *Confucian China and its Modern Fate*, vol. 1 (London, Routledge & Kegan Paul, 1965) pp. 98—100.
6. See the discussion in William Wallace, *Foreign Policy and the Political Process* (London, Macmillan, 1971) pp. 50—2.

7. For a challenging analysis of the factional alignments related to the conflict over the tilt to the United States in 1971, see Thomas M. Gottleib, *Chinese Foreign Policy Factionalism and the Origins of the Strategic Triangle* (RAND Report R-1902-NA, 1977).

8. For a discussion of these differences, see Alexander Eckstein, *China's Economic Revolution* (Cambridge University Press, 1977) pp. 125—7.

9. For the classic account of these reformers who would not have thought of themselves as modernisers, see Mary C. Wright, *The Last Stand of Chinese Conservatism: The Tung Chih Restoration 1862—1874* (California, Stanford University Press, 1957).

10. *Ibid.*, chapter XII, pp. 300—12.

11. See the argument in Wang Gung-wu, *China and the World since 1949: The Impact of Independence Modernity and Revolution* (London, Macmillan, 1979) p. 19.

12. See 'Introduction' in Stuart R. Schram (ed.), *Mao Tse-tung Unrehearsed: Talks and Letters 1956—1971* (Harmondsworth, Penguin, 1974) pp. 34—36.

13. Mao's 24 August 1956 Talk to music workers, *ibid.*, p. 88.

14. See the discussion in A. Eckstein, *China's Economic Revolution*, pp. 279—80. Also see the stimulating essay by Lyman P. van Slyke, 'Culture and Technology'; paper presented to conference on *Sino-American Relations in Historical and Global Perspective* held in Wisconsin, March 1976.

15. For an argument that Chinese foreign policy after 1949 was 'encumbered by the politics of foreign dependence' and that it was largely 'reactive to the (usually hostile) initiatives of external powers', see John Gittings, *The World and China 1922—1972* (London, Eyre Methuen, 1974) pp. 10—12.

16. Henry Kissinger, *The White House Years* (London, Weidenfeld & Nicolson, 1979) pp. 1058—63. Strobe Talbott (trans.) *The Khrushchev Memoirs*, vol. 1 (London, Sphere Books, 1971) pp. 424—40; vol. 2 (Harmondsworth, Penguin, 1977) pp. 282—343.

17. See Yahuda, *op. cit.*, pp. 171—82.

18. Based on interview with senior academician of Chinese Academy of Social Sciences held in Peking in April 1980.

19. Franz Schurmann, *The Logic of World Power* (New York, Pantheon Books, 1974) pp. 278—84.

20. See Harold P. Ford, 'The Eruption of Sino-Soviet Politico-Military Problems 1957—1960', in Raymond L. Garthoff (ed.), *Sino-Soviet Military Relations* (New York, Praeger, 1966) pp. 100—13.

21. On the military aspects, see Harry Harding and Melvin Gurtov, *The Purge of Lo Jui-ch'ing: The Politics of Chinese Strategic Plan-*

ning (RAND Report R-548-PR, February 1971). For my own interpretation, see 'Kremlinology and the Chinese Strategic Debate 1965–1966'. in *China Quarterly* (no. 49, March 1972) which takes issue with the interpretations of Uri Ra'anan, 'Peking's Foreign Policy "Debate", 1965–1966' and Donald S. Zagoria, 'The Strategic Debate in Peking' — both in Tang Tsou (ed.), *China in Crisis*, vol. 2 (University of Chicago Press, 1968) pp. 23–71 and pp. 237–68 respectively.

22. The documents on the Lin Biao affair are conveniently assembled in *Chinese Law and Government*, vol. 5, nos. 3–4 (Fall–Winter 1972–73). See also *A Great Trial in Chinese History* (Beijing, New World Press, 1981).

23. The best account is still Donald S. Zagoria, *The Sino-Soviet Conflict 1956–61* (Princeton University Press, 1962).

24. See, for example, Mao's comparison of China with the Soviet Union of December 1955 in which he asserted that 'we will be faster . . . ', *Miscellany of Mao Tse-tung Thought* (Joint Publications Research Service, Virginia, 20 February 1974) vol. 1, p. 29.

25. See *Resolution on CPC History 1949–81* (Beijing, Foreign Languages Press, 1981), also in *Beijing Review*, no. 27 (6 July 1981).

26. See John Gittings, *The World and China*, chapter 8. See also Gerald Segal, 'China and the Great Power Triangle', *China Quarterly*, no. 83 (September 1980) p. 491.

27. Speech at the Tenth Plenum of the Eighth Central Committee, 24 September 1962 in Schram, *Mao Tse-tung Unrehearsed*, p. 191.

28. See John Gittings, *Survey of the Sino-Soviet Dispute* (Oxford University Press, 1968) pp. 17–19 and his *World and China*, pp. 184–7.

29. Speech at the Group Leaders' Forum of the Enlarged Military Affairs Committee of 28 June 1958 in Schram, *Mao Tse-tung Unrehearsed*, pp. 128–9.

30. Political Report by Zhou Enlai to the Second Session of the Second National Committee of the Chinese People's Political Consultative Conference on 30 January 1956 in 'Supplement' to *People's China*, no. 4 (1956) pp. 5–6.

31. The best analysis of the interplay of these factors is by Roderick MacFarquhar, *The Origins of the Cultural Revolution: Contradictions Among the People*, vol. 1 (London, Oxford University Press, 1974).

32. For discussion of the concept of diplomatic style, see F. S. Northedge, 'The Nature of Foreign Policy' in his (ed.) *The Foreign Policies of the Powers* (London, Faber & Faber, 1968) pp. 21–3.

33. For the best analysis of these issues, see Allen S. Whiting, *The*

Chinese Calculus of Deterrence (Ann Arbor, The University of Michigan Press, 1975) chapter 6, 'Indochina and PRC Deterrence', pp. 170—95.

34. 'Chou En-lai's Report on the International Situation, December 1971', in *Issues and Studies* (Taiwan), January 1977, p. 116.

35. For more extensive analyses of this see Gottleib, *op. cit.*; Greg O'Leary, *The Shaping of Chinese Foreign Policy* (London, Croom Helm, 1980); Richard Wich, *Sino-Soviet Crisis Politics* (Harvard University Press, 1980). For my account, see *China's Role in World Affairs*, chapter 8.

36. Eckstein, *China's Economic Revolution*, p. 241 gives the approximate figure of $2.5 billion for 1972—74. I have taken the figure of a Chinese economist for 1973—76 of $3.5 billion. See Chen Weiqin, 'The Direction of introducing technology should be changed', in *Jingji Guanli (Economic Management)* no. 4 (15 April 1981), translated in *SWB/FE/W1139/C/1*.

37. See John Bryan Starr, 'From the 10th Party Congress to the Premiership of Hua Kuo-feng: The Significance of the Colour of the Cat'; John Gittings, 'New Material on Teng Hsiao-p'ing'; and Edward E. Rice, 'The Second Rise and Fall of Teng Hsiao p'ing' all in *China Quarterly*, no. 67 (September 1976).

38. Stuart R. Schram, 'To Utopia and Back: A Cycle in the History of the Chinese Communist Party', in *China Quarterly*, no 87 (September 1981).

Chapter 2: Chinese Society and Foreign Relations

1. For the most extensive account of these, see John Gittings, *The World and China 1922—1972* (London, Eyre Methuen, 1974), chapters 1—6.

2. See Stuart Schram's introductory essay to his edited *Authority Participation and Cultural Change in China* (Cambridge University Press, 1973), pp. 1—108.

3. For an account of this endeavour, see Raymond F. Wylie, *The Emergence of Maoism: Mao Tse-tung, Ch'en Po-ta and the Search for Chinese Theory: 1935—1945* (Stanford University Press, 1980).

4. See James Reardon-Anderson, *Yenan and the Great Powers: The Origins of Chinese Communist Foreign Policy 1944—46* (Columbia University Press, 1980), pp. 40—1.

5. A point made in J. R. Levenson, *Confucian China and its Modern Fate: The Problem of Intellectual Continuity*, vol. 1 (London, Routledge & Kegan Paul, 1958), p. 134.

6. See Ishwer J. Ojha, *Chinese Foreign Policy in an Age of Transition: The Diplomacy of Cultural Despair* (Boston, Beacon Press, 1969).

7. *SW*, vol. 5, p. 17.

8. *SW*, vol. 3, p. 309.

9. See, for example, the summary of different arguments on the subject in Song Yuanqiang, 'A Symposium on the Sprouts of Capitalism in China', in *Social Sciences in China* (Beijing, China Social Science Publishing House) December 1981, no. 4, pp. 5—20.

10. *SW*, vol. 3, p. 310.

11. See the discussion in Alexander Eckstein, *China's Economic Revolution*, pp. 125—7.

12. See Reardon-Anderson, *op. cit.*, pp. 39—45.

13. For an account see David D. Barrett, *Dixie Mission: The United States Army Observer Group in Yenan 1944* (University of California Press, 1970). See also Gittings, *The World and China*, chapter 5, pp. 90—115.

14. Mark Selden, *The Yenan Way in Revolutionary China* (Harvard University Press, 1971). See especially chapter 6, 'The Yenan Way'.

15. Cited in Reardon-Anderson, *op. cit.*, p. 41.

16. *Ibid.*, p. 135.

17. Stuart R. Schram, *The Political Thought of Mao Tse-tung* (Harmondsworth, Penguin Books, rev. ed., 1969), p. 127.

18. Reardon-Anderson, *op. cit.*, p. 56.

19. *Ibid.*, p. 94. See also John Gittings, *The World and China*, chapter 5.

20. *SW*, vol. 4, p. 413.

21. D. C. Watt, 'Britain and the Cold War in the Far East 1945—58', in Yonosuke Hagai and Akira Iriye (eds), *The Origins of the Cold War in Asia* (Columbia and Tokyo University Presses, 1977) pp. 92—3.

22. This is well known, but for a sensitive account which gives many examples of this from the thirties onwards, see Stuart R. Schram, 'The Cultural Revolution in Historical Perspective', in his edited volume, *Authority Participation and Cultural Change in China* (Cambridge University Press, 1973) pp. 1—108.

23. Watt, *op. cit.*, p. 93.

24. See the many scathing references to these 'dogmatists' who return from abroad and who are only good for reciting 'a stock of undigested foreign phrases' and yet cannot till the land, practise a trade, fight or provide practical leadership' in Boyd Compton, *Mao's China* (Seattle, University of Washington Press, 1952).

25. See O. B. Borisov and B. T. Kolosov, *Soviet—Chinese Relations 1945—1980*, 3rd supplemented edition (Moscow, Mysl Publishers,

1980). This is regarded in Russia as 'a definitive study' of the subject — see review in *Far Eastern Affairs* (Moscow, Institute of the Far East, USSR Academy of Sciences) no. 3, 1981, p. 139.

26. For Mao's eulogies of Stalin, see three extracts from Mao's published writings from 1939 to 1956 in Stuart R. Schram, *The Political Thought of Mao Tse-tung* (New York, Praeger, 1963) pp. 293–9.

27. Mao could have referred, for example, to Soviet assistance in Manchuria following the Japanese surrender although there had also been friction with the Soviet Red Army and the assistance was by no means unqualified. For the extent of the assistance see Tang Tsou, *America's Failure in China 1941–1950* (University of Chicago Press, 1963) pp. 327–40 and for evidence of friction with the Soviet occupying forces, see John Gittings, *Survey of the Sino-Soviet Dispute* (Oxford University Press, 1968) p. 41.

28. It would be futile to try to list even the main studies, but reference may be made to two relatively recent biographies of Mao which utilise the available evidence to good effect. See Dick Wilson, *Mao, the People's Emperor* (London, Hutchinson, 1979) and Ross Terrill, *Mao* (New York, Harper & Row, 1980).

29. 'Some Points in Appraisal of the Present International Situation', in *SW*, vol. 4, pp. 87–8. The note is on p. 88.

30. See John Gittings, *The World and China 1922–72* (London, Eyre Methuen, 1974) pp. 141–2 and Charles B. McLane, *Soviet Policy and the Chinese Communists 1931–1946* (New York, Columbia University Press, 1958) pp. 176, 180–1, 195. See also the analysis by Okabe Tatsumi, 'The Cold War and China', in Nagai and Iriye (eds), *The Origins of the Cold War in Asia*, pp. 231–3.

31. *Qun Zhong* ('*The Masses*'), January 1946.

32. See account and documentation in Gerald Segal, 'China and the Great Power Triangle', in *China Quarterly*, no. 83 (September 1980) p. 491.

33. See note 27.

34. Mao noted 'Stalin was very fond of Gao Gang and made him a special present of a motor-car. Gao Gang sent Stalin a congratulatory telegram every 15 August'. Stuart R. Schram (ed.), *Mao Tse-tung Unrehearsed* (Harmondsworth, Penguin, 1974) p. 100. Khrushchev's memoirs stated that Stalin told Mao that Gao was his man. Gao was later purged in 1953–54 for his conspiracy 'almost certainly' to replace Zhou Enlai and Liu Shaoqi. See Roderick MacFarquhar, *The Origins of the Cultural Revolution 1: Contradictions Among the People 1956–1957* (Oxford University Press, 1974) p. 47 and Frederick G. Teiwes, *Politics and Purges in China* (New York, M. E. Sharp Inc., 1979) chapter 5. See especially

pp. 191—4 which play down the Soviet connection. In the absence of evidence it can only be a matter for speculation as to whether his Soviet association was a factor in his purge. Interestingly, Mao at various points linked him with Beria, the Russian Secret Police chief who was killed by his colleagues very soon after Stalin's death.

35. It was not until the mid-1950s that Mao began to express irritation at the slavish attitude of some of his compatriots towards the Russians. See Schram, *Mao Tse-tung Unrehearsed*, pp. 98—9. Yet this was something which he had not only countenanced but had actually encouraged in 1953 when he exhorted his countrymen to 'set going a tidal wave of learning from the Soviet Union' (7 February). Five years later he recounted to a high-level Party conference how he could not have eggs or chicken soup for three years because of an article in the Soviet Press warning against them. Later another article claimed that they were all right. Mao commented: 'It didn't matter whether the article was correct or not, the Chinese listened all the same and respectfully obeyed.' While this may have been meant humorously, it suggests that Mao too 'respectfully obeyed'.

   For Mao's admission of his limited understanding of economic construction, industry and commerce and only a 'relative' understanding of agriculture, see *ibid*., pp. 173 and 175.

36. See Table 7—1 on China's foreign trade in Alexander Eckstein, *China's Economic Revolution*, p. 246.

37. Jan S. Prybyla, *The Chinese Economy* (University of Southern California Press, 1978) p. 183 claims this proportion for 1975 which represented the highest point of China's foreign trade until that point. See also Christopher Howe, *China's Economy* (London, Elek Books, 1978) Figure 1, pp. xxiii and 137—9.

38. See Howe, *China's Economy*, p. 140 on which this paragraph is based.

39. *Ibid*., pp. 137—8.

40. Feng-hua Mah, *The Foreign Trade of Mainland China* (Edinburgh University Press, 1972).

41. Schram, *Mao Tse-Tung Unrehearsed*, pp. 198—9.

42. See Ann Fenwick, 'Chinese Foreign Trade Policy and the Campaign Against Deng Xiaoping', in Thomas Fingar (ed.), *China's Quest for Independence: Policy Evolution in the 1970's* (Boulder, Colorado, Westview Press, 1980).

43. Alexander Eckstein, *China's Economic Revolution*, p. 260.

44. Alexander Eckstein, *Communist China's Economic Growth and Foreign Trade* (New York, McGraw-Hill, 1966) p. 167. The analysis here of the balance of advantages of Soviet aid and trade with China is largely based on chapters 4 and 5 of this book.

45. *Ibid.*, p. 137.
46. Frederick C. Teiwes, *Politics of Purges in China*, pp. 417–20.
47. For a note on these texts and their available translations, see Schram, *Mao Tse-tung Unrehearsed*, pp. 49–57.
48. Mao Tse-Tung, 'Talks at the Chengtu Conference' (March 1958), in Schram, *Mao Tse-tung Unrehearsed*, p. 98.
49. Stuart Schram, *Mao Tse-tung* (London, Pelican, 1974) p. 293.
50. For accounts of these campaigns see John Gardner, 'The Wu-fan Campaign in Shanghai: A Study of the Consolidation of Urban Control', in Doak A. Barnett, *Chinese Communist Politics in Action* (University of Washington Press, 1969) pp. 477–539 and various chapters in Doak A. Barnett, *Communist China: The Early Years* (London, Pall Mall Press, 1964).
51. Theodore H. E. Chen, *Thought Reform of the Chinese Intellectuals* Hong Kong University Press, 1960).
52. Roderick MacFarquhar, *The Origins of the Cultural Revolution: Contradictions Among the People 1956–57* (Oxford University Press, 1974) p. 311. See also Part Four, pp. 261–310.
53. Schram, *The Political Thought . . .* , p. 16.
54. Schram, *Mao Tse-tung Unrehearsed*, pp. 35–6.

Chapter 3: Mao's Legacy of Geopolitical Thought

1. See Mao's statement of 20 May 1970 on the occasion of the American/South Vietnamese invasion of Cambodia in *Peking Review* 'Special Issue', 23 May 1970, p. 9.
2. For a recent Chinese assessment to this effect see the article on Zhou Enlai's diplomatic style in *Journal of International Issues* July 1981 reprinted in the *People's Daily* over several days during that month and translated in *SWB/FE/6774, 6776* and *6779*.
3. For an analysis of Liu Shaoqi's alternative foreign policy vision in 1963–66 and of Lin Biao's challenge in 1968–71, see Yahuda, *China's Role . . .* , pp. 176–87 and 220–4 respectively.
4. Even Mao's famous essays on classes in Chinese society have been more concerned with identifying this role in the revolutionary process than with their position in the political economy of China. The opening paragraph of his *Selected Works* begins with the two questions 'Who are our enemies? Who are our friends?', and his analysis of classes were fundamentally designed to answer those questions.
5. This point is made forcibly by John Gittings, 'The Statesman', in Dick Wilson (ed.), *Mao Tse-tung in the Scales of History* (Cambridge

University Press, 1977) pp. 266–7. For an example of Mao's ignorance of African conditions see his 'Conversation with Zanzibar Expert M. M. Ali and his Wife' of 18 June 1964 in JPRS, 61269–2, (20 February 1974) pp. 361–71.

6. In Schram, *Mao Tse-tung Unrehearsed*, p. 108.

7. 'Talk on Questions of Philosophy' of 18 August 1964: 'The unity of opposites is the most basic law, the transformation of quality and quantity into one another is the unity of the opposites quality and quantity, and the negation of the negation does not exist at all', *ibid.*, p. 226.

8. For an analysis of this see Frederic Wakeman, *History and Will: Philosophical Perspectives of Mao Tse tung's Thought* (Berkeley, University of California Press, 1973) pp. 229–37 and 295–301.

9. For a social–scientific analysis of Mao's attempt to transform China's political culture along revolutionary lines, see Richard H. Solomon, *Mao's Revolution and the Chinese Political Culture* (Berkeley, University of California Press, 1971). Frederic Wakeman, *History and Will* presents a more philosophical analysis.

10. Mao's 'Talks on Questions of Philosophy', in Schram, *Mao Tse-tung Unrehearsed*, pp. 227–8.

11. Mao, 'On Dialectics', 1959, in *JPRS* (5079, 23 June 1970) pp. 30 and 32.

12. Michel Oksenberg, 'The Political Leader', in Dick Wilson (ed.), *Mao in the Scales of History*, pp. 74–7. The essay should be read as a whole for its unique insights into the complexity of Mao's concepts and use of power.

13. For the best analysis of Mao's theories and practice of (international) united fronts, see J. D. Armstrong, *Revolutionary Diplomacy* (Berkeley, University of California Press, 1977).

14. Cited in 'Chairman Mao's Theory of the Differentiation of the Three Worlds Is a Major Contribution to Marxism–Leninism', Editorial Department of *People's Daily* in *Peking Review*, no. 45, (4 November 1977).

15. See John Gittings, *The World and China 1922–72*, chapters Two and Three. The quote from Mao is in *SW*, vol. 1, p. 63.

16. Oksenberg, *op. cit.*, pp. 82–6.

17. For a good account of the genesis of 'Mass Line' and a sympathetic treatment of its application in the early 1940s, see Mark Selden, *Yenan Way*, chapter 6. For the best accounts of Mao's position on 'Democratic Centralism', see Schram, *The Political Thought of Mao Tse-tung*, chapter 6; the same author's introductory essay to his (ed.) *Authority, Participation and Cultural Change in China* (Cambridge University Press, 1973) and his introduction to *Mao Tse-tung Unrehearsed*, pp. 11–18.

18. See in particular, 'Problems of Strategy in China's Revolutionary War' (December 1936); 'Problems of Strategy in Guerrilla War Against Japan' (May 1938); 'On Protracted War' (May 1938) and 'Problems of War and Strategy' (November 1938) in *Selected Military Writings of Mao Tse-tung* (Peking, Foreign Languages Press, 1963).

19. 'On Protracted War', *ibid.*, p. 198.

20. *Ibid.*, p. 201.

21. See Yahuda, *op. cit.*, pp. 43 ff., 114 ff. and 153.

22. Mao Tse-tung, 'Talk with Anna Louise Strong', August 1946 in *SW*, vol. 4, pp. 99—100. For a fuller and more vivid version, see A. L. Strong, 'World's Eye View from a Yenan Cave', *Amerasia* April, 1947.

23. See, for example, Frank E. Armbruster, 'China's Conventional Military Capability', in Tang Tsou (ed.), *China in Crisis* (University of Chicago Press, 1968) vol. II.

24. Apart from Soviet officially inspired propaganda, see the poem by Yergeni Yevtushenko comparing the Chinese to the hordes of Genghis Khan cited in Yahuda, *op. cit.*, p. 226. Dissident writers as divergent as Solzhenitsyn and Amalrik have also depicted the Chinese Communists in terrifying terms.

25. See John F. Copper, *China's Foreign Aid* (Lexington, Mass., D. C. Heath, 1976), chapter 6.

26. The quotations are from Hedley Bull in his enumeration of what he considers to be the main elements of international society. See his *Anarchical Society*, p. 13.

27. See the discussion in Wang Gung-wu, *China and the World Since 1949: The Impact of Independence, Modernity and Revolution* (London, Macmillan, 1977), pp. 9—12.

28. For an argument to the contrary see Joseph Camilleri, *Chinese Foreign Policy: The Maoist Era and its Aftermath* (Oxford, Martin Robertson 1980) Part One and especially Chapter One.

29. See note 3.

30. Edgar Snow, *The Long Revolution* (New York, Random House, 1972) pp. 19—20.

31. For a list of the American nuclear threats against China in the fifties, see John Gittings, *The World and China*, note p. 203.

32. *SW*, vol. 4, p. 428.

33. Cited in Gittings, *The World and China*, p. 225.

34. Cited in *ibid.*, p. 224.

35. *JPRS*, 61269-1 (20 February 1974) pp. 108—9.

36. See reconstruction of Mao's 1957 speech in Moscow by John Gittings, *Survey of the Sino-Soviet Dispute*, pp. 81—2. See also his speech of 17 May 1958 in *JPRS*. 61269-1, pp. 108—9.

37. Cited in Gittings, *The World and China*, p. 231.
38. Editorial, 3 August 1963, in *People of the World, Unite for the Complete, Thorough and Total and Resolute Prohibition and Destruction of Nuclear Weapons* (Peking, Foreign Languages Press, 1963), p. 95.
39. See Yahuda, *op. cit.*, pp. 171–5.
40. See Allen S. Whiting, *The Chinese Calculus of Deterrence* (Ann Arbor, University of Michigan Press, 1975), chapters 1–5. See also Melvin Gurtov and Byong-Moo Hwang, *China Under Threat: The Politics of Strategy and Diplomacy* (Baltimore, The Johns Hopkins University Press, 1980), chapter 4.
41. See also the analyses by Richard Wich, *Sino-Soviet Crisis Politics* pp. 80–1 and by K. S. Karol, *The Second Chinese Revolution* (London, Jonathan Cape, 1975) pp. 390–5.
42. In *Peking Review*, no. 36 (1968) pp. 6–7. See also account in Richard Wich, *Sino-Soviet Crisis Politics*, pp. 59–62.
43. His authorship of the theory was claimed posthumously in Editorial Department of *People's Daily*, 'Chairman Mao's Theory of the Differentiation of the Three Worlds is a Major Contribution to Marxism-Leninism', *Peking Review*, no. 45 (4 November 1977), p. 11.
44. See studies by Whiting and Gurtov and Hwang cited in note 40.
45. The subsequent account is based on the analysis by Gurtov and Hwang, *op. cit.*, Chapter 6; Richard Wich, *op. cit.*, chapters 6–9; Neville Maxwell, 'The Chinese Account of the 1969 Fighting at Chen Pao', *The China Quarterly*, no. 56 (October–December 1973) pp. 730–9. The account by Thomas W. Robinson, 'The Sino-Soviet Border Dispute', *American Political Science Review*, December 1972, pp. 1175–1202, is perhaps the best documented, but it is ambiguous as to the course of the conflict. My account has also benefited from Allen Whiting's insights into Chinese patterns of deterrence such as 'the best deterrence is belligerence'. See his *Calculus of Deterrence*, especially chapters 7 and 8.
46. See note 42.
47. Maxwell, *op. cit.*
48. 'Talk at the First Plenum of the Ninth Central Committee of the Chinese Communist Party', 28 April 1969, in Schram (ed.), *Mao Tse-tung Unrehearsed*, pp. 285–6.

Chapter 4: Chinese Society and Foreign Relations After Mao

1. Frederick K. Teiwes, *Politics and Purges in China* (New York, M. E. Sharp Inc., 1979). See especially chapter 5.
2. *SWB/FE/6794/B11/7* (6 August 1981).

3. For an excellent analysis of the condition of the armed forces in the new period, see Ellis Joffe, 'The Army After Mao', in *International Journal*, vol. XXXIV, no. 4 (Autumn 1979) pp. 568—84.

4. For an account of aspects of these developments, see Frank Ching, 'The Current Political Scene in China', *China Quarterly*, no. 80 (December 1979) pp. 691—715.

5. For eyewitness accounts, see John Fraser, *The Chinese* (Toronto, Collins, 1980) and Roger Garside, *Coming Alive — China after Mao* (London, André Deutsch, 1981). For commentary and translations of the main writings of the activists of the movement, see David S. G. Goodman, *Beijing Street Voices: The Poetry and Politics of China's Democracy Movement* (London, Marion Boyars, 1981).

6. See review of World Bank Report in China in *The Economist* (London) 20 June 1981, p. 36. The Bank identified two options: a 5 per cent growth and $4 billion in loans by 1985 or 6 per cent growth and $10 billion in loans by the end of the decade.

7. See the argument by Bruce Reynolds in 'China in the International Economy', Draft Paper presented to conference on China's foreign policy to be published shortly under the editorship of Harry Harding by the United States Council on Foreign Relations.

8. The figure varies with estimates of the total GNP. Chinese official statistics use the lower figure, but estimates by some Western economists suggest higher figures.

9. See *Beijing Review*, no. 1 (4 January 1982) Special Report on Shanghai, *People's Daily*, 16 April 1979 for statement that 100 million peasants had not improved their standard of living since 1949 and they were still undernourished.

10. 'A Conversation with a PLA Divisional Commander', in *Zheng Ming Daily*, 14—24 July 1981 in *SWB FE/6801*.

11. For recent articles and statistics on China's population, see Liu Zheng, Song Jian *et al.*, *China's Population: Problems and Prospects* (Beijing, New World Press, 1981).

12. For the extent of the rail networks of China, Germany, France and India, see John Franklin Cooper, *China's Global Role* (Stanford, Hoover Institution Press, 1980) Tables 4—10, p. 66.

13. Quoted in Ross Terril, *Mao* (N.Y., Harper & Row, 1980), p. 402.

14. For a discussion of these and related problems, see Thomas Fingar, 'Recent Policy Trends in Industrial Science and Technology', in Richard Baum (ed.), *China's Four Modernisations* (Boulder, Colorado, Westview Press, 1980), pp. 61—101.

15. For an analysis of the difficulties in delineating the responsibilities of organisations and personnel in China, see Audrey Donnithorne, 'Aspects of Neo-Liuist Economic Policy', in *Australian Journal of Chinese Affairs*, no. 5 (January 1980).

16. A text of the draft was published in *Beijing Review*, no. 19 (10 May 1981).

17. See Donnithorne, *op. cit.*, p. 81.

18. The above paragraph relies very much on the arguments of Bruce Reynolds, *op. cit.*

19. *Ibid.*

20. See The Economist Intelligence Unit, *Quarterly Economic Review of China, Hong Kong and North Korea*, Annual Supplement, 1981, p. 19.

21. Table A1 in *Chinese Economy Post Mao*, A Compendium of Papers submitted to the Joint Economic Committee of the Congress of the United States, Washington, 9 November 1978, p. 733.

22. *China Business Review*, March/April 1982, p. 59.

23. State Statistical Bureau, 'Communiqué on the Fulfillment of the 1981 National Economic Plan', in *Beijing Review*, No. 20 (17 May 1982) p. 22.

24. Robert Delfs, 'Gaining Ground', in *Far Eastern Economic Review* 7 May 1982, p. 56.

25. *Beijing Review*, no. 21 (24 May 1982), p. 14.

26. Alexander Eckstein, *China's Economic Revolution* (Cambridge University Press, 1977), p. 234.

27. *Ibid.*, pp. 234–5.

28. Su Xing (an economic editor of *Hong Qi*), 'Price Stabilization in China' (Paper presented to the Seminar of the Centre for Asian Studies, the University of Adelaide, May 1982. See especially pp. 2–4.

29. For the figures regarding Hong Kong, see *China Business Review*, March/April 1982, p. 59. For those on Shanghai, see *Beijing Review*, no. 1 (4 January 1982) p. 21.

30. Economist Intelligence Unit, *Quarterly Economic Review of China, Hong Kong and North Korea*, Annual Supplement 1981, p. 14.

31. *Ibid.*, p. 5.

32. Christopher Howe, *China's Economy, A Basic Guide* (London, Elek Books, 1978) p. 152.

33. See Ian Wilson, 'China's Diplomacy in the Second World: The Australian Case', in Kuang Sheng Liao (ed.), *Modernisation and the Diplomacy of China* (Chinese University of Hong Kong Press, 1981).

34. See note 20.

35. Kuo Chi, 'Foreign Trade: Why the "Gang of Four" Created Confusion', in *Peking Review*, no. 9 (25 February 1977) p. 18.

36. Economist Intelligence Unit, *Quarterly Economic Review of China, Hong Kong and North Korea*, Annual Supplement, 1977, p. 21.

37. *International Herald Tribune*, 2 March 1979.

38. *SWB FE*/W1021/A/15, 7 March 1979.
39. *SWB FE*/W1023/A/15, 21 March 1979.
40. Ji Chongwei, 'Prospects for China's Capacity to Absorb Foreign Investment', in *Beijing Review*, no. 17 (26 April 1982) p. 20.
41. *SWB FE*/6950/B11/4, 10 February 1982.
42. *SWB FE*/6945/B11/5, 4 February 1982.
43. *SWB FE*/6961/B11/7 and 8, 23 February 1982.
44. Robert Delfs, 'A Choose Chinese Drive', in *Far Eastern Economic Review*, 7 May, pp. 54–6.
45. Cheng Weiqin, 'The Direction of Introducing Technology should be Changed' in *Jing Ji Guan Li (Economic Management)*, no. 4, (15 April 1981) in *FE*/W1139/C/1.
46. *Workers' Daily*, 26 May 1979.
47. *People's Daily*, 15 April 1979.
48. *Workers' Daily*, 26 October 1979.
49. David Bonavia, 'The Jobless Generation', in *Far Eastern Economic Review*, 6 March 1981, pp. 30–1.
50. Robert Delfs, 'Socialism's New Look', in *Far Eastern Economic Review*, 28 May 1982.
51. *Xinhua News Agency*, 18 January 1982.
52. See note 5.
53. Robert F. Dernberger, 'Economic Consequences of Defence Expenditure Choices in China', in *China: A Reassessment of the Economy*, puts it at $100 billion. For a similar assessment, see Lawrence Freedman, *The West and the Military Modernisation of China* (London, Royal Institute of International Affairs, 1980).
54. See Mao's 'Ten Great Relationships', in *SW*, vol. 5 and the version in Schram, *Mao Tse-tung Unrehearsed'*, See also Ellis Joffe, *op. cit.*, and Harry Harding Jnr., 'The Making of Chinese Military Policy', in William Whitson (ed.), *The Military and Political Power in China in the Seventies* (New York, Praeger, 1972).
55. See Ellis Joffe, 'The Chinese Army After the Cultural Revolution: The Effects of Intervention', in *The China Quarterly*, no. 55 (July/September 1973) and 'The Army after Mao', *op. cit.*
56. See Angus M. Fraser, 'Military Modernisation in China', *Problems of Communism*, vol. XXVIII, nos. 5–6 (September–December 1979) p. 37. Much of the information in the remainder of this paragraph is drawn from this article in which Fraser has drawn on confidential sources.
57. See Harlan Jenks, 'China's "Punitive" War on Vietnam"', *Asian Survey*, vol. 19, no. 8 (August 1979). See also Jonathan Mirsky, 'China's 1979 Invasion of Vietnam: A View from the Infantry', in *Royal United Services Institute*, vol. 126, no. 2 (June 1981).

58. See Gerald Segal, 'China's Security Debate', in *Survival*, March/April 1982.

59. For a careful survey of these and related issues, see Richard Breeze, 'China, The Wide Blue Yonder,' in *Far Eastern Economic Review*, 11—17 June 1982, pp. 21—6.

Chapter 5: Strategic and International Politics Since Mao

1. Derek Davies, 'Comment', in *Far Eastern Economic Review*, 23 March 1979. For a contrary Chinese view see Xinhua Commentary of 15 March 1982, 'Can Compromise with Hanoi break up the Soviet—Vietnamese Alliance?', in *SWB/FE/6980/A2/2-3*.

2. On the question of diplomatic style, see F. S. Northedge, 'On the Nature of Foreign Policy', in his (ed.), *The Foreign Policies of the Powers* (London, Faber & Faber, 1968) pp. 21—3.

3. Thomas W. Robinson, 'Chinese—Soviet Relations in the Context of Asian and International Politics', *International Journal*, vol. XXXIV, no 4 (Autumn 1979) p. 631.

4. Henry Kissinger, *Years of Upheaval* (London, Weidenfeld & Nicolson, 1982). See the extracts in *Time Magazine*, 15 March 1982 and *The Weekend Australian*, 27—28 March 1982.

5. Zhou Enlai, 'Political Report to the Tenth National Congress of the Communist Party of China', 24 August 1973, in *Peking Review*, nos. 35—36 (1973).

6. See for example, Deng Xiaoping's 15 November 1981 discussion of the significance of the Soviet invasion of Afghanistan in *SWB/FE/6585* and articles by the international editors of *Beijing Review* in issues no. 17 (27 April) and no. 20 (18 May) 1981.

7. For an extended analysis of these themes, see Jonathan D. Pollack, 'Chinese Global Strategy and Soviet Power', in *Problems of Communism*, vol. XXX, no. 1 (January—February 1981) pp. 54—69.

8. See the Xinhua Newsagency commentary, 'Is the Soviet Union Declining?', in *Beijing Review*, no. 3 (18 January 1982).

9. For different analyses of the interplay of these factors, see Thomas M. Gottleib, *Chinese Foreign Policy Factionalism and the Origins of the Strategic Triangle* (RAND Report R-1902-NA 1977); Greg O'Leary, *The Shaping of Chinese Foreign Policy* (London, Croom Helm, 1980) and Kenneth Lieberthal, 'The Foreign Policy Debate in Peking as seen through Allegorical Articles, 1973—76', in *The China Quarterly*, no. 71 (September 1977) pp. 528—54.

10. The first public statement was in Deng Xiaoping's speech to the Sixth Special Session of the General Assembly in *Peking Review*, Special Supplement no. 15 (12 April 1974). It was later claimed

that Mao had first enunciated the theory in a talk with President Kaunda of Zambia on 22 February — see Editorial Department of the *People's Daily* (1 November 1977), 'Chairman Mao's Theory of the Differentiation of the Three Worlds is a Major Contribution to Marxism-Leninism' in *Peking Review*, no. 45 (1977) p. 11.

11. Reported interview by G. Rowbotham, *East is Red*, October 1971 (York Society for Anglo-Chinese Understanding), pp. 6—10, cited by John Gittings, 'China's Foreign Policy: Continuity or Change?', in *Journal of Contemporary Asia*, vol. 2, no. 1.

12. Interviewed by Neville Maxwell in *Sunday Times*, London, 19 December 1971.

13. See interview by a delegation from the Australian National University cited as appendix in J. I. Armstrong, 'The United Front Doctrine and China's Foreign Policy', Ph.D. thesis, Australian National University, Canberra (July 1975) pp. 330—40.

14. For its genesis, see Michael B. Yahuda, *China's Role in World Affairs* (london, Croom Helm, 1978) chapter 9.

15. See Harry Harding, Jnr., 'The Domestic Politics of China's Global Posture', in Thomas Fingar (ed.), *China's Quest for Independence: Policy Evolution in the 1970's* (Boulder, Colorado, Westview Press, 1980) pp. 99—102.

16. For further elaboration see Michael B. Yahuda, 'Chinese Foreign Policy After the Victories in Indo-China', *The World Today*, July 1975, pp. 293—5.

17. See Yahuda, *China's Role* . . . , pp. 255—6.

18. *SWB FE/6618/A1/1* Zhang Mingyang, 'Multipolarization of the World and Unity Against Hegemonism', from *People's Daily*, 2 January 1981.

19. Huang Xiang, 'Western Economy in the 1980's', in *Beijing Review*, no 17 and no. 18 (27 April and 4 May 1981).

20. 'Chronicle and Documentation', in *China Quarterly*, no. 85 (March 1981) pp. 211—12.

21. Huang Hua, in the context of an exchange of views with Japan's Foreign Minister Masayoshi Ito, *Xinhua News Agency*, Bulletin 1, 3 December 1980.

22. *Beijing Review*, no. 25 (22 June 1981).

23. See the argument and documentation in Jonathan D. Pollack, 'Chinese Global Strategy and Soviet Power', *op. cit.*, especially pp. 58—61.

24. *Ibid.*, pp. 67—9.

25. See Gerald Segal, 'China's Security Debate', in *Survival*, March/April 1982 for documentation and analysis, pp. 68—70.

26. Xinhua Correspondent Tang Tianri in *SWB/FE/69/6/A2/1—2*.

27. *Beijing Review*, no. 40 (5 October 1981) p. 23.

28. In interview with AFP quoted in *Morning Star* (London) 24 October 1977.

29. *Beijing Review*, no. 11 (16 March 1979) p. 27.

30. For the Berlinguer visit see 'Chronicle and Documentation', in *China Quarterly*, no. 83 (September 1980) pp. 636—7.

31. *Beijing Review*, no. 8 (23 February 1981) pp. 5—6.

32. *SWB FE*/6921.

33. These figures are largely drawn from the statistical tables presented in Appendix 4 of Rudiger Machetzki, 'China—EC: Economic Developments in Perspective', in Kuang-Sheng Liao, *Modernization and Diplomacy of China* (The Chinese University of Hong Kong, 1981), pp. 97—106.

34. *Ibid.*, pp. 94—5.

35. See Michael B. Yahuda, 'Chairman Hua's Grand European Tour', in *World Today*, December 1979.

36. *Financial Times* (London), 3 May 1978.

37. See the analysis of Roderick MacFarquhar, *The Origins of the Cultural Revolution, Part I: Contradictions Among the People* (Oxford University Press, 1974).

38. See article by Edwina Moreton, 'The Triangle in Eastern Europe', in Gerald Segal (ed.), *The China Factor* (London, Croom Helm, 1982) pp. 126—51.

39. See Yahuda, *China's Role in World Affairs*, pp. 133—44 and 182—211.

40. See 'Chronicle and Documentation', *China Quarterly*, no. 73, (March 1978) and *Peking Review*, no. 6 (1978).

41. See 'Keng Biao's Report on the Situation of the Indochinese Peninsula', in *Issues and Studies* (Taiwan), vol. XVII, no. 1 (January 1981).

42. Jonathan D. Pollack, 'China's Potential as a World Power', in *International Journal*, vol. XXXV, no. 3 (Summer 1980) p. 581.

43. For a recent example of the differences between North Korea and China to which this gives rise, see 'Intelligence', in *Far Eastern Economic Review*, week 16—23 July 1982, p. 13.

44. See 'Chronicle and Documentation', in *China Quarterly*, no. 64 (December 1975), sections on Soviet Union and Thailand.

45. Ren Guping, 'Repulse the Wolf at the Gate, Guard Against the Tiger at the Back Door', *People's Daily*, 29 July 1975 in *Peking Review*, 8 August 1975.

46. 'Chronicle and Documentation', *China Quarterly*, no. 72 (December 1977), section on the United States.

47. See Pollack, 'Chinese Global Strategy and the Soviet Union', *op. cit.*, pp. 60—1.

48. Machetzki, 'China—EC . . . ', *op. cit.*, p. 68.

49. Special commentator, 'The Soviet Strategic Intention as Viewed from the Vietnamese Authorities' Anti-China Activities', *Red Flag*, August 1978 in *SWB/FE/5881*.

50. 'Appeasement — Its Manifestations and Adverse Effects', in *Peking Review*, no. 30 (28 July 1978) p. 36.

51. Hsu Hsiang-chin (Xu Xiangjian), 'Heighten Our Vigilance and Get Prepared to Fight a War', in *Red Flag*, 1 August 1978 in *Peking Review*, no. 32 (11 August 1978).

52. *SWB FE/5965* and *Peking Review*, no. 45 (1978), pp. 3—4.

53. 'Keng Piao talks on "a turning point in the China-US diplomatic relations" ' (speech delivered on 24 August 1976 at the graduation ceremony of the Peking Institute of Diplomacy), published in *Issues and Studies*, 13, no. 1 (January 1977).

54. See note 41.

55. First issue of *Time Magazine*, January 1979.

56. Gromyko, quoted in *Daily Telegraph* (London), 27 February 1979 and *Pravda* in *International Herald Tribune*, 6 March 1979.

57. For the text of Brezhnev's speech, see *Soviet News* (London), 30 March 1982. For China's official response, see *Beijing Review*, no 14 (5 April 1982) p. 7 and Xinhua Commentary, p. 11.

58. 'Where does the Crux of the Sino-U.S. Relationship Lie?', in *Beijing Review*, no. 15 (12 April 1982) pp. 13—18 and 28.

59. Joseph Camilleri, *Chinese Foreign Policy: The Maoist Era and its Aftermath* (Oxford, Martin Robertson & Co., 1980), p. 192.

60. See account of the Brown visit in *Beijing Review*, no. 3 (21 January 1980) and *International Herald Tribune*, 26 January 1980 for an account of the agreement reached.

61. See *International Herald Tribune*, 29 and 31 May, *SWB/FE/6433* and 6437. For an account of Holbrooke statement, see 'Chronicle and Documentation', *China Quarterly*, no. 83 (September 1980) p. 627 and for the Chinese response see *SWB/FE/6444*.

62. *Washington Post*, 11 September 1980.

63. See Frank S. H. Hsiao and Lawrence R. Sullivan, 'The Politics of Reunification: Beijing's Initiative on Taiwan', in *Asian Survey*, vol. XX, no. 8 (1980).

64. The Act was passed on 13 March. Foreign Minister Huang Hua protested to the American Ambassador Woodcock on 16 March and thereafter followed a stream of Chinese protestations and articles protesting the wisdom and legality of the Act. Chinese protests intensified in 1981 and 1982 as it became clear that the Reagan Administration intended to sell arms to Taiwan. For non-polemical articles giving the substantive Chinese case, see that by the Chinese

scholars, Zhuang Qubing, Zhang Hongzeng and Pan Tongwen, 'On the US "Taiwan Relations Act" ' in *Journal of International Studies* (Peking), vol. 1, no. 1, translated in *Beijing Review*, nos. 36 and 37 (7 and 14 September 1981), and interview with Professor Chen Tiqiang, 'U.S. Arms Sale to Taiwan Violates International Law', in *Beijing Review*, no. 6 (8 February 1982).

65. For a discussion of Soviet policy divergences on the Chinese factor and détente see Gerald Segal, 'The Soviet Union and the Great Power Triangle', in his (ed.) *The China Factor* (London, Croom Helm, 1982) pp. 64–7 and 68.

66. This was implied in the book by the Soviet-based journalist, Victor Louis, *The Coming Decline of the Chinese Empire* (New York, Times Books, 1980).

67. For examples of this see Wolf Mendl, *Issues in Japan's China Policy* (London, Macmillan, 1978), especially pp. 44–52 and 99–101.

68. See 'Chronicle and Documentation', *China Quarterly*, no. 62 (June 1975). For more extended analysis see G. T. Hsiao, 'Prospects for a New Sino-Japanese Relationship', in *China Quarterly*, no. 60, December 1974.

69. See Wolf Mendl, 'China's Challenge to Japan', in *World Today*, July 1979, pp. 278–86.

70. *Ibid.*, p. 280.

71. For Gu Mu's remarks see Xinhua Newsagency Bulletin, 6 September 1979. For Deng Xiaoping's see his interview with a Yugoslav correspondent, FE/6905.

72. See Allen S. Whiting, *The Chinese Calculus of Deterrence*, chapter 6. See also 'More on Hanoi's White Book', *Beijing Review*, no. 48. (30 November 1979) p. 14.

73. For example, *Peking Review*, no. 35 (29 August 1969).

74. See Wang Gungwu, 'Early Ming Relations with Southeast Asia: A Background Essay,' in J. K. Fairbank (ed.), *The Chinese World Order* (Harvard University Press, 1967). See especially pp. 48–9 and 55.

75. Edgar Snow, *Red Star Over China* (London, Pelican; new and enlarged edition, 1972) p. 505

76. Dennis Duncanson, 'China's Vietnam War: New and Old Strategic Imperatives', in *World Today*, June 1979.

77. See declaration of Premier Hua Guofeng on the normalisation of Sino-American relations, *Beijing Review*, no. 51 (22 December 1978).

78. For an argument that Sino-Vietnamese relations did indeed deteriorate without careful control by either side, see Lucian W. Pye, 'The China Factor in Southeast Asia', in Richard H. Solomon (ed.),

The China Factor (Englewood Cliffs, New Jersey, Prentice-Hall, A Spectrum Book, 1981), pp. 226–42.

79. See Gareth Porter, 'The Sino-Vietnamese Conflict in Southeast Asia', in *Current History*, vol. XLV (December 1978).
80. In conversation with the former British Prime Minister Edward Heath in 'Chronicle and Documentation', in *China Quarterly*, no. 64 (December 1975) p. 813.
81. See Hoang Van Hoan, 'Distortion of Facts About Militant Friendship Between Vietnam and China is Impermissible' in *People's Daily*, 27 November 1979 in *Beijing Review*, No. 49 (7 December 1979) p. 17.
82. Michael Leifer, 'Post Mortem on the Third Indochina War', in *The World Today*, June 1979, p. 249.
83. Nayan Chanda in the *Financial Times*, 9 March 1979.
84. For an account of many of these see Bruce Burton, 'Contending Explanations of the 1979 Sino-Vietnamese War', in *International Journal*, vol. XXXIV, no. 4 (Autumn 1979).
85. See note 41.
86. Nayan Chanda in *Far Eastern Economic Review*, 6 April 1979.
87. For an excellent account see Harlan W. Jencks, 'China's "Punitive" War on Vietnam: A Military Assessment', in *Asian Survey*, vol. XIX, no. 8 (August 1979).

Select Bibliography

Armstrong, J. D., *Revolutionary Diplomacy* (Berkeley, University of California Press, 1977).

Barnett, Doak A., *China and the Major Powers in East Asia* (Washington, Brookings Institution, 1977).

Borisov, O. B. and Kolosov, B. T., *Soviet–Chinese Relations 1945–1980* (Moscow, Mysl Publishers, third supplemental edition, 1980).

Brugger, Bill (ed.), *China Since the 'Gang of Four'* (London, Croom Helm, 1980).

Camilleri, Joseph, *Chinese Foreign Policy: The Maoist Era and its Aftermath* (Oxford, Martin Robertson, 1980).

D'Encausse, H. Carrere and Schram, Stuart R., *Marxism and Asia* (London, Allen Lane, 1969).

Eckstein, Alexander, *China's Economic Revolution* (London, Cambridge University Press, 1977).

Ellison, Herbert J. (ed.), *The Sino-Soviet Conflict: A Global Perspective* (Seattle and London, University of Washington, 1982).

Fairbank, John K. (ed.), *The Chinese World Order: Traditional China's Foreign Relations* (London, Oxford University Press, 1969).

Fingar, Thomas (ed.), *China's Quest for Independence: Policy Evolution in the 1970s* (Boulder, Colorado, Westview Press, 1980).

Gittings, John, *The World and China 1922–1972* (London, Eyre Methuen, 1974).

Goodman, David S. G., *Beijing Street Voices: The Poetry and Politics of China's Democracy Movement* (London, Marion Boyars, 1981).

Gottleib, Thomas M., *Chinese Foreign Policy, Factionalism and the Origins of the Strategic Triangle* (Santa Monica, RAND Report R-1902-NA, 1977).

Gurtov, Melvin, *China and South East Asia: The Politics of Survival* (Lexington, Mass., Heath Lexington Books, 1971).

Gurtov, Melvin and Hwang Byong-Moo, *China Under Threat: The Politics of Strategy and Diplomacy* (Baltimore, The Johns Hopkins University Press, 1980).

Harding, Harry and Gurtov, Melvin, *The Purge of Lo Jui-Ching: The Politics of Chinese Strategic Planning* (Santa Monica, RAND R-548-PR, 1971).

Hellman, Donald C., *China and Japan: A New Balance of Power* (Lexington, Mass, Lexington Books, 1976).

Howe, Christopher, *China's Economy: A Basic Guide* (London, Elek Books, 1978).

Kim, Samuel S., *China, The United Nations and World Order* (Princeton University Press, 1979).

Kissinger, Henry, *The White House Years* (London, Weidenfeld & Nicolson, 1979).

Kissinger, Henry, *Years of Upheaval* (London, Weidenfeld & Nicolson, 1982).

Levenson, J. R., *Confucian China and its Modern Fate* (London, Routledge & Kegan Paul, 1958–1965, 3 vols).

Lieberthal, Kenneth, *Sino-Soviet Conflict in the 1970's : Its Evolution and Implications for the Strategic Triangle* (Santa Monica, RAND R-2343-NA, 1978).

MacFarquhar, Roderick, *The Origins of the Cultural Revolution: Contradictions Among the People* (Oxford University Press, 1974).

Mao Tse-tung, *Selected Works* (Peking, Foreign Languages Press, 1960–77, 5 vols).

Maxwell, Neville, *India's China War* (London, Jonathan Cape, 1970).

Mendl, Wolf, *Issues in Japan's China Policy* (London, Macmillan, 1978).

Ojha, Ishwer, C., *Chinese Foreign Policy in an Age of Transition: The Diplomacy of Cultural Despair* (Boston, Mass., The Beacon Press, 1969).

Reardon-Anderson, James, *Yenan and the Great Powers: The Origins of Chinese Communist Foreign Policy 1944–46* (Columbia University Press, 1980).

Schram, Stuart R., *The Political Thought of Mao Tse-tung* (Penguin, Revised edn., 1969).

Schram, Stuart R. (ed.), *Mao Tse-tung Unrehearsed: Talks and Letters 1956–1971* (Harmondsworth, Penguin, 1974).

Schram, Stuart R. (ed.), *Authority, Participation and Cultural Change in China* (Cambridge University Press, 1973).

Schurmann, Franz, *The Logic of World Power* (New York, Pantheon Books, 1974).

Segal, Gerald (ed.), *The China Factor* (London, Croom Helm, 1982).

Solomon, Richard H. (ed.), *The China Factor* (Englewood Cliffs, N.J., Prentice, Hall, A Spectrum Book, 1981).

Taylor, Jay, *China and South East Asia: Peking's Relations with Revolutionary Movements* (New York, Praeger, 1974).

Teiwes, Frederick K., *Politics and Purges in China* (New York, M. E. Sharp Inc., 1979).

Teng, Ssu-yü and Fairbank, John K. (eds), *China's Response to the West: A Documentary Survey, 1839–1923* (New York, Athenium, 1965).

Terrill, Ross, *Mao, A Biography* (New York, Harper & Row, 1980).

Van Ness, Peter, *Revolution and Chinese Foreign Policy: Peking's Support for Wars of National Liberation* (London, University of California Press, 1970).

Wakeman, Frederic, *History and Will: Philosophical Perspectives of Mao Tse-tung's Thought* (Berkeley, University of California Press, 1973).

Wang Gung-wu, *China and the World Since 1949: The Impact of Independence, Modernity and Revolution* (London, Macmillan, 1979).

Whiting, Allen S., *The Chinese Calculus of Deterrence* (Ann Arbor, University of Michigan Press, 1975).

Whiting, Allen S., *China Crosses the Yalu* (University of Michigan Press, 1960).

Wich, Richard, *Sino-Soviet Crisis Politics* (Harvard University Press, 1980).

Wilson, Dick (ed.), *Mao in the Scales of History* (Cambridge University, Press, 1977).

Wright, Mary C., *The Last Stand of Chinese Conservatism: The Tung Chih Restoration 1862—1874* (California, Stanford University Press, 1957).

Yahuda, Michael B., *China's Role in World Affairs* (London, Croom Helm., 1978).

Zagoria, Donald S., *The Sino-Soviet Conflict* (Princeton University Press, 1962).

Index